Therapeutic Metaphors
for Children
and the Child Within

Other Titles Available by the Authors

CARTOON MAGIC
How to Help Children Discover Their Rainbows Within

SAMMY THE ELEPHANT AND MR. CAMEL
*A Story to Help Children Overcome Enuresis
While Discovering Self-Appreciation*

Therapeutic Metaphors
for Children
and the Child Within

by

Joyce C. Mills & Richard J. Crowley

In collaboration with

Margaret O. Ryan

BRUNNER/MAZEL, *Publishers*
A member of the Taylor & Francis Group

USA	Publishing Office	Brunner/Mazel A member of the Taylor & Francis Group 325 Chestnut Street, Suite 800 Philadelphia, PA 19106 Tel: (215) 625-8900 Fax: (215) 625-2940
	Distribution Center	Brunner/Mazel A member of the Taylor & Francis Group 7625 Empire Drive Florence, KY 41042 Tel: (800) 634-7064 Fax: (800) 248-4724
UK		Brunner/Mazel A member of the Taylor & Francis Group 11 New Fetter Lane London EC4P 4EE Tel: +44 (0) 171 583 9855 Fax: +44 (0) 171 842 2298

THERAPEUTIC METAPHORS FOR CHILDREN AND THE CHILD WITHIN

Library of Congress Cataloging-in-Publication Data available from Publisher.

Cover design by Glynis Scaramuzza.
Cover illustration: © Hallmark Cards, Inc. Reproduced with permission.

1st printing, 2001

ISBN 1-58391-370-X

This book is dedicated to the discovery of the teachings of Milton H. Erickson, to the delightful children and families with whom we have worked, and to the rediscovery of our own child within.

Return to the beginning;
Become a child again.

— Tao Te Ching

Contents

CONTENTS

Acknowledgments

We would like to extend our deepest appreciation to the following people who have provided both mental and emotional support to us throughout the conception and actualization of this book: ·

Gail Alsen
Paul Carter
John Paul Crowley
Stephen Gilligan
Jeanne Gordon
Steven Heller
Bernie Mazel
Dorothy Mc Gehee
Ernest L. Rossi
Charles J. Weingarten
Jeffrey Zeig

and to Margaret Ryan, whose guidance, editorial abilities, original contributions, along with her emotional involvement and love, permeate this book.

An acknowledgment to the memory of my mother and father, Anne and John Crowley (and the Sisters of St. Joseph), who must be delighted in knowing that all their hard work finally paid off.

Special appreciation and love are offered to my husband, Eddie Mills, and sons, Todd and Casey, for the personal love, support and understanding they so generously gave throughout the writing of this book, as well as to my mother Rose for her enduring love.

Foreword

Joyce Mills and Richard Crowley have written a book with heart, daring, and mind that is a therapeutic experience in itself to read. Their contribution to new ways of creating and utilizing therapeutic metaphors goes well beyond their excellent work with children; it opens the door to a new understanding of the entire process of problem-solving and growth facilitation in psychotherapy.

It is clear to most professionals that we are currently in a renaissance of new attitudes and methods. Mills and Crowley are on the growing edge of this new breakout. They use the work of Milton H. Erickson as an important resource, but add much original thinking of their own. They respectfully integrate their new methods with Freud and Jung, as well as with modern Neuro-Linguistic Programming, behavior, and cognitive theories. They are at their best when they use their own case material to illuminate their approaches.

I found myself intrigued by the theoretical complexity yet methodological simplicity of applying their ideas in practical daily psychotherapeutic work. In this book they introduce a variety of new methods, such as the *Inner Resource Drawings* and the *Pain Getting Better Book,* which utilize a three-step healing process. I found myself using this three-step process in new variations with my adult clients. Most people, for example, find it fairly easy to see a picture or have a feeling about their problem as they currently experience it, and they enjoy visualizing what it will be like when the problem is resolved. Then comes the surprising third step: getting a picture of the healing process itself, of how to go from the current problem to its already visualized solution.

This three-step procedure is disarming in its simplicity yet surprisingly effective in its rapid resolution of the client's sense of being mired in a hopeless muddle. This is probably the key to the usefulness of the approaches being developed by Mills and Crowley: They very rapidly move the client into a position of strength and self-efficacy.

Whatever the readers' background and training, they will welcome the freshness of these approaches, which have novel and effective applications with adults, as well as with children. This beautifully written book itself evokes the readers' own creativity, enabling them to view their clients' problems from a continually expanding therapeutic perspective. I hope to continue learning with Mills and Crowley into the rewarding future they are constructing for their clients and themselves.

Ernest Lawrence Rossi
Malibu, 1986

Introduction: Beginnings

For centuries pieces of colored glass, mirrors, and tubes were readily available. To some they were just bits and pieces. To others they were the ingredients to transform their world of colors and shapes into fantasies and new visions . . . the kaleidoscope.

In the last decade many volumes have been written by professionals in several related fields in an effort to comprehend and clarify the therapeutic approaches of psychiatrist Milton H. Erickson. Many of these volumes have been written by individuals who were privileged to have trained personally with Erickson. Certainly Erickson's personality was in itself a powerful learning tool, and all who worked with him were stimulated by this caring and crafty genius to reach beyond themselves in ways still unknown to many of them. Indeed, Ernest Rossi, who worked closely with Erickson from 1974 until Erickson's death in 1980, has only recently come to a full understanding of the unusual and complex learning techniques Erickson merrily devised to spur him on (Rossi, 1983). In direct ways and indirect ways, in humorous ways and serious ways, in didactic ways and metaphorical ways, Erickson continually strove to expand the mentalities, the viewpoints, the abilities of those who trained with him.

Given the sheer dynamism and ingeniousness of Erickson's personality, how much hope is there for "second-generation" students? Can therapists who have not worked directly with Erickson legitimately expect to integrate his brilliant techniques of therapy in personally creative ways?

The question to be answered is: To what degree was Erickson's phenomenal success as therapist and teacher contingent upon subjective elements—his unique combination of abilities, characteristics, and life experiences—or, to what degree was it contingent upon the objective elements of veracity and classicism contained in the ideas and insights he conceived? Ironically enough, it will be the second-generation students—those of us who never worked with Erickson—who will in the end provide an answer to this question.

The very fact that we have written a book describing our own applications of Erickson's approaches in the specific field of childhood disorders indicates that second-generation students can indeed experience the veracity of his approaches in a compelling and effective manner. Indeed, the glow of excitement we felt at our first Ericksonian workshop several years ago has only deepened with the passage of time and continued study. We now realize the excitement has endured precisely because it was not just in response to Erickson's creativity, but was rather a direct outcome of the creativity his approaches stimulated in our own work. There was a certain "domino effect" set in motion through which each new flash of insight seemed to inevitably spark another.

Before our introduction to Ericksonian approaches, we had accumulated approximately 25 years as practicing psychotherapists between the two of us. Certainly, the work had been satisfying for the most part, and the various therapeutic methods of insight-analysis, behavior modification, family therapy, and gestalt principles had been effective. Yet we both felt that a vital dimension or level of treatment was clearly missing. We began to explore current non-traditional approaches in the field and attended a Neurolinguistic Programming (NLP) workshop led by Richard Bandler and John Grinder. The colorfully presented theories and techniques captured our interest and we decided to continue exploring these concepts in a small group learning setting with an NLP trainer. Something, however, was still missing. We found ourselves getting stuck with the "which-step-goes-where" dilemma, and experienced our creativity being somewhat blocked by such a structured approach.

It was at that time we had our first exposure to Erickson's ideas and techniques in an exciting and entrancing workshop given by Paul Carter and Stephen Gilligan in March, 1981. Although the Bandler and Grinder techniques were derived from some of Erickson's approaches, we found that the Carter and Gilligan workshop captured the essence of Erickson's spontaneous, innovative methods in a way better suited to our own personalities and proclivities. It was in this workshop that the vital missing element for us as therapists became clear.

Actually it was more than a missing element; it was more like a sweeping shift in dimension and focus. In Erickson's work we saw how the psychology of pathology that had historically dominated psychotherapy was unobtrusively transformed into a *psychology of potentials;* how the traditional authoritarian approach of the therapist was mellowed with respect and care into a *utilization approach* of patient potentials; and how the ever-revered edifice of analysis and insight was nudged off the pedestal in favor of *creative reframing* and *unconscious learnings.*

Even more important than these conceptual innovations, however, was the personal element of respect and dignity that infused the work—even without the benefit of Erickson's presence. We had both received training in traditional hypnosis, yet we had found it to be artificial, limiting, and authoritarian. It also had seemed disrespectful of the patient who was, after all, being told to enter some strangely disconnected state in which he or she would be the passive recipient of someone else's suggestions. In the Carter and Gilligan workshop, however, just the opposite occurred: Trance became a natural inner movement of concentration and focus, and hypnotic suggestion became a natural outer means of evoking one's own solutions. Each time we went into trance during the workshop, it was as if something profound and personal was being touched within each of us. Like a window shade that suddenly lifts upward and allows the sunlight to enter and brighten a darkened room, Erickson's approaches lifted our awareness just as suddenly and brightly toward another, more creative way of working. We emerged from the workshop literally enlightened by the experience.

It is one thing to be dazzled by the light of discovery, but it is quite another to anchor that light into one's life in a personally relevant way. We soon discovered that the *vision* of what was to be accomplished was only the starting point of the process. Translating that vision into a *reality* then required many long months of work, practice, and study. We continued our learning by attending another intensive workshop presented in August of 1981 by Carol and Steve Lankton in which additional Ericksonian approaches were presented. We strove to expand these new hypnotherapeutic strategies through our own research and through our exploratory application of the strategies with our clients and ourselves.

With our introduction to Steven Heller in 1982 we took our next step forward. His concept of "unconscious restructuring" (Heller & Steele, 1986) extended the Neurolinguistic theory of communication by introducing a new model of mental functioning which included what he termed an *out-of-conscious system*. Heller's emphasis on the use of metaphor to integrate the out-of-conscious system gave us an even more focused approach to therapeutic intervention. This collaboration continued for some two years.

During this time we benefited from the guidance and encouragement of several leading teachers in the Ericksonian field, in particular Jeffrey Zeig, Director of the Milton H. Erickson Foundation. Jeff was not only emotionally supportive of our work, but also played an active role in bringing this book to fruition. It was through his networking efforts that we met Margaret Ryan, who has been invaluable to us not only as a collaborator on this project, but indeed as a dear friend in our lives. Through Margaret we then met Ernest Rossi, who generously contributed the Foreword to this volume. Finally, Jeff put us in contact with Brunner/Mazel, who became our publisher.

Learning to use Erickson's techniques (as well as techniques based on his approach) is always challenging and often disconcerting. In the beginning it is not unusual to feel clumsy and self-conscious. We found it awkward, for example, to interrupt an adult patient in mid-sentence with the unexpected lead-in, "and that reminds me of a story." Yet we did it because we intuitively believed in the validity of telling a metaphor to get across a point that ordinary conversation or discussion could not. Our fear that a client would become annoyed and say, "I'm not paying this kind of money to hear stories," never came true. What did come true was our growing confidence as patients responded favorably, and soon it seemed perfectly natural to be "telling stories" to children as well as adults.

Children, of course, are generally receptive to such an approach. In most cases they *prefer* hearing stories to being talked at by some adult. Indeed, children often provide the best training ground for the development of Erickson's metaphorical approaches, precisely because metaphor is such a familiar (though unconscious) reality for most of them. Part of childhood identity in our culture is woven out of bits and pieces of fairy tales, cartoons, and movie heroes that have most affected the child. Even the role modeling of parents can be viewed as a metaphorical process whereby the child learns to act "as if" he or she were the parent.

Given this natural receptivity to metaphor that characterizes childhood, we found that a conscious and directed application of a therapeutic metaphor via storytelling produced effective and gratifying results. Certainly storytelling is not a new or unique form of child therapy, but the particular combination of techniques used to create the story can result in something quite special. When this happens, the story as experienced by the child is an effortless flight into an inner world. As crafted by the therapist, however, the story is a complex interweaving of observations, learnings, intuitions, and goals which ultimately leaves the child with a very important message.

This volume is an exploratory and empirical examination of the work we have developed with children since our introduction to Ericksonian psychotherapeutic approaches. It is our intention to illustrate one way in which those approaches have been integrated and expanded in a manner that has been consistently exciting and effective. In our presentation, we have attempted to blend right- and left-brain functions by providing didactic information within a framework that hopefully stimulates the reader's own unique associations and experiences. That is, after all, what Erickson did with consummate skill. He never attempted to teach static or structured principles of therapy; he never attempted to present *a right way* to work. Rather he sought to help the therapist discover *the way that was right for him or her.*

A little child discovers a box of crayons with all its magical colors. She empties the box all over the floor, picks a color and starts to draw. Just scribbling at first, she delights in the blend and flow of colors. A scribble of blue can represent a rock, a dog, the sky, or any other wonderful thing she wishes to imagine.

As the child grows, she still happily uses her crayons in school but is now carefully instructed, "Today we will draw butterflies." Scribbling again, the child begins to create her image of a butterfly. As she is drawing, a voice from over there may interrupt to say, "That is not how you draw a butterfly. This is how." She may even be presented with a paper depicting a mimeographed butterfly.

"Color within the lines," she is told, "and then it will look like a real butterfly."

She tries to color within the lines, but again she goes out of the lines.

"No," she is reminded. "Stay within the lines."

Imagine now the teacher who provides the child with paper and colors and simply says, "Enjoy creating your picture in your own way. Let me be your guide, not your hand."

How many times have we as therapists or teachers heard those words, "Stay within the lines," in one form or another? How paradoxical. We are taught to stay within the lines, and yet we are expected to be creative and original at the same time. Erickson sidestepped this paradox by recognizing and respecting the abilities and resources he knew to be intrinsic to every individual. He facilitated these abilities and resources, not with a carefully prescribed formula or belief system, but by providing innovative frameworks which stimulated each person's unique internal processes. We certainly found that happening within ourselves as we moved into an intensive study of his work. Even without the benefit of his physical presence, we found layer after layer of our own creativity and originality thawing out and finally bearing fruit. We felt in the end that we indeed had been taught directly by Erickson—in his uniquely indirect way!

We have attempted to provide an approach that can be used by professionals in a variety of environments ranging from individual, family, and group therapy situations to classroom and hospital settings. To accomplish this, we begin with a discussion of the history and nature of metaphor in order to provide a deeper understanding of the dynamics involved in the use of metaphor as an innovative approach. Next we provide a bridge from understanding the potency of metaphor in its historical contexts to its application in the field of child and family therapy.

With this foundation in place, we then turn our attention to the multifaceted process of creating therapeutic metaphors. Here the ingredients of storywriting provide a guideline for creating original stories that later will incorporate unique inner resources gleaned from the observation and utilization of each child's unconscious language of minimal cues.

Expanding the metaphorical process into the dimension of artwork is our next focus in which we show how a variety of drawing strategies contribute yet another level of learning and intervention for the child in therapy.

Finally, the use of cartoon characters and their worlds are demonstrated as "ready-made" metaphors that can be used to help children cope with problems ranging from common childhood difficulties to the gravely serious issue of child abuse that faces our society today.

While it is necessary for didactic purposes to analyze the technique of metaphorical creation, it must be remembered that, ironically, the very potency of the metaphor as a therapeutic tool lies in its refusal to be completely analyzed. However thoroughly we may decipher its components, however carefully we may discern the myriad internal factors that compose it, still a certain ineffable quality remains. It is this ineffable quality which contains the transformational power of the metaphor. On the Eastern form of metaphor, the koan, Kopp aptly writes (1971, p. 67):

> The koan may seem straightforward in tone, or it may be openly bewildering. It turns out to be paradoxical, impenetrable by logic. The disciple may spend months or even years trying to solve the problem until it occurs to him that there is no problem to be solved. The only solution is to give up trying to understand, because there is nothing to be understood, and to respond spontaneously.

Responding spontaneously is what most children do best. They do not try to figure out the story being presented; they simply enter into it with the full force of their imaginative powers. These imaginative powers are the critical substance of change and healing, once they are activated. The metaphor can act as flame to candle, igniting the child's imagination to its brightest valence of strength, self-knowledge, and transformation.

This book is meant for all those seeking an approach for bringing out the best in the children and families who touch their lives. Through metaphor, you can add an incredibly powerful tool to the techniques and knowledge you have already acquired. And through metaphor, you can allow your own child within to emerge as a creative force in communicating with the children in your care.

Therapeutic Metaphors
for Children
and the Child Within

A Child's Fantasy

Beyond the nebulous reality of life
  Is the depth of your being to bridge my walk
And create a trance to return to me
    To my forgotten other world . . .
Simply known as "A Child's Fantasy"

Once I shed the shroud of proprieties and rigidities
  I entered again and forever
The garden of my earlier and happier days

Be with that child
  Play with that child

Either in the fantasy of toys and memories
  Or even in the solitude of an empty room
Experience the presence of the child's own magical love
  And share within it again

All may have gone unnoticed
  Unless I venture to risk
And returned to the child again. . . .

PART ONE

Prisms of Metaphor

1

The Nature of Metaphor

As the potter places clay in the center of the wheel and slowly begins to spin it, he combines water and a gentle but firm hand to guide the shape of the clay, until a unique object emerges to be appreciated and used in many different ways.

Metaphor is a form of symbolic language that has been used for centuries as a method of teaching in many fields. The parables of the Old and New Testaments, the holy writing of the Kabbalah, the koans of Zen Buddhism, the allegories of literature, the images of poetry, and the fairy tales of storytellers—all make use of metaphor to convey an idea in an indirect yet paradoxically more meaningful way. Recognition of this special power of the metaphor has also been grasped by every parent and grandparent who, observing the forlorn features of the young child, seeks to bring consolation and nurturance by relating an experience to which the child can intuitively relate.

This chapter will provide a spectrum of theories which scan philosophical, psychological, and physiological viewpoints regarding the nature of metaphor. Our purpose in presenting this range of views on metaphor is to communicate a portion of its long and rich history among the best minds of our past and present.

Metaphor and Eastern Masters

The young monk asks, "How shall I see the truth?" The Master replies, "Through your everyday eyes."

We begin this chapter with a glimpse into the Eastern Masters because the essence of their philosophies metaphorically parallels the development of the child. The Eastern Masters teach that interaction with life and nature is the way (Tao) to learn, grow, and solve problems. This interaction with life and nature is also the very way in which the infant and child take in information and gradually synthesize it into a cohesive world view. In this sense the teaching approaches of the Eastern Masters and the developmental processes of the young child can be viewed as analogical.

Eastern Masters from many orientations have long made use of metaphor as a primary vehicle for teaching (Kopp, 1971). Recognizing that most students would approach their learning from a logical, rational perspective—and that this perspective in itself would form a barrier to progress—the Masters sought more indirect means. For example, rather than attempting to explain such concepts as the unity of man, nature, and the universe in logical thinking terms, Taoist Master Chuang Tzu used stories, parables, and fables to help his students discover and experience their meaning metaphorically (Kopp, 1971, p. 61):

> There was once a one-legged dragon named Kui, whose envy of a centipede led him to ask, "How can you possibly manage a hundred legs, when I manage my one leg with difficulty?" "It is so simple," replied the centipede. "I do not manage them at all. They land all over the place like drops of spit."

In Zen Buddhist approaches these stories and fables developed into concise, carefully crafted *koans*. Koans are paradoxical riddles impenetrable by logic. One type of koan uses direct, simple statements that are actually indirect and quizzical (Kopp, 1971, p. 67):

> Tell me the sound of one hand clapping,
>
> *or*
>
> The flower is not red, nor is the willow green.

Another type of koan uses the traditional question-answer format but in a nontraditional way. Typically a student asks an expected or predictable question of a Master, who then gives an unexpected and completely inscrutable answer (Kopp, 1971, p. 67):

> The young monk asks, "What is the secret of
> Enlightenment?"
> The Master replies, "When you are hungry, eat;
> and when you are tired, sleep."
>   *or*
> The young monk asks, "What is Zen?" The Master
> replies, "Boiling oil over a blazing fire."

The power of this approach lies in its *enigma,* which serves to provoke a deeper quest for knowledge on the part of the student.

In some Zen Buddhist sects, the koan is the primary teaching vehicle. Rossi and Jichaku (1984) explain that the koan's importance comes from the fact that solving its riddle requires the student to bypass or transcend normal dualistic modes of thought. Right and wrong, black and white, lion and lamb must fuse into a unity if the koan is to be solved. In this way, the enigmatic, cryptic, and metaphorical quality of the koan forces the mind to reach past itself for solution. In this very reaching, however, the search for solution crumbles into the spontaneous flow of Enlightenment—which was there all along. Rossi and Jichaku quote Master Hakuin's description of his own Enlightenment experience, which begins with an all-consuming, restless absorption and culminates with a seemingly paradoxical insight (Yampolski, 1971, p. 118):

> All my former doubts vanished as though ice had melted away. In a loud voice I called: "Wonderful, wonderful. There is no cycle of birth and death through which one must pass. There is no enlightenment one must seek. The seventeen hundred koans handed down from the past have not the slightest value whatsoever."

"Enlightenment" for the Eastern Masters is always with us. It is not something we have to learn or seek. However, we *do* have to remove the clutter that stands between enlightenment and our personal experience of it, and one way to do that is through the metaphor of koans, stories and fables. An excerpt from *The Garden of Anecdotes* (Xianyi & Yang, 1981) best relates this point:

"Hui Zi is forever using parables," complained someone to the Prince of Liang. "If you, sire, forbid him to speak in parables, he won't be able to make his meaning clear."

The prince agreed with this man.

The next day the prince saw Hui Zi.

"From now on," he said, "kindly talk in a straightforward manner and not in parables." "Suppose there were a man who did not know what a catapult is," replied Hui Zi. "If he asked you what it looked like, and you told him it looked just like a catapult, would he understand what you meant?"

"Of course not," answered the prince.

"But suppose you told him that a catapult looks something like a bow and that it is made of bamboo—wouldn't he understand you better?"

"Yes, that would be clearer," admitted the prince.

"We compare something a man does not know with something he does know in order to help him to understand it," said Hui Zi. *"If you won't let me use parables, how can I make things clear to you."*

The prince agreed that he was right. (Italics added)

Enlightenment is typically an adult concept of an adult experience. What then does it have to do with children? Perhaps we could say that the child's experience of the world *is* Enlightenment, pure and interactional. Repeatedly in Zen and mystic writings of many orientations, children are viewed as natural possessors of Enlightenment. Adults are encouraged to become like children in order to achieve the advancement they seek. This is because children live in the moment, intimately connected to their sensory experience of what is occurring. They are not fettered by the probings of adult concerns (Kopp, 1971, p. 89):

[The child] seems in a state of grace when it comes to matters of the spirit. Totally involved in living his life, he has neither time nor perspective in which to struggle with questions of identity or purpose or the meaning of it all.

This is the same "state of grace" Master Hakuin achieved in his moment of Enlightenment when the value of the koan crumbled in the experience of the value of life itself. It seems we have to come full circle: from the innocence, freshness, and unselfconsciousness of the child, through the laboring of an adult mind striving to understand itself, and returning in the end to the spontaneity and simplicity of the child—but with the added dimensions of consciousness and maturation.*

A child can be viewed metaphorically as what Taoist Hoff (1982, p. 10) described as the "Uncarved Block":

> The essence of the principle of the Uncarved Block is that things in their original simplicity contain their own natural power that is easily spoiled and lost when simplicity is changed.

The special gift of childhood consciousness is this power of simplicity. It is a power that can be surprising to us as modern therapists raised within a cultural atmosphere of adult supremacy. When we find ourselves disconcerted by a child's swift grasp of a complex interpersonal situation, we have little in our training that tells us what to do with such insight. If we are supposed to know more, if *we* are supposed to be the guides, how is it that this child is so in touch? So comprehending? How can we at once support the power (and fragility) of children's simplicity while teaching them better ways to adapt to their complex worlds? It can be difficult unless we relax into the understanding that we as therapists have the ability to draw upon two special sets of resources: resources acquired by the evolution of adult perceptions, and resources lived long ago in our own childhood, which now reside in our unconscious, waiting, as *the child within*.

The Family of Nature

With full attentiveness, I listened as a mother tearfully related her sad and insecure feelings about her teenage son who had recently overcome a drug-addiction problem. She talked about her inner turmoil of not knowing when to let go, when to pull back and not rescue him, and when to offer help. She questioned how much to give of herself and how to cope with the feelings of helplessness that arose in

---

* Jung termed this process individuation (1960), and viewed it as the single most important task of modern consciousness.

her as she watched her son struggle with his new learnings. As she spoke, I suddenly recalled an experience from my own life which beautifully paralleled her concerns.

At one point, she sighed and seemed to relax as her shoulders dropped and her body melted into the overstuffed chair in my office. At that moment, I looked directly and meaningfully into her eyes and began my story:

A few months ago I took a river rafting trip. One morning I awakened quite early, before my companions, and walked down to the river only a few yards from where I had slept. It was such a quiet, peaceful time that I sat down on a log which jutted out a bit over the river's edge and began to look all around. I noticed a beautiful, large tree nearby. On one of its branches was perched a small bird with colorful feathers. I noticed the bird was looking intently towards an alcove in a rock that was approximately twenty feet away and somewhat lower than the branch. I then noticed another bird flying back and forth, landing first in the alcove and then flying up to another branch of that same tree.

A tiny baby bird was crouched in the alcove as if afraid to come out. As I realized the importance of what was taking place in this "family," I became intently curious. What are the parents trying to teach their baby? I stayed and watched this ritual for some time as the one bird flittered back and forth between the two points.

I then went away for an hour or so. When I returned to check on my "family of nature," I found the baby bird still inside the alcove, the mama bird still flying back and forth, and the papa bird still watching and chirping his message. Finally, mama flew once again to her branch and this time remained perched. After a while the baby bird began to flap its little wings and began its venture into the world. It got so far and fell. Mama bird and papa bird watched.

Instinctively I wanted to rush to the tiny creature and offer it help, but restrained myself, knowing to trust nature in this age-old learning adventure.

The birds remained where they were. The baby struggled, flapping its wings and falling; flapping its wings and falling. At that point, "papa" instinctively realized that baby bird was not ready for such a big learning. Papa flew down to the baby and chirped several times. Returning to the tree, he now landed on a branch that was much lower and more accessible to the baby. This tiny, jewel-like creature joined its father on the lower branch. Shortly after, the mama bird joined them.

After a long pause the mother in my office smiled and said, "Thanks, I guess I'm not such a bad mother after all. My 'bird' still needs my love and guidance but ultimately he has to learn to fly himself."

Metaphor and Western Psychology

CARL JUNG

The landmark work of Carl Jung has provided a much needed bridge between Ancient and Modern thought—between the Eastern Masters and modern-day psychologists, between Western religions and modern-day seekers. At the cornerstone of Jung's framework is the *symbol* (Jung, 1912/1956, 1964). Symbols, like metaphors, represent or suggest something beyond their immediate appearance. Jung believed that symbols mediated the entire landscape of our psychic life. The lowest to the highest aspects of the "Self" are made manifest through the use of symbols. Jung's definition of the symbolic is strikingly similar to the definitions of metaphor presented in the next two sections of this volume (Jung, 1964, pp. 20–21):

A word or an image is symbolic when it implies something more than its obvious and immediate meaning. It has a wider 'unconscious' aspect that is never precisely defined or fully explained. Nor can one hope to define or explain it. As the mind explores the symbol, it is led to ideas that lie beyond the grasp of reason.

For Jung, the most important role of the symbol was in its portrayal of the archetypes (Jung, 1958, 1959, 1961). Archetypes are inherited elements of the human psyche which reflect common patterns of experience throughout the history of human consciousness. Another way to say this would be to say that archetypes are *metaphorical prototypes* representing the many milestones in mankind's evolution. There are the mother and father archetypes, the masculine and feminine archetypes, the child archetypes, and so on. For Jung the archetypes were "living psychic forces" as real as our physical bodies. The archetypes were to the spirit what our organs are to the body.

Archetypes are expressed or portrayed in many ways. The most common sources of depiction occur in dreams, myths, and fairy tales. In these special arenas of the human mind, an intangible archetype is given tangible shape and set into action. It presents the conscious mind with a story or sequence of some kind, the point of which is fully grasped only on an unconscious level. The archetype expresses itself through metaphors (Jung uses the term *parables*) which transcend the comprehension of normal waking consciousness in a way similar to the Eastern Koans (Jung, 1958, p. 119):

> What an archetypal content is always expressing is first and foremost a parable. If it speaks of the sun and identifies with it the lion, the king, the hoard of gold guarded by the dragon, or the force that makes for the life and health of man, it is neither the one thing or the other, but the unknown third thing that finds more or less adequate expression in all these similies, yet to the perpetual vexation of the intellect—remains unknown and not to be fitted in a formula.

Symbols are powerful because they are "numinous" in that they evoke an emotional response, a sense of awe and inspiration, in us. Jung was careful to explain that symbols are both images *and* emotions, for without the emotional valence, the numinous quality, a symbol is meaningless (Jung, 1964, p. 96):

> When there is merely the image, then there is simply a word picture of little consequence. But by being charged with emotions, the image gains numinosity (or psychic energy); it becomes dynamic, and consequences of some kind must flow from it.

Symbols for Jung had a life-sustaining function which was desperately needed by the psyche as a means of expressing and transforming life. Indeed, Jung saw the symbol as the vehicle for a modern-day spirituality which would grow out of the vitality of each person's own psychodynamic processes. As traditional authoritarian religions diminished in appeal, man would be left increasingly to draw upon his own psyche and its symbolic communications for faith, for "soul" (quoted in Edinger, 1973, p. 109):

Man is in need of a symbolic life. . . . Only the symbolic life can express the need of the soul—the daily need of the soul, mind you!

SHELDON KOPP

While reviewing the works of many noted psychologists and psychotherapists, the personal and scholarly writings of Sheldon Kopp began to nestle comfortably within our framework of thought and experience. In *Guru: Metaphors from a Psychotherapist* (1971), Kopp recounts the lifesaving role fairy tales played during his childhood and describes his later rediscovery of the teaching potency of myths and poetry. In his search for growth as a therapist, Kopp began to question the scientific world of research and theories which did not speak to his own personal feelings, experiences, and intuitions. The classic myths and metaphors from the many regions of the world, however, did reach him in a lasting and profound way (Kopp, 1971, p. ix):

> At first it seemed very strange to me that the readings that helped me the most to trust what went on in my works as a psychotherapist were tales of Wizards and Shammans, of Hasidic Rabbis, Desert Monks, and Zen Masters. Not the materials of science and reasons, but the stuff of poetry and myth instructed me best.

The richness of these metaphorical readings helped Kopp to clarify an important aspect of the therapeutic process which is often overlooked: the inner process of the therapist himself. For Kopp, this process now could be comfortably experienced as one of "emergent relatedness" and "inner unity" with his clients.

In examining the phenomenon of metaphor, Kopp notes our three basic modes of "knowing": the rational, the empirical, and the metaphorical. He suggests that both rational thinking processes and empirical sensory processes may be expanded and even superceded by the metaphorical mode (Kopp, 1971, p. 17):

> In this mode we do not depend primarily on thinking logically nor on checking our perceptions. Understanding the world metaphorically means we depend on an intuitive grasp of situations, in which *we are open to the symbolic dimensions of experience, open*

to the multiple meanings that may all co-exist, giving extra shades
of meaning to each other. [Italics added]

In a manner similar to Jung's view of symbols, Kopp speaks of metaphor as a means of communicating in which one thing is expressed in terms of another. This new expression, however, cannot be fully understood by the conscious mind. In Jung's terms, the "intellect" is perpetually vexed by the "unknown third thing," and in Kopp's terms we cannot depend on "thinking logically nor on checking out perceptions." In a following section, we shall see how Kopp's "multiple meanings" to which we are opened through metaphor are also a centerpoint of Milton Erickson's therapeutic approaches.

JULIAN JAYNES

Psychologist and historian Julian Jaynes extends Kopp's viewpoint by theorizing that the subjective conscious mind *is* the process of metaphor. It is "a vocabulary or lexical field whose terms are all metaphors or analogs of behavior in the physical world" (Jaynes, 1976). In Jaynes's formulation, metaphor is a primary experience that serves a twofold purpose of (1) describing experience, which may then (2) generate new patterns of consciousness that expand the boundaries of subjective experience. In other words, we may begin by attempting to describe a particular experience as it occurred—to provide an "objective" report of it—but in the very process of describing it, new correspondences are generated which *in themselves* expand the original experience beyond what it was at the time.

A humorous example of Jaynes's point might be the "fish-that-got-away" story in which an original experience of mediocrity is transformed in the telling of it into a grandiose experience of accomplishment. A more productive example is the process of therapy itself in which a person comes to new insights simply through the narration of his own life story. In everyday life, too, we have all had the experience of recounting an event to a friend and discovering, in the telling of it, far more details, richer textures, more intricate connections than were recognized at the time. According to Jaynes, this process of enrichment occurs as a result of the generative powers of metaphor within the human mind.

If this view of metaphor as a natural generator of new patterns of consciousness is correct, then it follows that metaphor would be a particularly helpful means of communication in precisely those very situations of therapy, teaching, and counseling that seek new understandings as their goal.

ERICKSON AND ROSSI

Throughout the span of a brilliant 50-year career, Milton Erickson created more metaphorical stories than could be counted. Many of his metaphors were based on the personal life experiences of home, school, and work (Rossi, Ryan & Sharp, 1983;* Zeig, 1980). Indeed his always innovative use of metaphor in therapy was regarded by many to be nothing short of masterful. Erickson himself remained atheoretical on the matter of how and why his metaphors worked until his collaboration with pyschologist Ernest Rossi in the last decade of his life. As Rossi sought to delineate the components of Erickson's metaphors and indirect suggestions, a theory based on recent neurological research in hemispheric functioning began to come together (Erickson & Rossi, 1979).

This theory provides an important link between metaphor, symptoms, and therapeutic intervention. In the following section on metaphor and physiology we shall describe research indicating that the right hemisphere is activated in processing metaphorical types of communication. Since the right hemisphere is also more involved than the left in mediating emotional and imagistic processes (Luria, 1973; Galin, 1974), it is believed likely that psychosomatic symptoms are processed by predominantly right-brain functions. In other words, the right brain may be the "home" of both metaphorical language and psychosomatic symptomatology. Erickson and Rossi theorized that since "symptoms are expressions in the language of the right hemisphere, our use of mythopoetic language may thus be a means of communicating directly with the right hemisphere in its own language" (Erickson & Rossi, 1979, p. 144). They suggested that this right-hemispheric mediation of both symptomatology *and* metaphorical meaning would explain why metaphorical approaches to therapy were less time-consuming than

---

* See in particular pages 42–44 of the biographical sketch in Rossi, Ryan, and Sharp, 1983.

psychoanalytically oriented approaches (Erickson & Rossi, 1979, p. 144):

> This [use of metaphorical language to communicate directly with right hemisphere] is in contrast to the conventional psychoanalytic approach of first translating the right hemisphere's body language into the abstract patterns of cognition of the left hemisphere, which must then somehow operate back upon the right hemisphere to change the symptom.

Metaphor, on the other hand, goes straight for the target area—the right-brain processes.

Erickson was extraordinarily skilled at crafting what Rossi termed "two-level communication," which was a means of communicating simultaneously with both conscious and unconscious minds (Erickson & Rossi, 1976/1980). While the conscious mind is provided with one message (in the form of concepts, ideas, stories, images) which keeps it "occupied," another therapeutic message can be slipped to the unconscious mind via implication and connotation. Rossi notes that Erickson's interpersonal technique best illustrated the principle of two-level communication wherein specific, therapeutic suggestions are integrated within a larger context (a story, anecdote, joke, etc.). While the conscious mind is listening to the literal aspects of the anecdote, the carefully designed, interspersed suggestions are activating unconscious associations and shifting meanings which accumulate and finally "spill over" into consciousness (Erickson & Rossi, 1976/1980, p. 448):

> The conscious mind is surprised because it is presented with a response within itself that it cannot account for . . . Analogy and metaphor as well as jokes can be understood as exerting their powerful effects through the same mechanism of activating unconscious association patterns and response tendencies that suddenly summate to present consciousness with an apparently "new" datum of behavioral response.

This concept of metaphor as a type of two-level communication that can evoke new behavioral responses is well illustrated by Erickson's work with a man named Joe (Erickson, 1966/1980). After a vigorous and satisfying life with his own florist business, Joe suddenly found himself debilitated by terminal cancer. Unaccustomed to both pain and restrictions, Joe complained incessantly and battled against taking the disorienting medications prescribed for pain control. Aware that Joe disliked "even the mention of the word *hypnosis*," Erickson used a lengthy tomato plant metaphor as a vehicle for providing indirect and apparently nonhypnotic suggestions for hope, comfort, healing and happiness. Following is a brief excerpt (Erickson, 1966/1980, p. 271). [Italics are in the original and indicate interspersed suggestions]:

> Now as I talk, and I can do so *comfortably,* I wish that you will *listen to me comfortably* as I talk about a tomato plant. That is an odd thing to talk about. It makes one *curious. Why talk about a tomato plant?* One puts a tomato seed in the ground. One can *feel hope* that it will grow into a tomato plant that *will bring satisfaction* by the fruit it has. The seed soaks up water, *not very much difficulty* in doing that because of the rains that *bring peace and comfort* and the *joy* of growing to flowers and tomatoes. . . . Oh yes, Joe, I grew up on a farm, I think a tomato seed is a wonderful thing; *think, Joe, think* in that little seed there does *sleep so restfully, so comfortably,* a beautiful plant yet to be grown that will bear such interesting leaves and branches. The leaves, the branches look so beautiful, that beautiful rich color, *you can really feel happy* looking at a tomato seed, thinking about the wonderful plant it contains *asleep, resting, comfortably,* Joe.

Although Erickson was dealing with a fatal illness for which there was little realistic hope of cure, he did manage to achieve a significant degree of symptom amelioration. Despite the fact that the cancer continued to spread, Erickson's treatment helped relieve Joe's pain to such an extent that medications were no longer necessary. With his outlook much improved, Joe lived out his remaining months with a "vigor expressive of the manner in which he had lived his life and built his business."

While it cannot be "proven" that Erickson's tomato plant story "caused" Joe's improvement, it certainly appeared as though the metaphor had indeed activated "unconscious association patterns and response tendencies" that somehow "summated" to present Joe's consciousness with a new and better way of responding. The process might be depicted diagrammatically as follows:

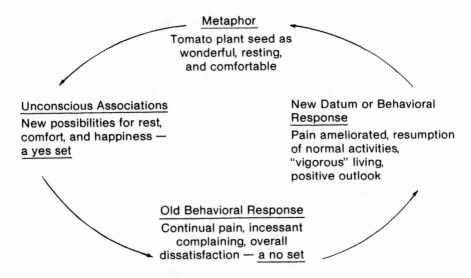

Figure 1: *Symptom Alteration via Metaphorical Intervention*

The input of the metaphor activates unconscious association patterns which interrupt the old behavioral response by generating new meanings, which in turn produce new behavioral responses.

Specifically in Joe's case, (1) the input of the tomato plant metaphor (2) activated unconscious association patterns of rest, comfort, and happiness which (3) interrupted Joe's old behavioral response pattern of pain, complaining, and dissatisfaction, eventually (4) summating in a new behavioral response of vigorous living and positive outlook. In diagramming this process, we have used a circular rather than linear representation to convey a sense of dynamic interaction. Certainly, change does not occur all at once, nor is the impact of the metaphor experienced all at once. Rather, a certain number of new meanings are generated, which in turn produce new behavioral responses—which in turn reinforce the metaphorical input to generate another series of new meanings. A cycle or circular flow of change is thus activated with a kind of built-in, self-generating feedback system.

BANDLER AND GRINDER

The last decade of Erickson's life was one of his most fertile teaching periods. Those who sought to learn his approaches were taught in many indirect ways that usually included elements of utilization, trance, and metaphor. Linguists Richard Bandler and John Grinder were among those who observed Erickson in his clinical work and from their observations developed a linguistically-oriented framework to explain how metaphor works (Bandler & Grinder, 1975).

In their formulation they propose that the metaphor operates on a kind of triadic principle by which its meaning moves through three different stages:

(1) The metaphor presents a *surface structure of meaning* in the actual words of the story,

(2) which activates an *associated deep structure* of meaning that is indirectly relevant to the listener,

(3) which activates a *recovered deep structure* of meaning that is directly relevant to the listener.

Arriving at Step 3 means that a *transderivational search* has been activated by which the listener relates the metaphor to himself: "Thus by a process of derivational search, the client generates the meaning which is maximally relevant for his ongoing experience (Bandler & Grinder, 1975, p. 22).

The widely acclaimed movie, *ET*, provides an example of this process. *ET* is a metaphor which evokes an entire spectrum of responses within audience members. One person watches with moist and watery eyes as ET and Elliott say farewell; another person sobs uncontrollably; others sit quietly, deep in thought; still others are unmoved. These differing responses to the same movie are a result of the differing levels of meaning evoked within each individual. These differing levels of meaning are experienced as viewers go on their own, unique *transderivational search*.

In the farewell scene of *ET*, a *surface structure of meaning* is presented to the viewer in the actual interactions between ET and Elliott as they say goodbye. This in turn activates an *associated deep structure of meaning* in the viewer which is generic or impersonal in nature. Thus the viewer may find himself pondering the sadness of partings between friends, or wondering what kinds of opportunities Elliott is passing up, or recalling another movie with a similar scene.

At some point, however, a more personally relevant connection will be made—the *recovered deep structure of meaning*—and the viewer may be reminded of the sadness he felt at his father's death, the sense of loss in the breakup of a marriage, or the poignancy of an unusually special friendship. It is, of course, this *recovered deep structure of meaning* which gives the metaphor (or movie) its potency. The storyline serves only as the visible bridge of connection between the listener and the message of the story. Without the invisible correlate of personal connection, the message will never make its way across the bridge. Once the personal connection occurs, however, an interactive loop is established between the story and the listener's inner world by which the story is enlivened and further extended. We could diagram this process in a way similar to Figure 1:

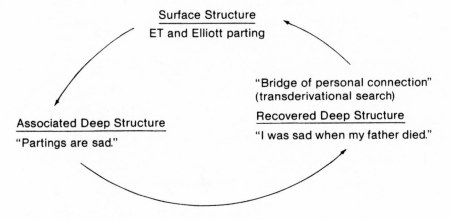

Figure 2: *Three-stage Process of Meaning in Metaphor*

The *surface structure* of the storyline in which ET and Elliott say farewell first activates an *associated deep structure of meaning* that is generic and impersonal, which in turn leads to the *recovered deep structure* of meaning that is specific and personal, which in turn provides a bridge of connection between the story and the viewer's private inner world.

If we were to integrate the main points of these various concepts on the nature of the metaphor, we could summarize that:

(1) Metaphor is a primary experience
               which
(2) is mediated by right-brain processes
               whereby

(3) unconscious association patterns summate to present consciousness with a new response
through
(4) a process of transderivational search.

Reviewing these theorists allows us to discover a common thread of
respect for the metaphor as a special and effective means of communicating. Jung's utilization of the symbol, Kopp's metaphorical view
of psychotherapy, Jaynes's theory of the mind as metaphor, Erickson's
transformation of simple, everyday experiences into therapeutic metaphors, Rossi's interest in discovering the linkage between symbolic
language, symptoms and therapeutic interventions, and Bandler and
Grinder's linguistic analysis of metaphor—all suggest that the metaphor
is a multifaceted approach which can be used in vastly different ways
toward the common goal of helping to expand human consciousness.

Metaphor and Physiology

Erickson and Rossi's theory regarding the possible connections between
metaphor, symptomatology and right-brain functioning seemed to turn
on an imaginative light for us. Finding out *why* metaphor is so powerful
and what happens on a physiological level led us to explore research
investigating the relationship between cerebral hemispheric activity and
symbolic or metaphorical language. To clarify the significance of this
possible relationship, it is first important to present a brief panorama
of recent history in brain research.

In the 1960s psychologist Roger Sperry and his colleagues Phillip
Vogel, Joseph Bogen, and Michael Gazzaniga were working together
investigating the relationship between the right and left hemispheres
of the brain. In his paper published in 1968, Sperry reported that
after Vogel and Bogen successfully performed an experimental and
unprecedented surgical procedure on Vogel's patients who suffered from
grand mal epileptic seizures,* Sperry and his colleagues discovered
unexpected alterations in their patients' behaviors which indicated that
the two hemispheres of the brain processed information in two fun-
damentally different ways (Sperry, 1968, p. 724):

---

* Vogel and Bogen devised the *commisorotomy,* a surgical procedure whereby the nerve
pathways of the *corpus callosum,* which connects the two hemispheres, are severed.

Instead of the normally unified single stream of consciousness, these patients behave in many ways as if they have two independent streams of conscious awareness, one in each hemisphere, each of which is cut off from and out-of-contact with the mental experiences of the other. In other words, each hemisphere seems to have its own separate and private sensations; its own perceptions; its own concepts; and its own impulses to act, with related volitional, cognitive, and learning experiences.

The significance of this discovery may well be lost on a generation accustomed to the idea of right- and left-brain differences. But until the split-brain discovery, it was assumed that both hemispheres functioned in an essentially similar, if not identical, manner.

The work of Sperry and his colleagues ignited research that has provided an increasingly complex profile of brain functioning. Within this profile are elements of *specialization* balanced by elements of *integration*. We now know that while each hemisphere of the brain has its own "style" of processing information (specialization), the hemispheres also function as a cooperative unit (integration). This is true even in the case of language, which was believed to be the private domain of the left hemisphere; research now indicates that *both* hemispheres interact synergistically in the intricate venture of language production and comprehension.

How each hemisphere processes language is the point at which brain research becomes excitingly relevant to an understanding and utilization of metaphorical communication. The left brain processes language sequentially, logically and literally, while the right brain processes it in a simultaneous, holistic and implicative fashion (Nebes, 1977). In other words, the left brain arranges all the individual puzzle pieces in the correct order, while the right brain perceives the total picture.

What does this have to do with metaphor? Since metaphor depends on *implication* rather than on *literal meanings,* it would seem likely that "more" right brain activity would be necessary to decode its meaning than would be involved in analytical, logical types of communication. Indeed, this has been demonstrated in two unrelated studies that investigated levels of left- and right-brain involvement in different types of language processing. Ornstein (1978) measured the brain-wave activity of medical students as they were performing various cognitive tasks. Highest *left*-hemispheric activity was recorded for the reading and writing of technical passages, while highest *right*-hemispheric activity was recorded for the reading of Sufi stories. The Sufi stories produced the same left-hemispheric activity as the technical *plus* a surge of involvement in the right hemisphere. Lamb (1980, p. 15) concludes:

> This is due to the fact that although the left hemisphere was still necessary to process the sequential coding of the printed word, right hemispheric involvement was necessary to generate the imagery and to process the metaphor in order to glean the meaning of the story.

Rogers and her colleagues (1977) compared the Hopi and English languages in terms of hemispheric activity. The same story translated into Hopi and English was played to bilingual Hopi elementary school children. EEG measurements were recorded. The results indicated that higher right-brain activity was involved in processing the story in Hopi than in its English version. The explanation for this difference was that Hopi is a far more *contextual* language than English. In Hopi, words do not have fixed meanings but are understood only in relation to the entire communication. This need for fluidity of *contextual understanding* is what produces greater right-brain involvement.

Pelletier (1978, p. 102) summarizes:

> Elements of these (right-brain) verbal constructions do not have *fixed definitions* but depend on *context* and can *shift meaning* when seen as parts of a new pattern. *[Italics added]*

Pelletier's concept of shifting meanings in right-brain processing coincides with what Kopp (1971) had termed the "multiple meanings [of metaphor] that may all co-exist," and with what Erickson and Rossi (1976/1980) termed the "two-level theory of communication."

While definitive conclusions cannot yet be drawn, initial research is confirming the intuitions of these theorists by paralleling the linguistic characteristics of metaphor with the physiological characteristic of right-brain functioning. Right-brain functioning is imagistic, implicative, contextual, and fluid; metaphor arises out of an interweaving of imagery and implication, the message of which can be gleaned only from a vantage point of context and shifting meanings. Indeed, metaphor appears to be *the* language of the right brain (Pelletier, 1978). If future research continues to affirm and refine what is being discovered, the precise patterns of hemispheric activity involved in processing differing types of language will provide us with a physiological basis for understanding and even quantifying the efficacy of metaphorical communication.

2

Metaphor in Child Therapy

In our real world, we perceive a horse as just a horse. Yet in the world of fantasy and mythology, with added wings, the horse becomes a Pegasus which can transport the beholder to all parts of the world in unlimited ways.

Contacting the Child Within

For those of us who work with children, "Return to the beginning, become a child again" can truly be a helpful passage to remember. We have found it invaluable to return to our own *child within* by recapturing pleasant memories and playful fantasies, or by observing children playing at parks, beaches, and schoolyards. This enables us to revivify those remembered or observed spontaneous moments and utilize them later as important therapeutic tools.

Volumes of material are available on the theory of what contributes to an effective therapeutic relationship with children (Axline, 1969; Freud, 1946; Gardner, 1971; Gardner & Olness, 1981; Oaklander, 1978; Russo, 1964). There is general agreement on the need for providing a safe environment in which the qualities of rapport, respect, and cooperation can be fostered. For us, *contacting the child within* is the pivotal element in building these many dimensions of the therapeutic relationship. Indeed it may even be the single most critical element in ultimately reaching the child. At times we as therapists have found that our own limitations and feelings of frustrations have occurred

27

when we momentarily forgot to allow ourselves to "enter the world of the child within."

Through a Child's Eyes

A colleague of mine called one day and asked if I would be able to see a client of his immediately—a mother with her four-year-old son, Mark. My colleague explained that Mark had been repeatedly sexually abused by his father, as reported by the mother. The mother was currently involved in a custody battle, trying to convince the courts of the father's abusive behavior. The child had been questioned and tested by many court-appointed therapists over the last few months. However, the process of decision-making was still in abeyance. In the meantime Mark's behavior and emotional status continued to deteriorate rapidly. The mother reported that he was awakening in the middle of the night with uncontrollable screams, and that he was extremely fearful during the day, manifesting numerous tearful outbursts.

I agreed to see the child and his mother the following morning. When this lovely mother walked into my office, she was carrying an entire armload of files and case material already amassed on her young son. Mark, a small, ash-blond boy with bright blue eyes and a hesitant smile, held onto the pocket of his mother's jeans with his tiny hand. Although the mother looked overwhelmed with emotion and distress, she bravely sat down on the couch and began ruffling through her files as efficiently as she could. Mark sat close to her, his fingers still looped through one of her pockets. I noticed his eyes scanning the many shelves of toys, games, stuffed animals, puppets, pictures, and drawing materials that were all around him.

Did I want to read the previous therapist's report first? Or did I want to glance through the extensive court report? For the first several minutes of this encounter I followed along with the mother's wishes, all the while peripherally observing little Mark. I glanced through the therapist's file, letting my eyes scan the key words. It seemed that there were endless psychodynamic explanations for what had occurred between the father and his child. I flipped through hefty court proceedings, and again a blur of suggestions and recommendations presented themselves. An inner awareness of feeling uncomfortable and distracted began to emerge in me. It felt as if 5,000 facts were all jumping up and down in the room, vying for my attention. The more "information" I took in, the further removed from the child I felt.

Meanwhile this little four-year-old boy before me, whom this barrage of information concerned, was sitting silently and sadly next to his mother. He moved very little, but his eyes continued to wander curiously about the room. Even though my review of the "pertinent information" was occurring within a short time-period of the session, I realized nonetheless that I could no longer continue in this manner. I became quickly aware that I had allowed this seemingly relevant material to interfere with the most essential element in the treatment of this child: making contact with Mark in *his own world*.

I put all the materials aside, explaining to the mother that it was important for me to just play with Mark for awhile so that we could get to know each other. I then went over to Mark, took his hand in mine, and with an uplifting tone in my voice said, "I've noticed you've been looking around this room, and I'll bet you'd like to get an even closer look." His eyes brightened as he nodded yes and began to move off the couch. As this shift took place, I noticed that my sense of discomfort and disconnection began to lessen.

As Mark looked around the room, I crouched down next to him and tried to look around the room through his eyes, not through the eyes of an adult therapist. I repeated the words he used to describe the toys and the games he saw. I also matched his childlike tonality and pronunciations, not only for the sake of making it sound like I was talking his language, but more for myself—to feel how my own four-year-old child within would feel being in yet another office with another therapist after such traumatic life experiences.

As therapists, we are trained to be concerned with such issues as objectivity and transference. However, we cannot really be objective about something until we know what it is the person is experiencing. This child had been objectively assessed to the point of accruing a combined psychological and court file that nearly outweighed him! Clearly there was an abundance of objectivity present in this case. Therefore, I felt strongly that it was vital for me to do just the opposite—to put aside temporarily all objectivity and really identify with Mark by allowing myself to feel my own child within. I knew I had to sense some of Mark's world before all the objective information would have any helpful meaning to me in terms of intervening.

Although Mark had been described by previous therapists as extremely reticent and unresponsive, in this first session he was able to begin giving expression to the many struggles in his life via artwork and storytelling. This occurred only after we had spent some thirty minutes mutually exploring the room and getting to know each other in the special way that only "children" can.

There are also times when we have searched for ways to help parents suspend their adult viewpoints in favor of the very real world of their child's problem. This suspension automatically requires parents to make at least a minimal connection to their own child within, for by agreeing to see the situation from their child's point of view they are actually seeing it from behind the lens of their own childhood life experiences. From this vantage point two important gains occur: (1) they can feel a greater empathy for what their own child is experiencing, and (2) they are simultaneously accessing a potential wealth of resources learned decades ago but not normally available to them from their adult perspectives.

The Monsters and the Cupcake

Daniele was a delightful eight-year-old girl who came to therapy with her mother for numerous complaints, including nervousness and chronic sleeping problems. For several years, Daniele had been afraid to go to sleep at night because she believed there were monsters in her bedroom. Her mother had rationally explained that monsters do not exist and that there was nothing to fear, but Daniele insisted that they did exist and tried desperately to convince her mother of this "fact." Daniele's initial fear of the monsters crystallized even more adversely when she was unable to convince anyone of their reality to her.

During the first session, I inquired about the monsters and learned what they looked like, if they made noise, if they made physical contact with the little girl, and so forth. Daniele became animated and excited as she responded to questions which acknowledged the reality of her world. Her mother appeared perplexed while Daniele and I interacted. She called me aside to tell me that she was irritated by my supporting Daniele's belief in monsters when she had spent painstaking years trying to dismiss such ideas in her child. I told the mother that before she could direct Daniele toward her way of thinking, she first needed to enter Daniele's reality, acknowledge her fears, and *then* lead her to other choices. I suggested that she herself just pretend she was an eight-year-old child terrified by monsters, and that she might learn something important as I continued working with Daniele. In the remaining time a metaphor was created which reframed Daniele's monsters and allowed her to create solutions that deflated her fears.

Daniele shook her head no when I asked if she had ever heard the "Untold Story of the Monsters and the Cupcake." Looking at her mother, I asked, "And you?" I received a shrug of her shoulders and a reply, "No."

Daniele was then told how monsters were really make-believe disguises for unhappy children who had no friends. Originally, these unhappy children, now disguised as monsters, tried to make friends in many ways, but the other children ignored them. Nobody would ever pay them the attention they truly wanted. The children became so sad that they just went off by themselves and felt bad. Then one day they finally figured out that they needed to create lots of attention in order to get the other children to like them. So they dressed up in a strange, strange fashion and behaved in a strange, strange way. They returned to the other children expecting to be greeted as friends. Instead the other children ran away scared and frightened, thinking that they had just seen monsters!

Now the unhappy children in the monster costumes were very confused and even frightened themselves. Since Daniele had seen the movie *ET,* she was asked at this time to remember how frightened Elliott and ET were when they first met in Elliott's backyard, and how Elliott had given ET a gift to become friends. "Reeses Pieces!" proudly interjected Daniele. "Yes, that's right," the therapist acknowledged enthusiastically. "Now, Daniele, I would like you to go home and give your monsters a gift that will change them into being friendly."

It was about this time that Daniele excused herself to go to the bathroom. Her mother looked at me with a smile on her face and commented, "You know, I could visualize everything you were saying and it made sense in some sort of crazy way. I had forgotten how I used to listen to stories on the radio when I was young and how I would imagine all sorts of exciting things. Thanks for reminding me."

The next week her mother reported that Daniele had made a cupcake especially for the monsters and had put it in front of the bedroom closet door where the monsters "lived." With one night's exception, Daniele slept soundly all that week.

During the course of the next three weeks, Daniele occasionally regressed into her fears before going to bed at night. It was her mother who then reminded Daniele about the cupcake, Elliott and ET, and Reeses Pieces. To her delight, Daniele's mother found herself becoming a storyteller lulling her daughter into sleep.

JUNG AND THE CHILD WITHIN

In his autobiographical book, *Memories, Dreams & Reflections,* Jung (1961) beautifully recalls his unexpected encounter with his own child within and the oddly enduring impact it had on his life. The chapter entitled "Confrontation with the Unconscious" describes a series of dreams which had left Jung feeling disoriented and "under constant inner pressure." So intense was his emotional disquiet that he suspected he had a "psychic disturbance." In the hope of finding the root cause of the problem, he began to search through his childhood memories. The search, however, led him only to an acknowledgment of his own ignorance and to a resolve to "simply do whatever occurs to me." The result was an activation of a vivid and moving image which became a memorable turning point in his life (Jung, 1961, pp. 173–174):

> The first thing that came to the surface was a childhood memory from perhaps my tenth or eleventh year. At that time I had had a spell of playing passionately with building blocks. I distinctly recalled how I had built little houses and castles, using bottles to form the sides of gates and vaults. Somewhat later I had used ordinary stones, with mud for mortar. These structures had fascinated me for a long time. To my astonishment, this memory was accompanied by a good deal of emotion. "Aha," I said to myself, "there is still life in these things. The small boy is still around, and possesses a creative life which I lack. But how can I make my way to it?" For as a grown man it seemed impossible to me that I should be able to bridge the distance from the present back to my eleventh year. Yet if I wanted to reestablish contact with that period, I had no choice but to return to it and take up once more that child's life with his childish games. This

moment was a turning point in my fate, but I gave in only after endless resistance and with a sense of resignation. For it was a painfully humiliating experience to realize that there was nothing to be done except play childish games.

Jung indeed "gave in" and began collecting the stones and materials needed to sculpt and build his creation—an entire village complete with castle and church. He worked on his "building game" without fail everyday after lunch, and then again in the evenings after his last session. Although he continued to question what he was doing and why he was doing it, he also simply trusted the yearning and proceeded on a vague inner sense of value (Jung, 1961, pp. 174–175):

> In the course of this activity my thoughts clarified, and I was able to grasp the fantasies whose presence in myself I dimly felt. Naturally, I thought about the significance of what I was doing, and asked myself, "Now, really, what are you about? You are building a small town, and doing it as if it were a rite!" *I had no answer to my question, only the inner certainty that I was on the way to discovering my own myth. For the building game was only a beginning.* [Italics added]

Jung's contact with his own inner child played a crucial part in releasing the extraordinary creative energies that culminated in his theory of the archetypes and the collective unconscious.

As mentioned previously, Jung described many different archetypal figures—mother, father, child, hero, villain, temptress, trickster, and so forth. Pertinent to this chapter is his lucid discussion of the unique importance of the child archetype—the child within—in a chapter entitled, "The Psychology of the Child Archetype" (Jung, 1949/ 1958).* For Jung the child archetype was a living symbol of future potentialities that brings balance, unity, and vitality to the conscious personality. Through the inner child, opposite qualities within the personality are synthesized and new possibilities are freed (Jung, 1958, pp. 125–128):

---

* This chapter is also included in Part I of Vol. IX of Jung's *Collected Works* (v. Jung, 1959).

The child-motif represents not only something that existed in the distant past but also something that exists *now;* that is to say, it is not just a vestige but a system functioning in the present. . . . The "child" paves the way for a future change of personality. In the individuation process, it anticipates the figure that comes from the synthesis of conscious and unconscious elements in the personality. It is therefore a *unifying symbol* which unites the opposites.

In another chapter entitled, "The Special Phenomenology of the Child Archetype," Jung states even more strongly (Jung, 1958, pp. 135–136):

It [the child-motif] is a personification of vital forces quite outside the limited range of our conscious mind; of ways and possibilities of which our one-sided conscious mind knows nothing. . . . It represents the strongest most ineluctable urge in every being, namely the urge to realize itself.

For Jung the child archetype was far more than a concept or a theory. It was a living force that helped to guide and sustain his adult personality. Indeed he continued to draw upon his special contact with the inner child as builder at difficult times throughout his personal and professional life.

ERICKSON AND THE CHILD WITHIN

Erickson also had a natural respect for childhood qualities, probably borne out of the mischievous and playful characteristics of his own adult personality. One delightful story well illustrates his willingness (albeit unconscious) to contact his inner child in order to help him solve an "adult" problem (Rossi & Ryan, 1985, p. 51):

There was a chapter that I just couldn't write for a certain paper. I couldn't figure out how to portray the illogic of one of my patients. I went into a trance wondering if I'd work on that case or another case, and I found out later that I had spent the time reading a whole bunch of comic books. I had used up the entire time reading a bunch of comic books.

The next opportunity I got to work on the paper, I was perfectly content to do it in a waking state. I came to the difficult section I hadn't been able to portray, and, that's right, Huey, Dewey, Louie, and Donald Duck had paraphrased that very situation, that particular type of logic! My unconscious mind had sent me to the box of comic books and had me search through them until I had found the exact paraphrasing that I had wanted to use.

Erickson tells yet another charming story that again demonstrates his connection to his own child within. A two-year-old child was waiting with her mother in an airport. Erickson was also waiting for a flight, and to occupy his time he engaged in his favorite pastime of observing human behavior. The little girl was restless and the mother was tired. The child spotted a toy in a nearby counter and quickly glanced back at the mother, who was absorbed in reading a newspaper. Methodically and repetitiously the child interrupted the mother by jumping up and down and racing about. Finally the exasperated mother got up to give the child some exercise, and, of course, the child led the mother straight to the toy counter. Without uttering a single verbal request, the child had managed to get exactly what she wanted. Erickson provides an appreciative summary which reflects his perception and respect of the world as viewed through the eyes of a child (Rossi & Ryan, 1985, p. 65):

And so that two-year-old, with all the wisdom of its infancy uncomplicated by the false learnings that society and convention force upon us reacted to its own understanding: "I want that toy; Mother often says no; maybe the best thing to do is to annoy her and give her a chance to quiet me down." I don't think the child thought all that out very clearly, but I watched the entire episode wondering just exactly how that child was going to get the toy. I thought—but then I'm an adult—that the child would simply take mother and lead her right over. But the child was a lot brighter than I was—she knew the right technique!

We as therapists can learn from the personal experiences of both Jung and Erickson who, in their individual ways, sustained a nourishing and creatively rejuvenating contact with their own child within. How each of us achieves this contact will be as varied and different as archetypes and comic books. The important element is not how the contact is manifested—in Jung's case via the building of a miniature city; in Erickson's case via the reading of comic books—but in how real and genuine the contact feels. For one person the child within may be lighthearted and capricious; for another it may be sensitive and perceptive; for another, openhearted and naive. Whatever the qualities, the adult therapist brings back from this special contact a perspective that adds an unequalled dimension of compassion and understanding to the child in therapy.

The Importance of Fantasy

One day at the beach I found myself watching a delightful little boy who had a severe neurophysiological impairment. I overheard him telling his father that the large rocks along the shoreline were really treasure chests filled with all kinds of hidden treasures. As he spoke, he pointed toward the rocks with his small, shaking arm. His eyes sparkled and the smile on his face spoke of a private pleasure—more, a private knowledge—that I could not help but envy.

Fantasy is the inner world of the child. It is also the natural, innate process through which the child learns to make sense of the world outside himself. Indeed fantasy is viewed by some as a genetic, biological function with a time clock of emergence that is necessary for healthy child development (Pearce, 1977). Pearce points out that there are two different types of play that are manifested by the healthy, growing child. One is imitative play, as when the child plays "Follow the Leader," and the other is "fantasy play" or "symbolic play," as when an object is turned into something different from its outer reality. For example, a large empty box in an attic becomes a fort, a castle, a boat; a saltshaker in a restaurant is turned into a racing car, a space missile, a submarine. In other words, the delimited reality of the box or the saltshaker becomes the unlimited springboard for imaginative fantasy and metaphor. This type of "child-created metaphor" appears to be one thread in the fabric of the child's inner learning process. The child turns what is learned into a spontaneous game or story, which in turn facilitates the integration of what is learned.

Dancing Shoes

When I arrived at the home of a Feldenkrais therapist for treatment of a back problem, her two-and-a-half-year-old daughter, Katie, was also present. Shy of strangers, Katie sat quietly on the couch, carefully tearing a piece of paper into small bits. Looking at a piece she had torn off, I inquired if it was a gift for me. Then, I reached out and she handed me the paper. I thanked her for her gift and put it in my pocket to protect it.

Toward the end of my session, I noticed through half-opened eyes that Katie and a twelve-year-old friend were watching their mother working on me. Without looking in their direction, I waved in a childlike fashion. When I finally opened my eyes and sat up straight, Katie and her friend were sitting quietly across from me. I smiled. Since my session had focused on balancing, Katie's mother now instructed me to walk slowly across the living room with my eyes closed. All the while Katie was observing. When I had finished, I thanked Katie again for the gift of the piece of paper and, for no conscious reason on my part, brought her attention to my shoes which I named "Dancing Shoes." I proceeded to move my feet quickly in place, spoofing a tap dance. I stopped and Katie smiled and giggled at me.

I commented, "All you have to do is tell my shoes to dance and they will do so."

I moved my feet quickly in place again. Then I suggested that she could request her shoes to become "Dancing Shoes" by telling them simply to "Dance." Katie did so, and began to shuffle and move her feet the way I had done. She giggled with the delight of her new found ability. I let her continue to make my shoes dance as I left her house and went down the stairs to my car.

The next week her mother reported that Katie, usually shy and quiet, had been dancing and showing everybody *her* "Dancing Shoes."

THEORIES OF FANTASY

There are many theories regarding the dynamics involved in the creative process of play and fantasy. Not surprisingly, some of these theories view fantasy negatively while others support its value and utility as a developmental and therapeutical tool.

Freud (1962) believed that fantasy developed out of deprivation and therefore expressed a need for wish fulfillment. As in the dream state, fantasy for Freud functioned primarily as a compensatory mechanism to help fill a gap or reverse a wrong. Bettelheim (1975) has added to the basic Freudian view by noting the critical developmental functions served by fantasy: Amidst the powerlessness and dependency of childhood, fantasy kindles hope and rescues the child from the despair of his failures. Furthermore, it can help the child deal with and "transcend" the emotional and psychological issues characteristic of the several Freudian stages of development.

Montessori (1914) took a surprisingly dim view of fantasy, considering it to be "a somewhat unfortunate pathological tendency of early childhood" that encourages "defects of character" (Gross & Gross, 1965). Piaget, on the other hand, believed that fantasy played an extremely important role in the cognitive and sensory-motor development of the child (1951). Symbolic games such as building a sandcastle or racing saltshaker cars could be seen as a means of improving motor performance and developing cognitive-spatial awareness. Piaget carefully noted and utilized the developmental phases of imaginative play in his work with children.

More recent investigators have noted that fantasy can function in both compensatory *and* creative modalities: Children can use fantasy as a way of changing unpleasant situations or gratifying unmet needs, and they also can use it as a means of developing purely creative capacities (Hilgard, 1970; Olness, 1978).

In direct opposition to the view that fantasy has a pathological influence on children is the view that its absence may be the real problem. Gardner and Olness (1981) speculate that our devaluation of fantasy in Western culture might contribute to the conflicts that emerge during adolescence.

Axline (1955) stresses the need for the therapist to be open to the free flight of a child's fantasy play "without ordering it into meaningfulness." She points out that what is meaningful and therapeutic for the child may be viewed as insignificant from the adult's point of view.

Providing a personal illustration of the value of fantasy, Oaklander (1978) recounts her own childhood experience of surviving the ordeal of a burn trauma by immersing herself in fantasy. Fantasy plays a central role in her work with children because of its important and diversified uses, both as a source of fun and as a mirror of the child's inner life process. Hidden fears can be expressed, unspoken desires depicted, and problems acted out, all through fantasy.

Erickson (1954a/1980) makes an interesting and useful differentiation between conscious and unconscious fantasy. *Conscious fantasy* is a simple form of wish fulfillment: We see ourselves performing great deeds or creating great masterpieces which we are in no way equipped to accomplish. *Unconscious fantasies,* however, are communications of actual potentiality from the unconscious mind; they are harbingers of what could be accomplished if the conscious mind gives agreement. "Unconscious fantasies . . . are psychological constructs in various degrees of formulation, for which the unconscious stands ready, or is actually awaiting an opportunity, to make a part of reality" (Erickson, 1954a/1980, p. 421).

The little handicapped boy on the beach mentioned at the beginning of this section knew that the rocks were really rocks; yet his unconscious mind wisely allowed the fantasy of hidden treasures to communicate an important metaphorical message about the child's own hidden abilities.

To a little child, the word *block* can evoke images of wonderful tools for building and exploring the world. Presenting the same word to an adult, however, would typically evoke images of obstacles. Children are able to turn simple wooden blocks into cities, buildings, cars, trains, airplanes. What does the child know about learning that we as adults often forget? Could it be the natural ability to use whatever is available—an image, an object, a sound, a texture—to create a wonderful experience of self-discovery?

Researching the Use of Metaphor in Child Therapy

In a framework as natural to the child as Saturday morning cartoons, the therapeutic metaphor safeguards its true purpose within the matrices of the story. The child is aware only of the actions and events being described to him. He does not look for hidden meanings, even as those hidden meanings are being communicated. While it is safe to assume that children will enjoy listening to therapeutic metaphors, is there any experimental evidence of effectiveness?

The last decade has witnessed a proliferation of research exploring the therapeutic use of metaphor and storytelling with both children and adults. In our overview of the literature dealing with children and adolescents, we located a wide variety of applications in which metaphor and storytelling served as either a primary or ancillary teatment modality. Following is a summary of these applications:

— Abusive parent (Lankton & Lankton, 1983)
— Bedwetting (Crowley & Mills, 1986; Elkins & Carter, 1981; Rogers, 1983)
— Classroom applications (Nickerson, 1973)
— Family therapy (Brink, 1982; Rule, 1983)
— Foster placement situations (Kagan, 1982)
— Hospitalization settings (Bassin, Wolfe & Thier, 1983; Becker, 1972; Schooley, 1976)
— Learning, behavior, and emotional problems (Allan, 1978; Arnott & Gushin, 1976; Elkins & Carter, 1981; Gardner, 1970, 1972a,b; Stirtzinger, 1983)
— Minimally brain-damaged children (Gardner, 1974, 1975)
— Oedipal problems (Gardner, 1968)
— Retarded children and adults (Hariman, 1980; Wildgen, 1975)
— School phobias (Elkins & Carter, 1981)
— Self-concept enhancement (Burnett, 1983)
— Sleep disorders (Levine, 1980)
— Thumbsucking (Lowitz & Suib, 1978)

In all of these reports, the use of metaphor was viewed as a successful communication tool that appeared to mediate therapeutic change in a pleasant and imaginative way.

Interesting studies utilizing metaphorical intervention with adults, couples, and groups were also reported (Adams & Chadbourne, 1982; Amira, 1982; Condon, 1983; Crowley & Mills, 1984b; Gindhart, 1981; Goldstein, 1983; Hoffman, 1983; Katz, 1983; Lankton & Lankton, 1983; Mazor, 1982; Naso, 1982; O'Connell, 1979; Papp, 1982; Pardee, 1984).

Several different strategies for creating the metaphors and stories reported in the literature were described. These strategies included eliciting the story from the child's own imagination (Bassin, Wolfe & Thier, 1983; Allan, 1978), or altering and retelling the elicited story as in Gardner's "Mutual Storytelling Technique" (Gardner, 1972a, 1972b, 1974, 1975). Standardized stories (Rogers, 1983) utilizing preordained themes from folktales (Brink, 1982), animal lore (Brink, 1982), and science fiction settings (Elkins & Carter, 1981) have been used; and "personalized fairy tales" paralleling psychodynamic factors and utilizing the child's favored activities and objects were reported (Levine, 1980). We will now describe several of these storytelling strategies in greater detail to highlight the scope of approaches to metaphor creation that exists in the literature.

Brink (1982) used metaphorical intervention as a conjunctive technique in family therapy situations, telling stories to the families at unexpected times during the session. The stories were based on either European-American folktales or Native-American folktales. He presented five cases in his report which were representative of similar work he had carried out with 23 other families. In all five cases, important positive changes occurred with varying degrees of endurance. Although it was difficult to separate the effects of the stories from the total therapeutic process, Brink speculated that certain changes appeared to be linked to the stories. In conclusion, he suggested that "metaphors can be used within the family therapy to provide insights and suggestions to the family in an indirect manner, one that avoids or overcomes the resistance of the family in dealing with fear of change" (p. 264).

Elkins and Carter (1981) used science-fiction based imagery as the primary treatment technique for children and adolescents between the ages of six and thirteen. In this approach the child is invited to go for a ride on a spaceship and take a science-fiction adventure "in his imagination." In the course of the space travel, the child encounters those characters and events which are needed to help resolve his problem. The authors reported (pp. 275–276):

> Preliminary trials with the "science fiction technique" have proven it to be an effective means of trance induction and treatment. The authors have employed the technique with satisfactory resolution of problems in eight out of ten cases of school phobia, five out of six cases of adverse chemotherapy reactions (i.e., nausea, pain and anxiety) in children, one case of fear of swallowing and choking in an anorexic adolescent female, three cases of secondary enuresis, and as an adjunct treatment of two cases of excessive motor activity associated with hyperactivity syndrome.

An obvious limitation of this technique (which the authors acknowledged in their discussion) is its reliance upon the singular theme of space travel, which may be frightening or of no interest to many children.

Levine (1980) reported the use of audio cassette recordings of personalized fairy tales in the treatment of two cases of childhood insomnia. The audiotapes were played at bedtime for six consecutive nights, producing successful results in both cases. The eight-year-old child responded positively to going to bed and falling asleep after only four nights of the audiotape, and seemed to be "more spontaneous and relaxed" during the day. The three-year-old responded positively after six nights of listening to her audiotape, often playing the story three or four times a night. The authors concluded that "these initial case studies seem to demonstrate the efficacy of treating childhood insomnia through the hypnotic suggestions of a personalized fairy tale" (p. 62).

Two techniques reported by different researchers came the closest to our approach; therefore we will describe them in greater detail.

Recognizing the enjoyment children experience in both telling and listening to stories, Gardner (1970, 1971) developed the Mutual Storytelling Technique as a means of utilizing storytelling therapeutically. In this method Gardner begins by using a predetermined introduction such as, "Good morning boys and girls, I'd like to welcome you once again to Dr. Gardner's Make-Up-A-Story Television Program." This is followed by an array of instructions to the child in regard to the story he is going to create. Gardner tells the child that the story: 1) should have adventure and excitement; 2) should not be about things on television or in movies, or actually experienced by the child; 3) should have a beginning, middle and end; and 4) should have a moral.

After being given these instructions, the child creates a story which the therapist "probes (for) psychodynamic meaning." The therapist then creates another story using the same characters and setting as created by the child but introducing "healthier adaptions" than those described by the child.

In our early work with children, we made use of Gardner's technique and definitely found it helpful. However, as our own individualities developed, we gradually shifted our focus off psychodynamic meanings and onto the behavioral subtleties actually taking place within the session. We then used these behavioral subtleties to create original metaphors that utilized a three-level communication process incorporating interspersed suggestions and a process of "sensory interweaving" into an engaging storyline (see Chapter 4).

Robertson & Barford (1970) reported the use of daily storytelling in the case of a chronically ill six-year-old boy. The child had experienced traumatic physical and psychological reactions after being separated from a respirator to which he had been attached for a year.

The stories were written specifically for the child and incorporated his perspectives as well as the medical team's procedures and goals. The authors recognized the needs of the child and utilized the therapist's empathy as a "basis for going into the child's world by means of stories." In the stories, a direct connection between storyline, character, and problem was made. For example, the child's name was Bob and the main character's name was also Bob. "Bob" went through the same procedures as the child, but with the added assistance of colorful characters, such as a friendly Green Dragon no bigger than a hand.

While Robertson and Barford reported the successful outcome of their storytelling treatment approach with this particular patient, we would like to offer variations of the procedure which would nudge it into a more indirect, metaphorical framework. For example, we would suggest using an entirely different name for the main character and changing the storyline so that it does not depict the actual, concrete events in the child's life. In essence, Robertson and Barford have *transposed* the actual problem situation into a storytelling format. We have found that *paralleling* the situation with less closely related metaphors is more effective because it facilitates dissociation from the problem area, which in turn enhances the child's ability to respond without the interference of conscious mental sets (Erickson & Rossi, 1979). This also brings the *story process* rather than its *content* into focus.

The Little Whale

When working with Megan, a little girl of seven who was experiencing difficulty with her breathing because of asthma attacks, the therapist told a story of a little whale who was having problems getting water through her spout. The whale was chosen as the metaphor because in previous sessions the child had described how much she loved seeing the dolphins and whales at Sea World. The story began by describing a little whale who used to play and romp about in the ocean so easily (reminding her of pleasant past memories). Then it seemed the little whale began experiencing difficulty with her spout—something would get stuck every time she tried to spout her water. Now an older whale was introduced who knew a lot about spouts and other wonderful things. For example, the older whale reminded the little whale of all the other times she had learned how to master something difficult. At times it is difficult to see in the water because of cloudiness, which makes it much harder to find food. Yet, the older whale pointed out, the little whale had learned to use her other senses to help guide her toward the food until the water became clear again. The story continued with the older whale reminding the little whale of all the abilities and resources she could use to help her learn how to use her spout.

Megan's breathing was still asthmatic by the end of the story. However, she was now sitting quietly on her mother's lap, smiling broadly. She said that she felt better.

The next day I phoned the mother to see how Megan was feeling. She reported that Megan had slept all night with only minor sleep interruptions. In a two-week follow-up session, Megan reported that she was feeling fine.

At a six-week follow-up, the mother said that Megan's attacks which were usually severe at that time of the year, requiring intermittent trips to the hospital, had now diminished to such a degree that only a mild medication, administered at home, was required.

Was it the metaphor that helped Megan? At the time I told the story I had my doubts. Yet Megan's reports of feeling better and her mother's reports of significant change seemed to indicate that indeed the story of the Little Whale had played an integral part in her improvement.

The Utilization Approach to Symptomatology

Erickson pioneered an approach of "utilization" whereby patients' presenting symptoms were accepted and incorporated into the treatment strategy. We have found the relationship between utilization and metaphor to be a vital and complementary one: An effective therapeutic metaphor must be crafted out of the many types of information and behavior presented, both consciously and unconsciously, by the child.

Since symptoms of one kind or another are usually the focus of therapy, it is important for therapists to clarify for themselves how they view symptomatology. Four major positions regarding the origin and treatment of symptoms now seem to dominate the field.

One theory is that symptoms are manifestations of traumatic past experiences, usually from infancy and early childhood, that can be resolved only by returning to the original cause. This return journey can be primarily cognitive and analytical in nature (the psychoanalytic approach), or its main thrust can be intensely emotional (Primal Therapy, Bioenergetics, Reichian Therapy). In either case, *connection to the original cause* is considered the pivotal agent of cure.

The second major position views symptoms as a result of faulty learning (conditioning) experiences, both past and present. The focus of treatment is on the present and revolves around *structuring cognitive experiences of relearning* (behavior modification, cognitive restructuring, reconditioning, repatterning). In this approach the concept of an original cause underlying symptomatology is viewed as irrelevant.

The third position takes a psychoneurophysiological view of symptoms by considering both their behavioral and organic components. In this framework, genetic and biochemical factors together with environmental influences are considered in determining the etiology of symptoms. Treatment approaches usually incorporate biochemical intervention.

The fourth position views the symptom as a message or "gift" (Ritterman, 1983) from the unconscious that can be utilized toward its own resolution, regardless of past causes. Erickson pioneered the basic premises of this fourth position with his multifaceted *utilization approaches* to hypnotherapy (see, in particular, Volumes I and IV of Erickson, 1980e; Erickson & Rossi, 1979). He was emphatic about the importance of relieving the symptom before any other psychodynamic factors were explored: "As a psychiatrist I do not think there is much to be gained from analyzing the underlying cause before you correct the symptomatic manifestation" (Rossi & Ryan, 1985, p. 168). After the symptom has been ameliorated, past causes can be sought when appropriate.

Utilizing the presenting symptom means that all approaches are pertinent, depending on the unique elements in each clinical situation. One patient might require a strongly cognitive intervention; another, a strongly cathartic experience; still another, a straightforward behavior modification technique. It is the patient's needs and symptomatology that determine the type of intervention, and an *ambience of utilization* that guides in the specific application.

The Storm

As a cotherapist I once worked with a couple who had each been married previously. They now had two babies from their current marriage. In addition, the husband had two teenage children from his previous marriage, Luke and Carolyn, who lived with their natural mother. When the mother's boyfriend seriously abused Carolyn, however, both children were sent to live with their father and his new wife.

Because Luke and Carolyn had many behavioral problems, there was a marked disruption in this new family. The father and stepmother initiated therapy because they were having difficulty deciding if they wanted to keep the older children, return them to the natural mother, or place them in a foster home.

During the session, the teenagers maintained their disruptive profile by bouncing from couch to couch, joking, throwing pillows, and interrupting with random questions and comments. The couple commented that this behavior was typical at home and upset their entire household. Meanwhile, the toddler was playing in the middle of the room with the other therapist, and the mother was holding the infant who was squirming restlessly in her arms. In total, the session included two therapists, an infant, a toddler, two teenagers, a father, and a mother/stepmother. Without some kind of cohesiveness, nothing but chaos and frustration would result.

At that point, as I watched the teenagers disrupting the session with such enthusiasm and skill, I realized that I had to get their cooperation in order to proceed in a therapeutic direction. Therefore, I directly asked them if what their parents had just said was true. They looked at each other with a mischievous glint in their eyes and replied, "Yeah!" Having interrupted their antics with my direct question, I now had their attention and decided to simply utilize their ongoing behavior as the background structure for a brief metaphor. I then began to talk about a recent storm that had hit Los Angeles. While the other therapist played with the toddler, I asked the kids if they remembered it and they nodded yes. I then continued in a slow, rhythmic voice, emphasizing the interspersed suggestions as I proceeded.

I talked about how the weather here had been calm for several months and then how the storm had hit us unexpectedly. I described lying in bed and hearing the crackling thunder and looking up to see the great flashes of lightning. I mentioned that no matter how old or young you were, you couldn't help but feel that the storm was out of control. I reminded them how the storm had knocked over trees and electrical poles, causing a great deal of disturbance in the community. The community knew it could not sustain any more major storms at this time. How difficult it was to rebuild anything until the storm finally stopped long enough for each worker to do his job! The residents certainly did not want to be flooded out of their homes into the unknown. They knew that everybody needed to calm down and do their job in their own way.

I spent about seven minutes developing this metaphor. At its end, the teenagers were sitting quietly, with a thoughtful expression on their faces. It seemed that the metaphor had helped to settle the session, as well as to activate an awareness of the important issues waiting to be addressed.

ERICKSON'S UTILIZATION APPROACH WITH CHILDREN

Erickson's case reports are replete with ingenious paradigms of utilizing the presenting symptom. For example, his charming utilization of thumbsucking behavior toward its own undoing illustrates how the utilization approach to symptomatology is both a *philosophy* and a *technique*. It is a philosophy of acceptance and validation, and it is a technique of delightfully credible alterations in how the problem is viewed. Working with a six-year-old child whose parents had brought him in for treatment because of a serious thumbsucking problem, Erickson begins by according the child the same degree of respect and self-responsibility he would an adult (Rossi, Ryan & Sharp, 1983, p. 263):

> Now let us get one thing straight. That left thumb of yours is your thumb; that mouth of yours is your mouth; those front teeth of yours are your front teeth. I think you are entitled to do anything you want to with your thumb, with your mouth, and with your teeth.

Having laid this foundation, he then proceeds to utilize the thumb-sucking behavior by paradoxically prescribing its increase in the form of giving the other fingers their rightful turn (p. 263):

> One of the first things you learned when you went to nursery school was to take turns. You took turns with this little girl and with that little boy in doing things in nursery school. . . . You learned to take turns at home. When Mother serves food she serves it first to one brother, and then it may be your turn, then it may be sister's turn, then it is Mother's turn. We always do things by turns. But I don't think you are being right or fair or good in always sucking your left thumb and never giving your right thumb a turn. . . . The first finger hasn't had a turn; not a single other finger has had a turn. . . . I think you really would like to give each of your fingers a proper turn.

Erickson's only judgment is the paradoxical one of admonishing the child for not "being right or fair or good in always sucking your thumb." In other words, the child is being told that he is not manifesting his problem behavior *enough*. Of course, the child soon tires of the "laborious task" of giving equal sucking attention to all ten fingers, and so gives up sucking the left thumb as well.

Although Erickson was not known specifically for his work with children, the cases he does report contain valuable principles and techniques which illustrate a utilization approach to therapy. Although he published only three papers dealing exclusively with child or adolescent therapy (Erickson, 1952/1980, 1958b/1980, 1962/1980), Erickson makes many references to cases in other papers (1954b/1980, 1958a/1980, 1959/1980, 1980a&b), in his seminars, workshops, and lectures (Rossi, Ryan & Sharp, 1983; Rossi & Ryan, 1985, 1986), and in his teaching sessions with other professionals (Haley, 1985). In our view, his philosophy and technique of utilization form the cornerstone of effective and respectful therapy with children. Central to the *philosophy* of utilization is a profound respect for the validity and integrity of the child's presenting behavior; central to the *technique* of utilization is a highly skilled ability to observe, participate in, and reframe what is presented.

For Erickson, a starting point in his work with children was in demonstrating a "reluctance to impose my personality" (Rossi & Ryan, in press). Implicit in this reluctance was a nonjudgmental attitude which viewed the symptom or behavior from an entirely novel vantage point: For Erickson it was neither right nor wrong—it was simply a message about the patient which he was only too glad to observe and utilize. With children, such nonjudgmentalism is particularly important since childhood is so much a time of judgments about what is right and wrong.

In Erickson's view, therapy with children involved the same basic principles as therapy with adults. In both situations the therapist's task is to *present ideas* that are comprehensible and that utilize each individual's unique life experiences. Erickson noted that because children have a natural "hunger for new experiences" and an "openness to new learnings," they are especially receptive to these new ideas. The challenge for the therapist is to find ways of communicating ideas that are "in accord with the dignity of the [child's] experiential background and life experiences" and that convey a full sensory experience that goes beyond the scope of the literal words employed (Erickson, 1958b/ 1980, p. 175):

> The mother croons a lullaby to her nursing infant, not to give it an understanding of the words but to convey a pleasing sense of sound and rhythm in association with pleasing physical sensations for both of them and for the achievement of a common goal and purpose. . . . Similarly in child hypnosis there is a need for a continuity of stimulation. . . . Hypnosis, whether for adults or children, should derive from a willing utilization of the simple, good, and pleasing stimuli that serve in everyday life to elicit normal behavior pleasing to all concerned.

APPLYING THE UTILIZATION APPROACH

In our approach to working with children, symptoms are viewed as the result of *blocked resources* (the child's natural abilities and potentials) rather than as manifestations of psychological or social pathology. Blockages arise from the child's perception or misperception of a myriad of experiences that occur. Family problems, friendship problems, school problems—any one of these issues can create an overload of pressures which block the child's natural functioning abilities and learning potentials. This in turn distorts the child into feeling or acting in ways other than his true self. When the child cannot be himself fully, those resources intrinsic to his personality are not readily available and other *limited solutions*—symptoms—are the result. We view the child's symptoms as a symbolic or metaphorical communication from the unconscious which is not only signaling distress within the system *but is also providing a graphic and utilizable depiction of that distress.* The symptom is the medium and the message. Heller (Heller & Steele, 1986) aptly stated:

> It is my belief that all presenting problems and symptoms are really metaphors that contain a story about what the problem really is. It is therefore the responsibility of the therapist to create metaphors that contain a story that contains the (possible) solutions. The metaphor is the message.

Erickson's specific technique of utilizing the symptom toward its own undoing provides one type of model whereby symptoms can be transformed into their own solutions. On many occasions we have successfully applied Erickson's approach of validating the symptom and then reframing it.

Sara's Favorite Things

A delightful eight-year-old girl, Sara, was having trouble controlling her bladder during daytime hours. With her mother present in the session, I asked Sara about all the kinds of "favorite choices" she could remember making, such as choosing her favorite ice cream flavors, her favorite dress to wear for the day, her favorite television program, and so forth. I then asked her to pick a favorite day on which she would like to wet her pants. At first Sara had a puzzled look which quickly turned to a broad smile as she said, "I like two days, Tuesday and Wednesday." I said, "Good!", also with a broad smile on my face. "Now what I would like you to do, Sara, is to be totally successful on Tuesday and Wednesday, and enjoy wetting your pants."

The next week Sara came in and told me how successful she had been that week by wetting her pants on Tuesday and Wednesday. We again began to talk about favorite choices and this time Sara was asked to pick out the favorite times of day she would like to continue wetting her pants.

Over a five-week period we added many different variations of favorite conditions for Sara to wet her pants. Each shift to a new "favorite" gave Sara the opportunity to simultaneously manifest her symptom *and* her control over it. By limiting her wetting to the new favorite condition (be it day of the week, time of the day, location, occasion, or whatever), she was gaining experience in the sensation of controlling her bladder and determining her time of urination. At the end of the five-week period, the novelty of our game had played itself out and Sara simply lost interest in wetting her pants.

An Angel's Apologies

In another case, a shy and naive teenage girl was referred for therapy because of lack of confidence in relation to her peers. Not surprisingly, Angel was timid and apologetic in therapy. Throughout the early part of the session she continued to respond with, "I'm sorry . . . Did I interrupt you. . . . I'm sorry. . . . I didn't make it clear. . . . I'm sorry. . . . I'm sorry." The therapist interrupted her as she was presenting a piece of information she believed had something to do with her lack of self-worth. She was asked if she was aware of her "I'm sorry's," and with embarrassment she commented, "Yes, and everybody reminds me that I do it but I can't stop it. I wish I could."

We agreed to use part of her session to help her stop the "I'm sorry's" while she continued to report what she was quite eager to discuss. I suggested that Angel consciously insert the words "I'm sorry" after every fifth word. She was eager to please me, smiled, and began talking. After her first five words, she proudly inserted "I'm sorry," then spoke five more words, "I'm sorry," another five words and, "I'm sorry." Eventually, however, she began to make mistakes, with six or seven words elapsing before the agreed-upon, "I'm sorry."

Because of these mistakes Angel became anxious and frustrated in completing her important story about a boy she liked.

I acknowledged how frustrating it must be and suggested that I would be willing to help her tell her story without her having to count the five words. I offered to move my left index finger after the fifth word so that she could continue more easily, added "I'm sorry," and then directed her back to the boy-girl vignette she was telling. She smiled and thanked me for the assistance. Within a few minute's time, however, Angel's face became redder and redder and her voice more and more tense until finally she exclaimed, "I'm sick of trying to say, 'I'm sorry,' all the time! I don't want to do it anymore!"

"What specifically don't you want to do anymore?" I naively inquired.

"I don't want to say, 'I'm sorry,' anymore!!" she exclaimed again.

"It's up to you," I said complaisantly. "I guess I'll have to think of another way to help you in that matter. Sometimes that technique isn't effective. Now tell me about the boy."

The following week Angel described how she would find herself laughing each time she said, "I'm sorry." She noted that she was using the phrase less and less because "It just felt dumb now." Previously, other concerned people in Angel's life (parents, teachers, friends) had urged her to stop saying, "I'm sorry," yet it had continued. The key was in allowing Angel herself to be the one to consciously and firmly choose to be in control of her own behavior. Structuring her use of "I'm sorry" in the initial session also helped to emphasize the tediousness of the behavior in the first place.

Erickson makes an important and subtle differentiation between *falsifying* versus *modifying* the child's reality in an example in which his daughter precociously corrects her doctor (1958b/1980, p. 176):

> . . . The surgeon who told four-year-old Kristi, "Now that didn't hurt at all, did it?" was told with bitter, scornful contempt, "You're poopid! It did, too, hurt, but *I* didn't mind it." She wanted understanding and recognition, not a falsification, however well intended, of a reality comprehensible to her. For one to tell a child, "Now this won't hurt one bit" is courting disaster. Children have their own ideas and need to have them respected, but they are readily open to any modification of those ideas intelligently presented to them.

Numerous cases illustrating this important distinction between falsification and modification are available in the Ericksonian literature. We will use one brief example in which Erickson first accepts the child's symptom (trichotillomania), enters her reality, and then offers a therapeutic alteration of that reality (Rossi & Ryan, 1985, pp. 169–170):

Acceptance of Symptom I can think of one little girl who had completely bare eyelids. Not a single eyelash. And I told her that a lot of people thought her eyelids looked homely—but

I thought that they looked interesting. And the girl was pleased, and she believed me. But I *did* think that her eyelids looked interesting, because I was viewing it from the child's point of view.

Modification of Symptom

Then I raised the question of would her eyelids look even more interesting if she had one eyelash here and one over here. And the next question was, what about one in the middle—three eyelashes? How long would they be, and would the middle one grow faster than the outside ones? . . . Well, how do you answer that question except by letting them grow?

The danger with this type of approach is that it is so unavoidably clever. Without doubt, it is very clever to gently scold the thumbsucking child for not sucking all of his fingers, or to suggest days for wetting one's pants, or to ponder different ways of pulling out eyelashes. It would be easy for the therapist to get so caught up in the ingeniousness of the idea used to modify the child's reality that the underlying, guiding principle of a "simple presentation of an earnest, sincere idea by one person to another" can be lost. Erickson firmly believed in the child's right to suck his thumb; he truly viewed the problem behavior as the child's own private business. It is only from such a vantage point of genuine respect and accord for the child's integrity that such an approach is beneficial. Rossi has speculated that it was this quality of genuineness in Erickson's work that was really responsible for the effectiveness of his brilliant therapeutic techniques (Rossi, Ryan & Sharp, 1983).

On one hand children can be easily dazzled by technique and clever cognitive manipulations. On the other hand, they are shrewdly perceptive of falsity, ingenuousness, and what we might call ego-centric cleverness. A very important and delicate balance between technique and philosophy must be discovered by each therapist.

The Sleeping Burglar

I gained personal insight into the importance of sincerity and conviction in working with clients two decades ago when I was a Captain in the Medical Service Corps in the 1960s. A teenage military dependent,

Delores, came to the outpatient clinic with the complaint of sleeping problems associated with fears of being burglarized at nighttime. Ten years ago her family's house had been burglarized but she had no memory of any sleeping problems associated with the trauma at the time. Delores proceeded to describe a ritualistic behavior that she currently performed every night prior to going to bed. First she made sure the front door and back door were securely locked; then she checked each and every window to be sure it was closed and locked; then she selected her clothes for the next day and put them together in one area in the event she needed to dress quickly.

At that time I was being supervised by a psychiatrist who devised a treatment plan based on Jay Haley's concept of paradoxical intention (Haley, 1963). I was unfamiliar with this type of unconventional approach and even laughed at his plan. He suggested that I treat Delores's sleeping problem by utilizing her ritualistic behaviors in specific ways. I was to have Delores perform her rituals in detail at bedtime and then have her go to bed. If she were still awake the next hour, she was to get out of bed and perform the tedious task of double-checking every lock in the entire house. This procedure was to continue all night long. Of course, the strategy of this approach was to provoke in her the unconscious conclusion that "If I fall asleep before the next hour, I can get out of this boring and tedious task of doing the same thing again!"

I found this irreverent way of dealing with her symptom to be the antithesis of my psychoanalytic training in Boston. So although I followed my supervisor's suggestions, I must have transmitted my own unconscious disbelief to Delores. For even though she agreed to such an unusual treatment plan, she had not implemented it when we met next. My supervisor criticized me for not being firm with the assignment. In effect, he told me, I was allowing her to discard an important prescription that would help her sleep. We talked at length about how *I* needed to accept such an innovative way of treating a client. Our discussion helped resolve some of my own disbeliefs about achieving a therapeutic outcome through such a "radical" approach (it was a radical approach at the time).

The following week I was able to present the assignment to Delores with conviction, enthusiasm, and an air of, "Don't waste my time and yours if you're not willing to overcome your sleeping problem." The subsequent week Delores reported that she had experienced five consecutive nights of sleep. By carrying out the "prescription," she had interrupted her own sleepless pattern. The issue of burglary was never mentioned again.

Flexibility in Utilization

Inherent in a genuine utilization approach to child therapy is the quality of flexibility. Utilization means responding to those realities that spontaneously present themselves. There is little room in such an approach for a strict adherence to conventional treatment procedures. Erickson was known for his willingness and flexibility in providing therapy wherever it was needed. If the patient could not or would not go to him, he would simply go to them. In one case (Erickson, 1959/1980, pp. 201–202), the parents of a nine-year-old girl contacted Erickson and explained that their daughter was failing in her school work and withdrawing socially to an alarming degree. They added that she had refused to go to his office for treatment. Therefore he visited her in her home every evening for over six weeks.

In talking with the child, he discerned her deep sense of inadequacy in relation to activities that required physical coordination. She hated the typical games of childhood that most children loved. Since Erickson's right arm was obviously crippled (from poliomyelitis at the age of 17), he challenged his patient to the effect that he could play a "more terrible" game of jacks than she could. The challenge was accepted and the girl and Erickson proceeded to play jacks for the next three weeks, by which time she had become an excellent player.

For the next two weeks the same procedure was carried out with roller skating. Since Erickson's right leg was also clearly crippled, he exclaimed that he could be much worse than she at roller skating. In two weeks' time the girl had mastered roller skating. Next Erickson asked her to try to teach him how to jump rope with one bad leg; in a week's time she had learned the skill herself.

Finally came bicycle riding. This time Erickson asserted that *he* could beat her in a race, because, as everybody knew, he was good at cycling. The girl accepted the challenge, stating that her accomplishments in all the other activities had made her feel better but that they didn't mean much because of Erickson's handicap. Cycling would be the real test, and she warned him that she was going to watch his legs to make sure he was trying his best. Erickson did try his best with both legs, which the girl could easily see, but she won anyway. The twist was that Erickson's good cycling was actually achieved by pedaling with his one good leg. When he tried to use both legs, he was indeed handicapped! The girl knew only that he was a good cyclist, that he had tried his best, and that she had beaten him.

Winning the race also marked the girl's last "therapeutic interview." She became an avid sports participant in school, and, of course, her grades also improved.

The delightful unorthodoxy of Erickson's treatment plan in this case illustrates how potent utilization can be and how important flexibility is in this utilization. Erickson did not deal with the "cause" of the child's problems, and he did not even deal directly with either of the two presenting problems: Studying habits were never addressed, nor was the issue of social interaction. Instead he realized that the focal problem was the child's lack of physical coordination and the humiliation that naturally followed.

Could these problems have been as adequately handled within the confines of a conventional office setting? It is unlikely. Erickson's willingness to go to the child's home territory and interact with her on her terms was probably as crucial to the child's recovery as was the actual treatment experience itself. Obviously, limits have to be set—therapists cannot be expected to go traipsing about town at any time. The important point is that flexibility in providing therapy can open dimensions of treatment otherwise not possible. I discovered this for myself through an unexpectedly touching experience.

In the Pink

In the initial session, six-year-old Steven was described by his mother as "being different" from her other three children. In addition to having sleeping problems, he was out of control much of the time. When other children were present, he would throw more tantrums so that he would have to be separated from them. Enjoyable activities for most children, such as riding in the car or playing in the sand, were not experienced as enjoyable by Steven.

After working with Steven and his parents for a month, I received a phone call from his mother requesting that I call Steven's teacher.

The mother was feeling very good about what she and her husband were learning in therapy and she wanted me to help her son in his classroom situation. It seemed that even though Steven was learning to express himself verbally rather than by acting out his reactions, the other children continued to view him within the old frame of reference. Because of the interest, motivation, and cooperation shown by both Steven and his parents, I was more than willing to broaden the therapeutic scope. I contacted the teacher and asked if I could visit the classroom and observe and interact with the children in order to help Steven and the other children accept his differences. She graciously accepted and asked if I would be willing to share any observations and suggestions I might have with her. Upon receiving the parents' written permission, we scheduled the day for my visit.

While observing Steven in both the classroom situation and outdoors at recess, I noticed that he had a very hard time demonstrating his abilities in a positive way. The other children made fun of him when he came close to where they were playing and called him names such as "Steven Shmeven the Weirdo." He tried to tell them how that made him feel, but they persisted.

The children were curious about my presence. They came up and asked me who I was and what I was doing there. Proudly I said, "I am a very special friend of Steven's and I've come here today to play with him." I intentionally introduced a new viewpoint of Steven—one of acceptance and valuation rather than rejection. Hoping to stimulate interaction with the other children, I picked up a football that was lying on the ground and asked Steven if he would like to play catch with me. He was delighted. He stood about ten feet away as we played. Close by another child stood and watched. The look on the child's face and his body movements (minimal cues) alerted me to the interest he was showing in wanting to play with us. After a few more passes I casually asked him his name.

"Matthew," he said.

"Would you like to play, too?" I asked.

His smile widened and he said, "Yeah!"

I then threw the football to Matthew; he threw it back to me. I threw it to Steven and asked Steven to throw it to Matthew. The chain had begun. Our play then engaged the interest of the other children and before long we had become a team, each individual interacting with the others.

After twenty minutes of play it was time to go inside and have a "quiet time." During this time the children would sit on mats and the teacher would tell them stories or talk to them about social subjects such as how to make friends. Knowing that the stage for change had been set, I asked the teacher if I might tell the story today. I had brought a tape recorder and I told her I would be happy to give her a copy of the tape. She was delighted.

As the children settled down on their mats, I told them how much I had enjoyed playing with them and that in appreciation for their kindness, I would tell them a very special story. Steven moved closer, as did the others, to hear this new tale. [Following is a verbatim transcription of the story created spontaneously for the group.]

Just imagine yourself going on an incredible, marvelously relaxing journey . . . a journey where you can just close your eyes and imagine all kinds of wonderful, exciting, beautiful things to see, feel, taste, smell and touch. That's right. And you can begin this journey by getting in a very comfortable position and allowing yourself all the room you need . . . and take a nice, slow, deep breath in through your nose and exhale slowly out through your mouth. That's right. And continue this breathing easily, comfortably, as the journey begins so easily for you now.

While you are on this journey you can imagine a wonderful place you'd like to be. Perhaps you'd like to float high above the clouds. I don't know where you would like to go, but with your wonderful imagination you can create whatever kind of place you would like to be in. And while you are floating and drifting and feeling comfortable, I'd like to tell you a story—a story about a little elephant who lived in a zoo. A little elephant who was somewhat different from the other elephants, you see, because he was pink. Most elephants, especially in this zoo, were all gray. There were a few white ones, a few even lighter in color, and a few darker; but this elephant, this little elephant, was *pink*.

He worried and worried because the other elephants really had a hard time accepting him. He wanted to be so much a part of the group, to be a part of the play. He wanted to run between the rocks, and he wanted to be able to play and throw the dirt back and forth to each of the other little elephants, especially the ones that were in his cave area. And elephants, as they are and as they do, love to roll around in the dirt; they love to splash water on their backs; and they all like to do their own kind of play. The only problem was this little elephant was different. He saw things differently, he felt things differently. Sometimes he even heard things differently. And occasionally he would get a shaky kind of feeling inside and he didn't even know what that feeling was.

Elephants don't know very much at times and they need to learn. Elephants need to learn so many things about themselves. One day, as this little elephant was just wandering around in the corner of his play area, another elephant—an older, wiser elephant—came over to him and said, "What seems to be the trouble today?" This little elephant said, "Well, you see I'm different. I can't play the same kinds of games and I don't like to do everything the way everyone else does. I'm worried about that, and besides, I'm pink and being pink is awfully hard to be when everyone else is gray."

At that moment the older, wiser elephant looked at the little pink elephant and said, "I wonder if you can remember a time when being pink, bright pink, was so important for you."

The little elephant thought and thought and thought to himself. Yes, I do remember a time, a long time ago, when I got lost. I was wandering around and it was dark, and all the keepers were out looking for me. That's right. They were looking for me and didn't know where to find me. It got later and later and I was very frightened. I thought no one would be able to find me. As I was wandering down the road, looking for my way back, trying to find the right path back to my home, all of a sudden a car pulled up and there were the keepers. They were able to find me! The keeper said to me, 'I'm so glad that you are pink, bright pink, because if you were gray we would not have been able to see you in the dark.' "

At that moment a twinkle appeared in the little elephant's eyes. He realized there was a time, there is a time, when it is so important to be different—when being different can even be wonderful.

The older, wiser elephant nudged him gently and said, "That's right. There are many, many times when being different is such a wonderful ability, like all the abilities you have now. And I wonder if you are able to teach some of those abilities, to share some of those abilities with the other little elephants who may not understand."

The little pink elephant thought and thought and thought with that same twinkle and said, "Yes, I certainly could."

He went back to where the other little elephants played and he began to show them three other abilities that he had. He wanted to share those three abilities so that they could experience him in a new and different way. He showed them how many things he could do by being pink. And they were amazed. They realized that being pink could be quite exciting and different, and they really tried hard themselves to become pink.

Well, for each of them, for each of those little elephants, they could not become pink—not the same color as this little elephant. But as they tried to become pink they realized something magical and wonderful was happening—the way they felt about each other and the way they saw each other also began to change. They began to see and hear and feel wonderful, magical abilities in one another, and how exciting and marvelous that felt! Soon the little pink elephant realized that it was getting very late and so he nudged each one of the other elephants gently and then sent a message with the twinkle in his eye as if to say: "I am your friend and we have many learnings yet to discover about each other." They all closed their eyes and went to sleep. That's right.

And as you drift and allow those wonderful, comfortable feelings, all of what we talked about and learned will come together for you in a new way, helping you to feel calm, relaxed, and peaceful. Allowing you the wonderful feeling of knowing how many things you can do so successfully, like when you learned how to tie your shoes; and how you know what one and one is and what two and two is; and you know how to read; and you know so many things that are such marvelous learnings. Just allow yourself to drift, returning to a comfortable, comfortable place at your own time and at your own speed. Allowing your eyes to open and taking with you only those pleasurable moments you want to remember, and allowing yourself to forget whatever you wish to forget so that you can continue to feel comfort and peacefulness and a wonderful, relaxing feeling. That's right. Just imagining and continuing to imagine, day after day, for all the moments you wish. That's right. And you can either drift into a comfortable sleep or you can allow your eyes to open now. Taking a nice deep breath, and stretching, and just returning to full awareness. Full comfort. That's right.

3

Ingredients of Storywriting

As the sun streamed its shimmering rays across the ocean, we noticed a large gray-and-white pelican out at sea. As we watched her graceful body lift off the water while scanning for food, we wondered how she knows where to search? We are not able to see where her source of nourishment lies out there. Yet what is beyond our realm of awareness is well within the sphere of awareness of a simple creature such as the pelican.

In subsequent chapters we will present a detailed framework for generating effective therapeutic metaphors from a clinical perspective: how to observe, evoke, and utilize a vast array of emotional and behavioral information that is incorporated into a story. In this chapter we will focus on the therapeutic metaphor as a storywriting experience, having much in common with the rich legacy of fairy tales we all remember from our childhoods.

Literary Versus Therapeutic Metaphors

Fairy tales are an excellent example of how metaphor can be used as both a literary and therapeutic device. The stories are told in colorful, image-filled language and contain an important psychological message

(Bettelheim, 1975). Not all metaphor is therapeutic, however, so it is necessary to understand the subtle elements that separate a purely literary one from a therapeutic one. The one element both types of metaphor have in common is *correspondence* (Jaynes, 1976): We must be able to experience an immediate synchrony between the ·metaphor and whatever it is describing (its "referent"). Correspondence can take place on many levels within the reader, however, and it is here that the pathways of literary and therapeutic metaphors diverge.

In a literary metaphor, the correspondence between the metaphor and its referent must be close enough to evoke a sense of *imagistic familiarity:* The reader must be drawn into the richness of the imagery, however remote or foreign the experience being depicted. For example, in the following passage by D.H. Lawrence which concludes his book *Sons and Lovers* (Lawrence, 1969), we see Lawrence's expert use of metaphor to connote the desolation of young Paul upon the death of his mother (p. 420):

> On every side the immense dark silence seemed to be pressing him, so tiny a spark, into extinction, and yet, almost nothing, he could not be extinct. Night, in which everything was lost, went reaching out, beyond stars and sun. Stars and sun, a few bright grains, went spinning round for terror, and holding each other in embrace, there in a darkness that outpassed them all, and left them tiny and daunted. So much, and himself, infinitesimal, at the core a nothingness, and yet not nothing.

In this passage, Lawrence uses metaphorical images for the purpose of describing an experience. The experience is set in a different time period and in a different country, which makes it experientially unfamiliar to most American readers. Furthermore, the actual details of the experience—the death of Paul's mother following a long and painful illness—may seem familiar to only a small number of readers. And certainly not everyone has experienced the vacuous desolation Paul is feeling. Yet the scene Lawrence describes is so beautifully drawn by the metaphors he creates that the reader enters into it through the richness of the images alone.

Where *description* is the main function of a literary metaphor, *altering, reinterpreting,* and *reframing* are the main goals of the therapeutic metaphor. In order to achieve these, the therapeutic metaphor must evoke both the imagistic familiarity of the literary metaphor and a *relational familiarity* based on a sense of personal experience. The story itself—the characters, events, and settings—must speak to the common life experience of those listening, and it must do so in language that is familiar. An example from a modern fairy tale might be *The Wizard of Oz* (Baum, 1900), which functions as a metaphor for the common theme of searching for magical solutions somewhere outside oneself. The images of a wicked witch, a good witch, a tinman, scarecrow, lion, and wizard all depict aspects of the listener's experience as mirrored in Dorothy. Even as adults viewing the original film version for the tenth time, we find ourselves still drawn into Dorothy's journey. Captivated, we watch as Dorothy's initial yearning for "somewhere over the rainbow" is transformed through a myriad of fantastic experiences into her departing heartfelt declaration, "There's no place like home."

Each major character in *The Wizard of Oz* carries an imagistic *and* therapeutic message. The grand and mighty Wizard, apparent bearer of magical solutions, turns out to be "just a common man" (Kopp, 1971) who guides the characters to solutions they hold within themselves—a therapeutic metaphor for reowning projected strengths and abilities. The Wicked Witch of the East, from whom Dorothy and her companions flee in terror and subservience, turns out to be completely water soluble—a metaphor for the ultimate impotence of negative viewpoints and actions. The problems each character brings so earnestly before the Wizard for resolution turn out to be mere oversights: The Lion always had courage, the Scarecrow always had a brain, the Tinman always had a heart, and Dorothy always had the ability to get back home. These are all metaphors for the basic therapeutic principle that answers, solutions, abilities, and resources lie *within* each individual.

The fact that *The Wizard of Oz* story has appeal for all ages points to the degree of *relational familiarity* it contains. The images in the story are encompassing enough to generalize to many different ages and life experiences, and yet they are personal enough to evoke immediate, private responses. Lawrence's night metaphor does not have such wide-ranging applicability, even though it clearly succeeds on a literary level. Ultimately, it is not enough in the therapy session, group session, or classroom to construct a metaphor that is imagistically rich, as in Lawrence's passage, if it fails to touch the listener in a personally relevant way.

Ingredients of Therapeutic Metaphors

The question could be asked, What does an effective metaphor *do* that makes it therapeutic? Possibly its most important function is to create what Rossi (1972/1985) termed a "shared phenomenological reality" in which the world created by the therapist's metaphor is experienced by the child. This creates a three-way empathic relationship between child, therapist, and story which then makes it possible for the child to develop *a sense of identification* with the characters and events portrayed. It is this sense of identification that contains the transformational power of the metaphor (Gordon, 1978). The child must create a bridge of personal connection between himself and the events of the story if he is to bring parts of the story back into his "real" life. In the effective therapeutic metaphor, this is facilitated by representing the child's problem accurately enough so that he no longer feels alone, yet indirectly enough so that he does not feel embarrassed, ashamed, or resistant.

Once identification is established between the child and the story, the child's *sense of isolation* about his own problem ("*Nobody* has my problem") is replaced with a sense of *shared experience* ("They had a problem like mine!"). Again, however, the connection between the metaphorical problem and the child's problem remains "not quite" conscious. Indeed this is the fine delicacy of a therapeutic metaphor: The story "hits home" but in a curiously removed way; it focuses on the problem but in a quietly diffused way; and it activates specific abilities and resources, but in a nonthreatening, generalized way. The fatherless child crying through the farewell scene of *E.T.* may never consciously think, "This is just like when Daddy went away." Yet on some level the sense of love and ultimate well-being suggested by the movie's ending may help the child experience his loss in a new and more healing way—and without his ever being aware of it.

How does one go about creating the shared phenomenological reality by which the therapeutic metaphor achieves its effect? If we look at the classic fairy tales, we can discern elements or ingredients of storywriting that are common to many of them. In one way or another, most classic fairy tales:

(1) Establish an overall theme of *metaphorical conflict* in relation to the protagonist;

(2) Personify *unconscious processes* in the form of heroes or helpers (representing the protagonist's abilities and resources), and villains or obstructions (representing the protagonist's fears and negative beliefs);

(3) Personify *parallel learning situations* in which the protagonist was successful;

(4) Present a *metaphorical crisis* within a context of inevitable resolution, by which the protagonist overcomes or resolves his problem;

(5) Develop a new sense of *identification* for the protagonist as a result of his victorious "hero's journey";

(6) Culminate with a *celebration* in which the protagonist's special worth is acknowledged.

THE UGLY DUCKLING AS THERAPEUTIC METAPHOR

Let's take a well-known example. In the fairy tale of *The Ugly Duckling*, a *shared phenomenological world* is created out of the common experience of feeling unwanted, unattractive, and different. Whether child or adult, the fairy tale displaces our sense of *isolation* in those negative feelings by drawing us into the poignancy of the Ugly Duckling's pain and rejection. We feel a sense of *shared experience* as we go with the little duck through his many travails, and the *identification* that arises out of this shared experience allows us to fully participate in the little duck's transformation into the beautiful swan.

All of this is brought about in *The Ugly Duckling** by Hans Christian Andersen's (unknowing?) use of our six classic ingredients. To begin with, the *metaphorical conflict* is depicted with the birth of the funny looking duckling. From its first moments out of the egg, the newborn duck looks different—and his brothers and sisters, and all the other barnyard companions, are quick and cruel to act upon this difference:

> The poor duckling, who was the last out of the egg and looked so ugly, got pecked and jostled and teased by ducks and hens alike. "The great hawk!" they all clucked. . . . The poor duckling didn't know where to turn; he was terribly upset over being so ugly and the laughingstock of the whole barnyard.

---

* All quotations from *The Ugly Duckling* are taken from the version translated by R. P. Keigwin and published by Charles Scribner's Sons (New York, 1965). (Pages were not numbered.)

Only his mother sees his good points. She acknowledges his potential for improvement and enumerates his *unconscious processes* in the form of abilities and resources:

> Look how beautifully he uses his legs and how straight he holds himself. . . . He's not pretty, but he's so good tempered and he can swim just as well as the others—I daresay even a bit better. I fancy his looks will improve as he grows up, or maybe in time he'll grow down a little.

Nonetheless the barnyard abuse only gets worse, so the little duckling flees "to the great marsh where the wild ducks live," hoping to find acceptance or at least respite. He finds neither but instead encounters the first *metaphorical crisis* in the story when the marsh is suddenly surrounded by hunters and their dogs. Other creatures are killed, but the Ugly Duckling manages to survive. When confronted by a "fearsome great dog with lolling tongue and grim, glittering eyes," the duckling fears his life is over—but the dog turns and leaves without even touching him. Here Andersen provides an example of reframing by having the duckling recognize that his supposed ugliness had served the very positive purpose of saving his life: "Thank goodness, I'm so ugly that even the dog doesn't fancy the taste of me!"

After this crisis is resolved, the duck finds his way to a cottage which unwittingly provides many *parallel learning situations* for him. Already the little duck has learned many important things: He has learned how to swim, he has learned how to take care of himself, and he has learned how to survive a crisis. Now safe in a cottage with an old woman, a hen, and a cat, the duckling is given the chance to choose between what he knows and wants, and what *others* think and want *for* him. Declaring his desire to leave the cottage and go back to the water, the duck is sorely admonished by the arrogant hen:

> "You must have gone crazy," said the hen. "Ask the cat about it—I've never met anyone as clever as he is—ask him if he's fond of swimming or diving! I say nothing of myself. Ask our old mistress, the wisest woman in the world! Do you suppose that she's keen on swimming and diving? . . . Surely you'll never try and make out you are wiser than the cat and the mistress— not to mention myself. Don't be silly child! . . . You're just

stupid, and there's no fun in having you here. You may take my word for it—if I say unpleasant things to you, it's all for your good; that's how you can tell which are your real friends.

Undaunted, the little duck replies, "I think I'll go out into the wide world!"

Now back in the "wide world," the duckling is still met with rejection and hardship. But as winter approaches and all the great birds begin their migrations, he is given his first glimpse of hope when the beautiful swans fly overhead. Here Andersen personifies the little duck's *unconscious potentials* in the form of the swan he is unknowingly to become:

Ah! He could never forget those beautiful, fortunate birds; and directly they were lost to sight he dived right down to the bottom and when he came up again, he was almost beside himself. He had no idea what the birds were called, not where they were flying to, and yet they were dearer to him than any he had ever known. . . . How could he ever dream of such loveliness for himself?

The swans disappear and the little duck is again left alone in a barren and cold winter. During this winter he undergoes another crisis when he freezes in the pond and is rescued at the last moment by a peasant. This crisis then leads to further learning, as the little duck teaches himself to fly in order to escape the peasant's besieging wife and children.

Still the winter cold brings further trials of conflict, crisis, and learning to the duck, who by this time was no longer so little. As spring warmed and colored the land, he found his wings had spread and gained in strength—and he flew quite well! Again he spotted a flock of swan, this time swimming in a pond, and he resolved to fly over and be with them—even if "they will peck me to death for daring, ugly as I am, to go near them." Now Andersen provides a lovely depiction of the process of discovering and owning unconscious potentials. With the reappearance of the flock of swans, who personify the Ugly Duckling's true beauty, the Ugly Duckling finally "sees for himself" when he beholds his reflection in the water—"no longer a clumsy greyish bird, ugly and unattractive—no, he was himself a swan!"

Next the duck goes through a period of joyful transition in which he synthesizes a new *identification* as a beautiful swan out of a thoughtful consideration of his past:

> He felt positively glad at having gone through so much hardship and want; it helped him to appreciate all the happiness and beauty that were there to welcome him. . . . He was too, too happy, but not a bit proud, for a good heart is never proud.

Finally a *celebration* occurs in which the Ugly Duckling's true and special worth is heralded, as children dance and clap their hands and "the old swans bow before him." His new identity is now fully accepted with his closing realization that he had come full circle: "[The Ugly Duckling] thought of how he had been despised and persecuted, and now heard everybody saying that he was the loveliest of all lovely birds."

And so the tale which begins in rejection and hurt ends in celebration and happiness, having brought its readers effectively through a series of events which mediated this transformation—and which may help mediate similar transformations in its readers. Following is a summary of how a "shared phenomenological reality" (Rossi, 1972/1985) is achieved in *The Ugly Duckling* via our "ingredients" of storywriting.

SHARED PHENOMENOLOGICAL REALITY

> *Feeling unwanted and different;*
> *Learning many new things;*
> *Overcoming hardships;*
> *Transforming into one's higher potential.*

Metaphorical Conflict	Birth of the funny looking duckling.
Unconscious Processes and Potentials	The duckling's mother defends him and cites his positive qualities; the Ugly Duckling gets his first glimpse of the swans.
Parallel Learning Situations	Learning how to swim, how to take care of himself, how to fly.

Metaphorical Crisis	Attack in the marsh; cold winter in the pond.
New Identification	The Ugly Duckling beholds his beautiful new image in the water. "He was too, too happy, but not a bit proud."
Celebration	"The old swans bowed before him."

Being able to create original stories that touch children such as *The Wizard of Oz* and *The Ugly Duckling* can be facilitated by an awareness of these six classic ingredients of storywriting. Of course, not all the ingredients will be used in each and every metaphor. The idea is not to present a rigid procedure that "must" be followed, but rather to provide a "latticework" of ideas that guide and stimulate. We have formulated the ingredients in conceptual terms here for teaching purposes, which might make them appear unfamiliar; yet in reality they are all natural and familiar to us from a long history of childhood fairy tales, movies, books, and our own inner fantasies. We all have an unconscious sense of drama—of how a good story develops and unfolds. Indeed if you were to make up a story in the next five minutes, you would probably find it contains several of our ingredients without any conscious effort on your part to recall or include them.

Another comforting factor we have discovered is the way in which we will unconsciously draw upon stories or fairy tales already familiar to us as a means of creating an "original" story for a child. For example, in the following Driftwood metaphor, a clear parallel can be seen between its theme and the theme depicted in *The Ugly Duckling*. Yet, curiously, we recognized this connection only as we were working on the chapter, months after the experience had occurred. From the vantage point of our conscious awareness at the time, the Driftwood metaphor was an entirely unique story spontaneously emerging from within as a response to the living realities of the child to whom it was being told. Perhaps, though, unconscious processes were also actively participating by accessing memories that could be quickly and effectively used.

Along a similar line, in response to reading our "Sammy the Elephant" metaphor in Chapter 6, a friend told us that it reminded her of Dumbo the Elephant. We looked at each other in surprise and amusement and said that we had never even thought of Dumbo the

Elephant. We realized how important it is to know that a "support system" of past knowledge and experience operates effectively within us on an unconscious level. There are times when we create stories that are completely original, and there are times when we consciously or unconsciously draw upon familiar elements of known stories. Even when that occurs, however, the therapeutic metaphor that results is "original" as long as it is fashioned in dynamic response to the ever-changing and always unique realities of the child before us.

Driftwood

On a late wintry afternoon I arrived at the home of a friend for a meeting regarding this very book. Her older daughter, Shannon, who was sixteen at the time, met me at the front door and informed me that her mother would be an hour later than expected. I could wait there, she told me bruskly. I couldn't help noticing that she seemed on the verge of tears. Her voice was tight and quavery, her eyes were watery, and her shoulders were slumped. When I asked her how her day had gone, she blurted out that she had unsuccessfully auditioned for an acting role in the school play. To make matters worse, four of the five students who had auditioned had been selected—which meant that she was the only one rejected.

Shannon was born with cerebral palsy. She has a mild case, relatively speaking, in that her speech is normal, her hand and arm coordination is almost normal, and she is able to walk unaided but with a conspicuously dragging gait. The less visible effects of the cerebral palsy include significant learning disabilities and an emotional identification with being different and disabled.

As Shannon told me about the rejection from the play, we moved into the living room and I began putting logs on the fireplace. It was almost dark by this time and I thought the warmth and light of the fire would help lift her spirits. I was wrong. Shannon's remarks were peppered with phrases such as "I'm worthless," "I'm no good," "I'll never amount to anything," "I'd be better off dead."

I had known Shannon for several years and in that time had seen her come home from school on many occasions in tears from being called "cripple," "retard," or "weirdo." Each time I had tried to console her directly by emphasizing her other abilities, I met with defeat. She didn't want to hear about what she could do when she was feeling so much pain over what she was being told she couldn't do. This time I tried a different approach. I enlisted her help in simply listening to a story, ostensibly for our book, that might or might not make sense to her. I had my tape recorder with me for the meeting with her mother and, since she liked tape cassettes, I offered her the finished cassette as a gift for listening. The logs and the fireplace served as my inspiration for the following story which is reproduced verbatim. As the fire crackled in the background, Shannon leaned back in her chair to listen.

As you are sitting there, maybe you can become aware of something outside of yourself . . . maybe something you can focus on comfortably . . . perhaps that vase over there.

I don't know what would happen if you closed your eyes and used your imagination while I talk to you *[pause]*. That's right, just adjust yourself until you find a position that feels good to you.

Perhaps imagining a fireplace . . . or watching the sound of the flames crackling . . . or becoming aware of the smell of smoke . . . or noticing the firewood over there which will be used for just a single purpose—important for a time—and then forgotten.

Crackling sounds have a melody all their own—soft, and only known by the fireplace.

And as you are watching the movement of the dancing of the flames, perhaps they can bring back another pleasant memory . . . *[long pause]*.

There was a story a long time ago about wood, lumber, and logs. There was this piece of wood, like a log, that felt terrible about itself. It was ridiculed by some and laughed at by others because it just didn't fit in. It just looked different.

(Metaphorical conflict) For many, many years this log felt sad from time to time, confused about why it was here in such a different way than all the other logs. Why was it twisted, worn, and curved when the other pieces appeared strong, firm and very useful?

(Metaphorical crisis) One day this certain piece of wood became very upset when it found itself in a pile of wood next to a fireplace to be burned and changed into

nothing but ashes, swept away, and never thought of again. Somehow it narrowly escaped becoming a burnt log in a fireplace. Instead it somehow found itself on a truck being taken to a factory to be turned into part of a piece of furniture. While riding on the truck it was difficult to conceal itself and everybody could see it. Even though there were some kind logs on board, it seemed that most of them were jealous or mean or wanted to make fun of it because they thought it was so different from them. Suddenly this certain piece of wood felt all the hurt for all those years, the laughs and jeers, the jokes about its shape, about it as a log, itself. It even had more humiliation as it fell off the furniture truck and bounced all over the road, until it landed over there, all alone. There was no purpose anymore if it couldn't even have the role of being made into furniture.

(Unconscious processes)

(Metaphorical conflict)

Time passed by and one day it was picked up by a dump truck to be thrown away. Nobody appeared to have any use for it, not even a fireplace. It was dumped onto a barge that carried garbage and useless objects to be disposed of. You could hear the old barge clanking along the road, taking the log and tons of other things to be tossed into the deepest part of the water to drift down and down and down. *[long pause]*

Well, this certain piece of wood just couldn't understand how that could be its purpose in life! It thought, "If this is the end, I would just rather be in control myself and drop off the barge by myself . . . under my own control . . . and fall down into the water and continue to go under in my own way *[long pause]*. It did, and as it was going under in its own way, it was surprised . . . and confused . . . to find itself floating on the surface . . . able to float in its own special way.

(New identification)

And as it looked around it saw many things. It saw the sound of the wind whispering through

(Parallel learning situations)

the sails of the sailboat, it saw the sound of a pelican in search of food, it saw other pleasant sounds that made it feel good inside again. *[pause]* After a while if found itself floating in with the sound of the waves that eventually brought it to shore. Now it was going nowhere again and it thought it might just stay there and dry up and disappear. What a sad purpose in life that would be! Soon, though, it fell asleep in the warm sun by listening to the rhythm of the soft waves. Just listening to the sound of the blue sky relaxed it even more, listening to the sound of the ocean as you could see white caps gently riding in.

Suddenly it was awakened from its rest by a pleasant caressing hand that held it and smiled and expressed acclamations of joy, saying, "You are fantastic, you are fantastic." It couldn't remember seeing such a loving look on someone's face . . . *[pause]* . . . nor remember words of praise from somebody's voice . . . *[long pause]* . . . nor remember being touched in such a special way, a pleasurable way. *[long pause]* It was confused, but before long it was whisked away with excitement and energy and taken to more people who were delighted to see the shape of this piece of wood in a unique and creative way. *[long pause]* And as it looked around, it read the sign on the door which said something about *driftwood*. It had been labelled *Driftwood* and held in high regard!

(New identification)

As a matter of fact, it was even given the distinct purpose of being the finest piece of driftwood ever.

(Celebration)

Eventually it won a contest and many, many prizes and was acknowledged all over the world for its beauty and warmth and much, much more. It soon found itself in a beautiful environment on a special mantle, where it relaxed during the day as it watched the smiling faces and heard words of praise from the passersby who would reach over

(Celebration) gently to touch—just to feel what it's like to be such a unique and beautiful piece of wood. And as it relaxed into its new, full life as a special piece of *driftwood,* it thought to itself, "Even though you worried for all that time, eventually you reached your destination, your purpose, in a relaxed way!" And it finally did reach its own destination and a purpose, a universal purpose that was acknowledged by all.

Frameworks for Metaphors: Real-Life Versus Fictional

In the research section of Chapter 2 we saw how therapeutic metaphors were created out of several different strategies: preordained themes from folktales or science fiction stories, original stories based on fairy-tale motifs, and original stories based on the child's (and/or therapist's) own imagination.

Another rich source of metaphor creation is real-life experience. While it certainly can be effective to use predetermined themes and motifs, as well as unconscious memories of known stories or themes, we have found that there need be no limitations to discovering original frameworks. Even everyday occurrences and events can provide the raw material out of which to create a unique therapeutic metaphor. In this section we will contrast metaphors generated out of real-life events with those sparked by our own imaginations and inner associations.

REAL-LIFE FRAMEWORKS

The Three-Legged Dog

For ten years the Allens were an intact family with four members. One day the father abruptly left the home and two weeks later demanded a divorce. At this point, Julie, an attractive 38-year-old woman, and her two daughters of eight and five, Sandy and Melissa, came in for help. The mother was not eating or sleeping well. She talked about feelings of anger and uselessness saying, "I just don't feel whole anymore." The two little girls also expressed their feelings of sadness and fear over the sudden loss of their father.

During the initial session, the family members were asked to draw pictures of some things they enjoyed doing. The little girls drew activities which included their hobbies, friends, and pets, while Julie drew pictures which depicted "a whole family" (four members) interacting. It was at this point my own personal experience of a three-legged dog came to mind and was immediately presented to the mother and her daughters:

Last week as I was driving down the street with my ten-year-old son Casey he suddenly said, "Mom, look over there!" He pointed excitedly to the left. "It's a three-legged dog!" he exclaimed in amazement.

"Yes," I said, "that's a three-legged dog all right."

"But, Mom," he protested, "look at what she's doing! She's playing ball, she's running, she's sitting, she's eating her bone. She's doing everything our dog does, but she has only three legs. How is that possible?" [pause]

Casey continued to question me curiously. "But Mom, how can she do all those things?" [pause]

"Well Casey," I answered, "I guess she learned how to adjust to not having that other leg, that fourth leg. I guess she learned how to have fun with the three legs that were left."

Again Casey questioned, "But don't you think that was hard to do?"

"Yes," I said, "probably in the beginning it was hard. It takes all of us a little time to learn something new. But once we learn it, that new learning is forever."

After a while Casey asked what had happened to the dog's fourth leg. I said I didn't know for sure—maybe she had been born that way, maybe she lost it as a pup, maybe she lost it recently. It really didn't matter. What mattered, I told him, was that the dog had lost something important and then learned how to use what remained in a new way.

Casey liked my answer and sat back comfortably in the car for the rest of the drive home. When he got home, he ran to tell his friend all about the amazing, three-legged dog.

The family was seen for a period of six months, during which time other storytelling and artistic metaphors were employed as key treatment approaches. Julie secured a good job and began entertaining thoughts about going back to college to further her career. She started dating and began feeling "quite whole again."

Within the first two months of therapy, Sandy and Melissa's overall emotional upsets had improved significantly, with their eating and sleeping patterns returning to normal. However they still complained occasionally of headaches, stomachaches, and not wanting to go to school. These problems seemed to coincide with visits with or phone calls from their father. After medical etiology was ruled out, the father was contacted and brought in for family counseling with his daughters. Through the therapy, he began to understand the importance of his role in their lives and responded with warmth and a willingness to help his children.

Some two months after therapy had ended, I received a delightful phone call from Melissa. She excitedly related how a three-legged dog had moved onto their block and how she and Sandy were teaching the dog lots of "fun things."

Vanessa's Garden

In the following case, an actual garden experience was used to structure a story for a young foster child. A young couple and their foster child, Vanessa, were referred for treatment by a social worker because the nine-year-old girl was to be transferred to another foster home—her third in less than two years. The foster parents were unable to care for her because of their own personal problems and Vanessa's constant need for attention.

While we were eliciting some of Vanessa's likes and dislikes, she mentioned that she received a weekly allowance for helping in the garden, which she liked to do. Her comment triggered a memory of an experience I had had with garden plants, so I used the memory as a basis for a story which would match her current reality and point toward a happier resolution.

A couple of years ago my neighbors sold their home. It was to be torn down and replaced with an apartment building. There was a period of time between the house being sold, the windows being boarded, the house being torn down, and the new construction beginning. I noticed that some of the bushes and plants around the house were wilting since nobody was watering them anymore. I contacted the new owner and was given permission to dig up and transplant whatever I wanted.

To begin with, I chose the plant that looked the saddest and needed the most help. I took it from the empty yard down the street to its new home. I told it that even though I knew a lot about caring for flowers, I still needed its help in letting me know what it needed—just like it let me know it needed help when it lived down the street by its wilted leaves.

After I transplanted it in a place I thought was best, I gave it plenty of water and plant food. But it wasn't enough. The plant didn't take root so I moved it out of the shady section down below to a separate pot all its own and said, "Now you can let me know if this is where you want to be." After a period of time it told me by its lack of blooming beautiful colors that it wasn't all right. I felt sad and the plant looked sad. If it could talk it might be saying, "Will I ever grow bigger and learn how to bloom all my colors?"

I pointed to my favorite rosebush that was doing so well by giving me its gift of beautiful red roses and the nicest fragrance I'd ever smelled and said, "It's hard to believe that I had to transplant that rosebush a number of times before it found the best soil and just the right amount of sun and shade and water and plant food. But as long as I was able to get help from gardening experts, I knew that it was just a matter of time. So let's get you out of that pot and into a new location. And your roots will take hold when you are in the best possible soil and condition for you. It's nice to know that a part of you knows what's best for you and what's not—even though you thought at first you'd be in that pot for a long, long time."

Vanessa had been in therapy for two months when she moved to her new foster home. Since there was a garden in the new home, I gave her cuttings of the hardiest plants I had in my garden: Creeping Charlies and Wandering Jews. My experience with these two plants was that it was next to impossible to kill them, as they are survivors under any conditions. Vanessa accepted the plants joyfully and took complete responsibility for giving them all the attention they needed. She knew that transplanting was an important event in any plant's life and that each plant needed special care every day.

Although Vanessa had been uprooted from several placements in the past, this time she "took root." The caring and nourishment of her new foster parents led to her own blossoming. The social worker continued making home visits and spent time with Vanessa in the garden as she continued to care for the plants she had been given.

In this metaphor I used a real-life personal experience as the background structure for the metaphor *and* as the primary means of matching Vanessa's problem. By personalizing the plight of the abandoned and transplanted plants via dialogue with them, Vanessa was able to identify safely and meaningfully, without feeling overwhelmed. This left her free to also participate in the positive ending of the story and to attempt to anchor it into her own life with the planting of my cuttings.

This contrasts with the following metaphors, which were based entirely on our own imaginative associations.

FICTIONAL FRAMEWORKS

Blue Sparkle

I worked weekly with a small group of children consisting of three boys and one girl between the ages of eight and nine. All the children had been referred for a number of behavior problems that centered around attention deficits and subclinical hyperactive behavior. Indeed, they wiggled and squirmed continuously! In our first group meeting I discovered that they all enjoyed watching cartoon shows (no concentration problems reported here!) and had all been to the aquatic shows at Sea World. They were quite lively in voicing their excitement at watching all the different kinds of fish jump and leap through the water. Since jumping and leaping was something they themselves did a great deal of the time, I had all the clues I needed to begin. I told them to close their eyes and pretend they were watching a cartoon show entitled "The Adventures of Blue Sparkle."*

Blue Sparkle was the story of a wonderful little fish who wiggled his tail so quickly that no one could catch him. That is a fine ability for a fish to have when it needs to race or protect itself, but Blue

---

* See Chapter 8 for a detailed presentation of the use of cartoons as therapy.

Sparkle was hardly ever still and never stopped long enough to enjoy all the treasures within the ocean. This made him sad when he heard other fish tell amazing stories of slowing down to see all the fascinating things in the ocean. But no matter how hard Blue sparkle tried, he still wiggled and swam too fast.

One day he found himself thinking about a time when the current of the water was slow and peaceful. He could really remember the slow, floating feeling of the slow current. As he was thinking these relaxing thoughts, he noticed his fin slowed down too! He was delighted with his discovery and was eager to see if it would work again. And it did. He then swam by a school of fish who were all gathered around a shimmering treasure chest. Once again Blue Sparkle remembered the slowness of the water's current and so he slowed down and began to learn so much. And all the other fish were surprised and happy to have Blue Sparkle swim and play and learn with them.

Stories such as Blue Sparkle and other fantasy adventures were told to the children as an integral part of each session. Our weekly meetings continued for a period of eight months. In general, the children demonstrated signs of overall improvement in behavior: They were able to concentrate longer in school and they were better able to interact with their peers.

A Work of Art

Carey was an eleven-year-old girl who was "caught in the middle" of a custody battle taking place between her divorcing parents. Because there was no possibility of altering or ameliorating the course this custody battle would have to run, therapy was focused on helping Carey gain a strong sense of her own beauty and self-worth despite the chaotic events taking place in her life.

During one of the sessions, Carey was told a story about a beautiful piece of artwork—indeed, a masterpiece—that was put up for auction. A great deal of time was spent describing in detail the uniqueness and beauty of this masterpiece. The activity of bidding was then introduced to metaphorically match the custody and visitation battle the child was experiencing. To underscore the reality of her parents' love even as they haggled over her, Carey was told, "Even though each person upped the bid in order to own this work of art, they each loved this masterpiece and felt they had a right to have it in their home."

The metaphor emphasized that the work of art always remained a masterpiece regardless of who owned it.

Since the masterpiece possessed a special beauty all its own, it would be appreciated and loved by many throughout the years ahead.

PART TWO

Creating Therapeutic Metaphors

4

Gathering Information

When I was a little child I watched my grandmother crochet a tablecloth. I remember noticing that she started by gathering a large, beige ball of thin yarn, her special crochet needle, a scissors, and the patterns she was about to follow—all contained in a lovely straw basket. I asked if she would teach me what she knew, and she nodded, saying yes.

Learning how to generate therapeutic metaphors involves a multi-faceted process for the therapist that can be learned one step at a time. In Part II we will provide a framework of the basic ingredients we have found helpful in creating metaphors that foster change and growth. First, ways of perceiving, evoking, and generating the different kinds of information that will be needed for creating the metaphor will be examined. This information includes both specific and nonspecific aspects of sensory and linguistic systems. We then will demonstrate how to utilize the information by weaving it into a story that contains a plot, characters, and action that match the child's presenting problem, inner resources, and desired solutions.

Eliciting and Utilizing Positive Experiences

Possibly the most important information which therapists can elicit from the child is that of positive experiences—those hobbies, movies, cartoon characters, playmates, animals, events, memories and so forth, which have had a beneficial effect. This focus on eliciting positive experiences differs from traditional approaches in which emphasis is placed on the problem area. As therapists, we are very aware of the power wielded by painful memories and traumas, yet we tend to minimize or simply overlook the corollary to this reality: An equally powerful valence can be associated with the positive. We have found that in most cases enough attention has been accorded the negative side of the scale. Therefore, it is helpful for both child and therapist to move toward a balance by focusing on pleasant memories and interests. These pleasant associations can function as a "ticket for admission" into the child's unique inner world of resources. In addition, they help form the "background structure" (Brink, 1982) of the metaphor, using scenes, activities, and occurrences already familiar to the child.

The events of Erickson's personal life helped to bring this fertile area of utilizing positive experiences into professional focus in terms that were tangible, human, and real. In a biographical sketch of Erickson, Rossi (Rossi, Ryan & Sharp, 1983) describes the ways in which Erickson achieved his own self-recovery from the paralysis of polio at the age of 17 by drawing upon his past sensory memories (p.12):

> In the weeks and months that followed [the attack of polio], Milton foraged through his sense memories to try to relearn how to move. He would stare for hours at his hand, for example, and try to recall how his fingers had felt when grasping a pitchfork. Bit by bit he found his fingers beginning to twitch and move in tiny, uncoordinated ways. He persisted until the movements became larger and until he could consciously control them. And how did his hand grasp a tree limb? How did his legs, feet, and toes move when he climbed a tree?

In a published conversation, Rossi probed Erickson to clarify just how he had achieved his recovery (Erickson & Rossi, 1977/1980, pp. 112–113):

> *Rossi (R):* In your self-rehabilitative experiences between the age of 17 and 19 you learned from your own experience that you

could use your imagination to achieve the same effects as an actual physical effort.

Erickson (E): An *intense memory* rather than imagination. You remember how something tastes, you know how you get a certain tingle from peppermint. As a child I used to climb a tree in a wood lot and then jump from one tree to another like a monkey. I would recall the many different twists and turns I made in order to find out what are the movements you make when you have full muscles.

R: You activated real memories from childhood in order to learn just how much muscle control you had left and how to reacquire that control.

E: Yes, you use real memories. At 18 I recalled all my childhood movements to help myself relearn muscle coordination.

Erickson's striking personal experience with the positive power of his own past memories naturally led him to evoke and utilize the same in his patients. This was one of the ways in which Erickson achieved his significant, paradigmatic shift away from pathology and onto potentials.

Following is a case example of a brief dialogue between therapist and child which demonstrates the process of eliciting positive memories and experiences.

Paulana, age 12, was the younger of two children. She was described by her parents as being a "model child who was always even-tempered and predictable." She was an A student and socialized well with her peers. The problem arose a few weeks after her older brother stormed out of the house, having had a "knock-down-drag-out" battle with the father. Paulana suddenly developed sleeping and eating problems, was unable to concentrate on her homework, and was described by her teachers as "daydreaming all the time."

After hearing the parents' version of Paulana's problems with Paulana present, the therapist then met with the child alone.

Therapist (T): It looks like a lot of things have changed in your life in a short period of time.

Paulana (P): Yeah. I really miss Bobbie. I'm so worried about what's happened to him. He's only called twice since he left, and I was at school both times. *[Paulana begins to cry.]*

[Everytime Paulana tried to remember Bobbie, she would relive that terrible night when her father and Bobbie yelled at each other, knocked the chairs over, and slammed doors. She said she had never seen such violent anger between them.]

T: What would it take for you to feel better?

P: Bobbie here, right now *[still crying]*.

T: And if he were here, what would be happening and how would you feel?

P: Bobbie would hold me tight and tell me he'll never leave again and then I'd feel happy inside *[tears have almost stopped now]*. *(Patient describes desired outcome.)*

T: What are some other things in your life that usually make you feel happy inside?
(Therapist elicits pleasant memories for background structure.)

P: Oh, I like music a lot. Is that what you mean?

T: Uh-huh. *[Nodding affirmatively.]* What else besides music?
(Therapist elicits additional favorite experiences.)

P: My doggie, Peddles. He's real silly. . . . Oh, and my mother taught me how to sew and I was making a dress—before Bobbie left *[saddened look]*.

[As a strategic intervention to prevent Paulana from slipping back into a negative trance by again focusing on her brother's departure, the therapist quickly threw a magic marker in her direction with instructions to use it for some artwork in a moment.]

(Therapist provides pattern interruption to maintain child in present and out of painful trance.)

T: Good catch, Paulana. Specifically, what is it about music that you like?

P: *[Face brightens]* When I *hear* my favorite groups play, I *bounce* to the music and *feel great*. I *don't think* of anything else.
(Identify sensory resources as kinesthetic and auditory precesses.)

More specifics were elicited about Paulana's relationship with her dog, her sewing abilities, and music. These experiences offered valuable resources of "feeling happy inside." They were later integrated into a therapeutic metaphor that provided her with new, more positive ways of responding to the loss of her brother.

It should be noted that this process of eliciting positive experiences is a "soft" one in which there is no A-B-C formula to follow. The therapist's questions may not always evoke a specific memory of a particular experience, as was the case with Paulana. One severely depressed child we treated could not think of anything that made him happy when we first questioned him. As we refined our questioning to probe for nonspecific associations, the little boy suddenly exclaimed, "Raindrops! I like the sound of raindrops against the roof!"

Memories, experiences, and associations are subtle, multidimensional phenomena and the process of evoking them can be equally as intricate. The memory of sitting by a fireplace and listening to the crackling sounds of burning logs or watching the flames flicker and dance can be as powerful a tool as the memory of having stories read at bedtime. The challenge for the therapist is one of finding ways to trigger whatever past positive associations can be meaningfully utilized in the child's therapy. Following is an example of how an elicited favorite object was used to form the background structure of a therapeutic metaphor.

Bobbie and the Toy Store

I first met Bobbie several years ago when he was only two-and-a-half years of age. At the time I was treating his mother, Annette, for clinical depression, she would bring Bobbie to the office when baby-sitters were not available. The father had abandoned the mother and child soon after the birth and the mother had not resolved the trauma. We worked well together and her depression lifted. A few years later Annette returned with some mothering issues regarding Bobbie and once again brief therapy was all that was necessary.

As Bobbie grew older, he began to blame his mother for the absence of his father. At age nine he arrived back in my office because his mother was frightened of his spontaneous outbursts of crying which would turn into screaming and uncontrollable tantrums of anger and fury. Annette could not communicate with Bobbie during these tumultuous states—he simply did not respond. The only piece of information that continued to surface in many indirect ways was that Bobbie missed having his father in his life. Bobbie denied this, however, and would become very withdrawn whenever I moved near a "Daddy issue."

I learned from Bobbie that he had his own dog, liked stuffed animals, and enjoyed wandering around a local toy store. Based on this information, I presented a metaphor about a special toy store in which stuffed doggies waited to be purchased and taken to new homes. In this toy store, some of the doggies were bought by children, others by a woman and man together, some by a man alone, and others by a woman alone. At nighttime all the doggies in the toy store would howl about who they wanted to take them home.

"I only want to be in a fun home," said one.

"I want to be in a mama home," explained another.

"I want to be with anybody who will love and care for me," said yet another.

But one doggie alone was stuck because he had only one type of home he thought he would ever be happy in. It was a Mama and a Papa home, and nothing else. Well, whenever a child saw him and wanted to take him home, the doggie would look so sad and unhappy that the child would change her mind. When a woman by herself would show delight in having him, the doggie's face would change suddenly into a ferocious snarl and the woman would quickly select another stuffed doggie. Little by little all the doggies were purchased except one—the one who remained behind because he refused to be happy and go to any home unless it was a Mama and Papa home.

One day the wizard puppet who lived across the aisle in the toy store said to the doggie, "There's a way to get over your problem. If you don't, you'll just be upset the rest of your doggie life. You'll have to let go of all that disappointment and annoyance and replace it with what you had so long ago—puppy love. I don't know why you decided to hold onto only one choice, one solution. My magic wand can change anything because it knows there are other choices. My wand would never hold onto being sad and mad all the time—they're so heavy—it wouldn't be able to lift and do its magic. Use my magic wand to allow yourself to be accepted by the one who *loves* you."

In addition to telling metaphors with this kind of theme, I also introduced a living metaphor. I decided to utilize Bobbie's own behavior instead of trying to stop it; I suggested the only problem was that he hadn't cried, screamed, and gotten angry *well enough*.

Bobbie was given the assignment of taking fifteen minutes each night to stand in front of a mirror and turn on a tape recorder. First he was instructed to see himself looking very, very sad; he was to make the sound his sadness made; and he was to feel what parts of his body felt the most and the least of the sadness. The same instructions were given for anger.

Two weeks later his mother reported how surprised she was that Bobbie was religious about practicing his assignment—all on his own. The uncontrollable outbursts had stopped for the most part. However, one day Annette was in the living room with Bobbie when he resumed the old behavior. She asked him nervously, "Bobbie, are you all right?" He unexpectedly snapped out of his tantrum, smiled and exclaimed, "I'm OK—I was just practicing what the doctor told me to do." Further therapy continued to reinforce Bobbie's new learnings about the specialness of his one-parent home. Gradually his tantrums subsided as he turned his energy toward normal, nine-year-old activities.

Recognizing and Utilizing Minimal Cues

As her fingers moved, delicately interweaving the yarn with the crochet needle, a flowery, lace circle began to emerge almost magically. I wondered to myself if I would ever do it so easily.

The importance of utilizing minimal cues for creating metaphors lies in the subtlety of the new information they can provide. Learning to recognize and utilize the child's minimal behavioral responses gives the therapist a better chance of creating a story that rings true to the child. Minimal cues, both verbal (conscious) and nonverbal (unconscious), can tell us which types of sensory experiences are most familiar to the child. In a way, minimal cues are the latticework over which the storyline is woven.

Theoretically the exact same storyline could be revised linguistically for every child to maximize the therapeutic possibilities. In each case the underlying latticework of minimal cues is subtly shifted to reflect each child's unique sensory and linguistic preferences, even as the main principal of the story remains the same. To an unattuned listener, the reworked versions would sound essentially the same. To a trained ear, however, important and sensitive differences could be detected.

What are minimal cues? We have all had a lifetime of experience in recognizing and responding to minimal cues. Parents, in particular, are an excellent example. They learn a highly complex and refined repertory of minimal cues within a few days of their baby's birth. Indeed, the infant is learning to communicate with the mother even before its birth. The mother feels its movement, its growth, its development, and can sense when it is comfortable or restless. As soon as the baby is born, its parents begin to learn a whole new type of language. A soft sound from the crib or a tiny movement can tell a parent that the baby is awakening. Parents quickly learn the difference between a sleeping movement and a waking movement. The nursing mother learns to sense when the baby is becoming satiated by a subtle decrease in the strength and frequency of the sucking motion. The mother can even discern her baby's mood by the quality of its sucking. Parents learn to respond to slight changes in facial expression that signal the beginnings of discomfort, and to sense the minute stiffening of their baby's body in their arms that signals its need to be put down.

Thus, although the baby has no language capacities during this period of time, a vast array of qualities, feelings, and needs are communicated. Indeed, through each stage of development—from infant to toddler to young child—a new and complex arrangement of minimal cues spontaneously emerges between parent and child.

Teachers in classroom situations also know a great deal about minimal cues. They often recognize a child's discomfort at forced class participation, or will pick up the underlying insecurity of the child who too readily participates. Changes in facial color, eye blinking, voice tones, and breathing patterns are knowingly or unknowingly recognized and responded to by the sensitive teacher.

Learning to recognize and respond to minimal cues as therapists is one of the most powerful therapeutic tools available because it provides a window into the child's personal experience. The child who manifests an asthma-type breathing pattern, for example, can be taught a more comfortable way to breathe once the therapist has herself recognized and utilized the breathing behavior by matching it. Similarly when a child is speaking in a very rapid and tense manner, matching and utilizing the speech pattern can help the therapist create her own internal experience of what the child may be feeling.

A child comes into a therapy session knowing she has been brought in for a problem. I ask the child, "I wonder if you know why you've been brought here today?" The child says, "No, I don't have any idea. Everything is fine." Yet I notice that the child's eyes are looking downward as she is talking; her breathing is shallow and she is curled up in the corner of the couch with her arms crossed tightly in front of her. After observing the child's subtle behaviors, I might direct my eyes downward, move toward the other corner of the couch, and match her breathing pattern for the purpose of providing myself with an experiential awareness of her state. I am communicating to the child's unconscious that *I see it, I hear it, I experience it; I do understand what it's like to be in that position.* I might then tell a story that matches the child's experience, based on what I myself am feeling, and then slowly lead the child out of the uncomfortable situation with the storyline.

> "As I'm listening to you, I am reminded of a time I saw my friend's little dog shaking in the corner because she was frightened by a storm. When she heard thunder and lightning, she put her head down and her eyes down, covered her ears with her paws, and began to tighten up into a little ball." The story would then introduce positive elements of safety and security until the child showed signs of a more relaxed and receptive mood.

Formal recognition of the importance of minimal cues came with the emergence of the body therapies in the 1960s (Lowen, 1965, 1967, 1975; Perls, 1969; Reich, 1949). Nonverbal body language then became a new and valid focus for therapists. As a result of this new focus, most of us have received some kind of training in perceiving the nonverbal behavior presented by client.

Specific approaches for recognizing and utilizing minimal cues are available in Erickson's original work (1964a/1980, 1964b/1980, 1980b, 1980c, 1980d) and have been elaborated by many of his students (Bandler & Grinder, 1975; Dilts, Grinder, Bandler, DeLozier, & Cameron-Bandler, 1979; Erickson & Rossi, 1979; Erickson, Rossi & Rossi, 1976; Rossi, 1982, 1986a). Erickson was quietly developing his own innovative way of observing and utilizing what he termed "minimal cues" long before the body therapy movement emerged. In his later years he received professional recognition for the skill and mastery with which he had demonstrated these abilities in clinical situations. Here again Erickson was not "inventing" a technique of observing and utilizing minimal cues, but was rather drawing upon past experiences from his own childhood and teenage years. In a sense, he simply elaborated and refined what had come naturally to him as a child.

Rossi points out that Erickson's early life, even before his bout with polio, was characterized by "constitutional differences and altered perceptions" (Rossi, Ryan & Sharp, 1983). Erickson was color-blind, tone deaf, arrhythmic, and dyslexic. His childhood curiosity was greatly stimulated by the fact that he apparently experienced the world in a way that was noticeably different from those around him. He initiated any number of "experiments" to gain information about how individuals perceived and responded to their world. These experiments engaged his natural penchant for minute behavioral observations and formed a solid foundation for the self-recovery work he would carry out in his late teens.

We have already described how Erickson utilized his own past memories and associations in his rehabilitation effort. The second major tool he brought into this process was his ability to perceive and utilize the *minimal cues* naturally occurring in his environment. Rossi narrates (Rossi, Ryan & Sharp, 1983, p. 11):

> Just how Milton recovered is one of the most fascinating stories of self-help and discovery I have ever heard. When he awakened after those three days he found himself almost totally paralyzed: he could hear very acutely; he could see and move his eyes; he could speak with great difficulty; but he could not otherwise move. There were no rehabilitation facilities in the rural community, and for all anyone knew he was to remain without the use of his limbs for the rest of his life. But Milton's acute intelligence continued to probe. For example, he learned to play mental games by interpreting the sounds around him as he lay in bed all day. By the sound of just how the barn door closed and how long it took the footsteps to reach the house, he could tell who it was and what mood he or she was in.

Erickson's ability to utilize a minimal cue that occurred in his own body proved to be the turning point of his difficult recovery. Again Rossi narrates (Rossi, Ryan & Sharp, 1983, pp. 11–12):

> Then came that critical day when his family forgot that they had left him alone, tied into the rocking chair. (They had fashioned a kind of primitive potty for Milton by cutting a hole in the seat of the chair.) The rocking chair was somewhere in the middle of the room with Milton in it, looking longingly at the window, wishing he were closer to it so that he could at least have the pleasure of gazing out at the farm. As he sat there, apparently immobile, wishing and wondering, *he suddenly became aware that his chair began to rock slightly. . . .* This experience, which probably would have passed unnoticed by most of us, led the 17-year-old lad into a feverish period of self-exploration and discovery.

It was during this "feverish period of self-exploration and discovery" that Erickson utilized the sensory memories mentioned previously to help him regain the use of his muscles. Rossi notes, however, that more than the introspection of remembered sensory experiences would be required if Erickson were to walk again. Erickson somehow recognized this and so began daily observation sessions of his youngest sister, who was herself just learning to walk. Methodically, he would observe and imitate all the micromovements that accompanied the more perceptible motions of getting up, standing, and walking. Erickson reiterates (Rossi, Ryan & Sharp, 1983, pp. 13–14):

> I learned to stand up by watching baby sister learn to stand up: use two hands for a base, uncross your legs, use the knees for a wide base, and then put more pressure on one arm and hand to get up. Sway back and forth to get balance. Practice knee bends and keep balance. Move ahead after the body balances. Move hand and shoulder after the body balances. Put one foot in front of the other with balance. Fall. Try again.

Erickson spent eleven months forging a recovery that resulted in his ability to enter college on crutches that fall. After the summer of his freshman year, he was walking unaided but with a noticeable limp.

Erickson's early life story is important to therapists because it so poignantly demonstrates the power of past positive memories and current minimal cues in bringing about significant emotional, behavioral, and psychophysiological change. Clearly, Erickson's recovery hinged on his innate abilities to perceive and utilize that which was not apparent. His later development of these abilities in the clinical setting helped to uncover a new fertile area of exploration and expansion for therapists on the growing edge of consciousness. Because Erickson's contribution to the therapeutic utilization of minimal cues was seminal, we will provide a short overview of his writings in this area.

Probably the most dramatic illustration of Erickson's facility with minimal cues was demonstrated by his spontaneous development of the pantomime technique of hypnotic induction in 1959 (Erickson, 1964a/1980). Invited to address a hypnosis group in Mexico City, Erickson was presented with a demonstration subject who neither spoke nor understood English. Erickson himself neither spoke nor understood Spanish. A completely mute demonstration ensued during which he relied solely upon nonverbal, behavioral, minimal cues to interact with (and hypnotize) his subject. In the paper he wrote describing his initial and subsequent experiences with the pantomime technique, Erickson concluded (Erickson, 1964a/1980, p. 338):

> A parallelism of thought and comprehension exists which is not based upon verbalizations evocative of specified responses, but which *derives from behavioral manifestations not ordinarily recognized or appreciated at the conscious level of mentation.* [Italics added]

In another important paper, Erickson (1964b/1980) described a demonstration involving one of his techniques that relied heavily upon his perception and utilization of the subject's minimal cues. An audiovisual recording was made of the demonstration. So subtle were the behavioral nuances utilized by Erickson during the demonstration that neither subject nor audience could account for the hypnotic trance that had clearly occurred. Several replays of the video were necessary to pinpoint the interplay between verbal and nonverbal behaviors that had culminated in the subject's trance experience. Later, a verbatim written transcription of the demonstration was found to be meaningless to students who had not attended the demonstration nor seen the video: "To the reader's eye it [the transcription] was abominably repetitious . . . The minimal cues of the total situation and of the author's behavior . . . were vital for any effective understandings" (Erickson, 1964b/1980, p. 357).

In a particularly delightful fragment written during the 1960s and published for the first time in 1980, Erickson (1980d) described his lifelong process of observations into the nature of verbal and nonverbal communication. With humor and wit he described his bewilderment at the inexplicable movements of hand clapping and foot tapping his grade school classmates would make whenever music was played. (He was arrythmic.) Adding to his confusion were the strange breathing patterns he observed them making whenever they opened their mouths to sing. (He was tone deaf.) Breathing patterns gradually became a compelling focus of interest for him. By his teens he had recognized that both humming and yawning were contagious and that he could induce such behaviors in his classmates by casually initiating one or the other. His high school observations on stuttering were critical in solidifying his estimation of breathing as a powerful if little recognized determinant of behavior (Erickson, 1980d, p. 364):

> When I encountered my first stutterer, I was completely bewildered by his breathing pattern when *he thought of talking* and *when he spoke*. It made me uneasy and uncomfortable, and I avoided it after copying the pattern a couple of times as well as I could to make a classmate uncertain and hesitant in reciting. This frightened me and served to convince me further that *people communicated with each other at "breathing" levels of awareness unknown to them. [Italics added]*

In his later years Erickson's own breathing patterns became almost as famous as his eyes in facilitating hypnotic experiences in his clients and subjects.

Still another paper (Erickson, 1980c) provides interesting observations on how we absorb and respond to minimal cues in our everyday environments, and on the role of minimal cues in relation to memory. Finally, the two-way significance of minimal cues in the therapeutic relationship is well described in a brief report (Erickson, 1980b) that focuses on how minimal cues given unknowingly by the therapist can influence the patient's responsiveness.

The concepts and empirical data presented in Erickson's writings on the multifaceted phenomenon of minimal cues can provide a solid foundation for understanding the dynamic interplay of nonverbal and verbal behavior that occurs between therapists and clients. In the sections that follow, we will describe specific techniques involving fairly refined perceptions of minimal cues. In the following example, however, we wish simply to stress how minimal cues can be perceived, utilized, and translated back to the child metaphorically in a spontaneous way.

Mikie's Blanket of Puppets

Six-year-old Mikie sat rather quietly on my big brown rocker and blanketed himself with many of the animal puppets in my office. I had worked with Mikie and his parents for some months prior to this session and had established a good rapport. Mikie was an energetic and inquisitive child. Usually he was rather active and chattery in our sessions, whether we were playing on the floor with toys or sitting at the art table. His quiet, somewhat subdued behavior today was uncharacteristic of our past encounters.

A few weeks prior to this session, Mikie's two-year-old sister, Janie, had showed him how she had been "poked here with a pen" (pointing to her rectum) by their babysitter. Mikie immediately told his mother and the incident was reported to the proper authorities. Mikie's mother told me how angry and upset he was that someone he trusted had hurt his sister. There were a number of individual sessions with Janie in which various drawing strategies were utilized as a primary treatment approach* to help her deal with her feelings of fear, hurt, and anger over the molestation incident. The family was also seen intermittently between the individual sessions. Janie soon returned to normal daily routines and was acting "her old, funny little self again," as her father reported during one of the sessions.

Mikie, however, was having a harder time dealing with his feelings of anger and insecurity. His mother reported that he would not stay with anyone except her or his father since the incident. She said he was even reluctant to go to a friend's house and play unless she stayed with him. She put it simply, "His trust was shaken by the incident."

---

* Drawing strategies are presented in detail in Chapter 7.

As part of our sessions, Mikie and I would always have a little snack. This time I noticed Mikie hesitate before accepting my offer of milk and chocolate chip cookies, which he usually accepted quite enthusiastically. His body also tensed slightly as I moved a bit closer to him. Among the soft, cuddly puppet animals on Mikie's lap was a black-and-tan striped kitten. The kitten, together with Mikie's minimal cues (puppets surrounding him, tenseness in his body, hesitancy before accepting snack, pensiveness) and his cup of milk sitting on the table, somehow shed a reflective light on an idea for a story.

I began by putting the kitten puppet on my right hand and stroking it with my left hand. I asked Mikie if I had ever told him the story about the kitten who wandered into my yard one day. Shaking his head, he said, "No."

"Well," I began softly and rhythmically, "One day, when I was in my house, I heard the sound of a kitten crying outside. I went out to the yard and there was this darling little striped kitten. I knelt down to pick it up but it snarled and hissed at me loudly. *[I made the sounds and motions with the puppet.]* I backed away quickly, realizing that the kitten was scared and needing to protect itself by hissing and snarling. I went back into my house and got a cup of milk *[letting my finger touch Mikie's cup of milk on the table]*. I put the milk down and moved behind a corner of my house and waited. Soon the kitty came out again and wandered over to the milk *[I moved the puppet over to his cup of milk]* and began to drink. I then went over to the kitty again and this time only touched the cup to let it know that it was safe here, and then moved away again. Finally, I knelt down by the kitty and put out my hand for it to sniff. This time the kitty licked my hand and looked up at me."

While looking into his eyes and petting the kitty puppet, I then said to Mikie, "Something must have scared the kitty once, and he learned how to protect himself by sounding and looking angry. That scary feeling must have made him forget how to trust. It was important for the kitty to *learn how to trust again*."

Mikie was completely entranced by the short story and the small movements of the kitten puppet on my hand. With the end of the story and the statement to him about learning to trust, he took a deep breath, sat back, and smiled. Within a few moments he picked up a big walrus and began talking to me, using the puppet. Then he picked up the little black bear, put down the walrus, picked up the cinnamon bear in his free hand, and then asked me to go get the big bear. He became increasingly animated and directive in his behavior. Rather than blanketing himself in the puppets, he now began to use them actively as a means of expressing himself—and also just for the fun of it. When his mother came for him at the end of the session, Mikie was hard at play and did not want to leave. He asked her if he could come back and play with the puppets again; when she said yes, he was willing to stop for the day.

Recognizing and Utilizing Sensory Preferences

Seeing the look on my face, Grandma seemed to understand my apprehension. She took out another crochet needle and some yarn from the basket, and began showing me how to hold the needle and yarn between my fingers—how to begin to crochet my very own cloth.

Each of us perceives, learns, and communicates in the world through our five sensory systems of visual, auditory, kinesthetic, olfactory, and gustatory processes. Sensory systems play a vital role in child development as the primary means of early learning during infancy and young childhood. Even the child's later cognitive development is shaped and colored by the experiences of his sensory-motor stage of development (Piaget, 1951). Our senses literally act as transmitters of information to the brain and as such help to influence the evolution of our overall level of intelligence (Pearce, 1977).

If we were to view child development through a lens of perfection, we would hope to see a synchronicity emerging among the sensory processes whereby each sensory system interacts in a balanced way with the others. In the course of normal growing processes, however, early life experiences, together with innate personality traits, affect the child in a way that produces a preference in sensory function: One system is used more readily than the others in a given task or experience.

For example, one child might rely *primarily* on her auditory sensory system to process music (becoming entranced in the sound of the melody), while when reading she would use *primarily* her visual sensory system (making pictures of the words). These are typical and expected sensory preferences. Another child, however, might engage his kinesthetic sensory system to process the music (responding *primarily* to the beat of the music and his own movement impulses), while when reading he might prefer to use his auditory sensory system by reading aloud (making sounds rather than pictures of the words).

We emphasize the word *primarily* because it is important to remember that in complex experiences such as reading or listening to music, all sensory systems are in operation on different levels of consciousness. One, however, is relied upon more dominantly. The two children just mentioned have different sensory strategies for processing the same experience of reading and listening to music. Teachers often see this difference in the classroom and parents often experience it in the home. One child will grasp a new concept most readily if it is explained to him vocally, while another will need a diagram or picture.

Sensory *preferences* become sensory *imbalances* whenever the preference results in a problem—be it emotional, behavioral, or psychosomatic. The child who *prefers* to read aloud develops a sensory imbalance when he can *only* read aloud. At this point, the preference has become crystallized into a fixed mode of responding which limits the child's choices and impedes his range of experiences. The consequences of sensory imbalances are most clearly manifested by learning disabled children in whom the imbalances are severe enough to produce observable difficulties. Because they experience the world in a different sensory-perceptual level, learning disabled children encounter barriers that are not experienced by others. The failures in cognitive and motor performance that occur because of this difference then lead to emotional and behavioral maladjustments which are only a symptom of the real problem. The following case highlights this dynamic but subtle interplay between sensory functioning and emotional well-being.

Mary's Spelling Bear

When eight-year-old Mary was brought to the office by her mother, she was shy and very reluctant to speak. According to her mother, Mary was having a very difficult time with spelling. It seemed that no matter how hard she tried, her efforts to spell turned out "wrong." Although she was doing very well in her other subjects, Mary's repeated failure with spelling was upsetting her a great deal. Her mother naturally feared that this cycle of failure would undermine Mary's progress in the other areas.

After working unsuccessfully with a tutor to help with the spelling problem, the school counselor suggested that an evaluation by a child psychotherapist would be helpful to determine if there were an emotional block.

The only information I could elicit from Mary was that she liked teddy bears and had a collection of them in her bedroom. By using the techniques described in the upcoming chapters, I then isolated the sensory imbalance that was creating the problem. Mary, it seemed, was a very visual person. She was able to describe her various teddy bears to me in vivid language. Her auditory sense, however, was less accessible. The problem was that her teacher was emphasizing *phonetics* in spelling, continually encouraging her to *"hear* how the word *sounds"* in order to learn how to spell it. But Mary needed to *see* how the word *looked* in order to remember it.

To help overcome the immediate problem in spelling, I suggested that Mary pick one word and imagine *seeing* the letters of that word going across the chest of her teddy bear—almost like a T-shirt insignia. Interestingly enough, Mary spontaneously chose the word *easy,* closed her eyes, and to her delight found that she could see the letters e-a-s-y going across her teddy bear. Since we could not retrain her teacher to use more visual techniques in teaching spelling to Mary, we simply made this game our secret. Each night Mary dutifully used her teddy bear as the background structure for learning her new spelling words.

Once the spelling problem was resolved, we focused on opening up Mary's restricted auditory system by eliciting positive areas of Mary's life in which *sounds* were her preferred or primary way of enjoying an experience. Such sounds as waves at the beach or her parakeet chirping in the morning constituted pleasant auditory experiences that could be utilized in subsequent metaphors to strengthen, broaden, and integrate Mary's auditory system into her daily life.

Although sensory imbalances may not appear to be the generating problem for all children, we have found that they do play a consistently pivotal role in determining how the child copes with the presenting problem. It could be said that some kind of sensory imbalance is inherent in any emotional or behavioral problem, which is why sensory systems are a predictable, reliable and utilizable focus of treatment. By disentangling sensory imbalances from their emotional ramifications, you can alter the entire psychodynamic constellation. Even when the presenting problem is not caused directly by a sensory imbalance, intervening on a sensory level will invariably re-order the dynamics in a positive direction.

A variety of sensory integration approaches to treating learning disabled children (Ayres, 1971; Cantwell, 1980) have been recognized as effective remedial techniques for increasing attention and concentration skills and improving overall learning abilities (Abrams, 1980). We have found that the concept of sensory integration or *sensory synchronicity* is also an effective focus for behavioral and emotional problems because the way in which children's sensory systems function in relation to the presenting problem *and* in relation to positive areas of their life will serve as both a critical diagnostic tool and as a valuable resource in resolving the problem. Learning to observe and utilize sensory imbalances therefore provides a core foundation for change on many different levels.

The concept of utilizing sensory dynamics in therapy as a standard clinical tool rather than as one specifically associated with learning disabilities was also modeled by Erickson. Rossi explains that as a self-acknowledged "visual type," Erickson would routinely explore his patients' early memories to ascertain whether they were "predominantly visual or auditory" (Rossi, Ryan & Sharp, 1983, p. 35). He would then utilize these predispositions in trance work as a means of dealing with the presenting problem, whatever that might be. Erickson cites an example of a man who was able to distract himself from pain by focusing on the memories of the sound of crickets which he had enjoyed in his childhood.

As was often the case with Erickson, the techniques he utilized with his patients were first developed in response to his own needs. Because he lived in almost constant pain during the last two decades of his life, he found ever new ways of utilizing his sensory memories and sensory preferences as a means of distraction from the pain. He recalled (Erickson, 1971/1980, p. 123):

> I was recovering the feeling of lying prone with my arms in front of me, head up and looking at that beautiful meadow as a child. I even felt my arm short as a child's. I went to sleep essentially reliving those childhood days when I was lying on my stomach on the hill overlooking the meadow or the green fields. They

looked so beautiful and so blissful and so peaceful. It was the gentle movement of the grass in the breeze, but the grass itself was not putting forth the effort.

It could be said that Erickson helped to pioneer the recognition and utilization of sensory dynamics as they relate to a wide variety of clinical problems. Later workers (Bandler & Grinder, 1975; Erickson & Rossi, 1979, 1981; Erickson, Rossi & Rossi, 1976; Grinder, DeLozier & Bandler, 1977; Gilligan, 1986; Haley, 1967, 1973; Lankton, 1980; Lankton & Lankton, 1983) have added system and theory to the groundbreaking approaches developed by Erickson.

Our goal in working with children is to facilitate an ongoing experience of sensory synchronicity that can provide the child with a rich and accessible "treasure chest" of inner resources. One easy and natural way to begin this process of sensory synchronization is through storytelling, an ancient tradition rooted in rich, poetic, sensory-filled language. Unlike the historical storyteller who creates classical stories of sociocultural traditions, however, the therapist-storyteller is creating tailor-made stories (metaphors) based on the personal, idiosyncratic, and psychodynamic qualities of the child. The starting point for the creation of these specially designed stories is in developing a sensitive awareness to the sensory preferences that reflect the otherwise elusive inner world of the child.

5

Learning the Language of the Child

At first my fingers fumbled the stitches. Frustrated,
I said, "This seems so hard to learn—will I ever be
able to do it?" Grandma reassured me in her own
soft way.

Language Cues: A Conscious Communication System?

When traveling to a foreign country, greeting a person in his own native language is an acknowledgment of respect that can lead to an immediate rapport. However, not having the skill to communicate in that foreign language can lead to confusion, frustration, and even alienation.

Language barriers can also exist *within* the same language. We all communicate our experiences, feelings, perceptions and thoughts in ways which utilize both verbal and nonverbal sensory descriptions. *How* we communicate reveals as much about us as *what* we communicate. Problems in communication often arise because the *what* of our communication conflicts with the *how* of our communication, or because the *style* of our communication conflicts with the *style* of the listener's communication. For example, a poetic writing style might spark a deep association for one reader while another reader more receptive to literal communication would be "turned off."

The same concept or idea can have a vastly differing impact depending on the linguistic style used to present it and on the linguistic preferences of the readers to whom it is presented. While each of us has our own personal style of communicating, all of us share the processes by which we communicate. Thus, while two different people choose two different ways to describe a shared experience, they both draw upon common *sensory preferences* in order to compose their descriptions.

What kind of language does a person select to describe his experience? Which sensory system does he use to perceive his experience? Learning to recognize and utilize these sensory preferences as manifested in language helps to establish rapport and familiarity in the therapy or teaching setting for the same reason that speaking the language of a foreigner leads rapidly to a sense of friendship. Since the effectiveness of a therapeutic metaphor depends on its ability to communicate a message to the listener, language preferences become particularly important to its creation. Indeed, the impact of a carefully created metaphor may falter solely because of a communication failure whereby the therapist unwittingly employs language preferences which are natural to herself but not to the patient. Then, despite a thorough and compassionate understanding of the problem, the therapist simply may not be able to reach the child who is "on a different wave length."

One model for observing and utilizing sensory preferences has been presented by Bandler & Grinder (Bandler & Grinder, 1975; Dilts, Grinder, Bandler, DeLozier & Cameron-Bandler, 1979; Grinder, DeLozier & Bandler, 1977) who observed and analyzed Erickson's work in the 1970s. As linguists, they focused on Erickson's meticulous skill in using language as a therapeutic tool. They sought to uncover "patterns" or didactic systems in his approach that could be easily taught. As a result of their work they developed the *Neuro-Linguistic Programming* (NLP) approach to therapeutic intervention. We have found that the "bare essentials" of the NLP approach can provide an easy and immediate entrance into the patient's private inner world of sensory processing. Therefore, we will discuss this approach briefly and then illustrate our own applications of it with children.

In the NLP model, the sensory language a person uses serves as a *conscious, verbal representation* of the internal neurological process being accessed in the communication. To simplify, one child might say:

(Visual)   ". . . . Let me *show* you how many different *colored* dresses I have for my dolly."

                                                (Six-year-old Margie)

". . . . I *imagine* being in a big rocketship *watching* planet Earth in the distance."

(Nine-year-old Philip)

While another:

(Auditory) ". . . . I can *listen* to that group *sing* all day long."

(Fifteen-year-old Steven)

". . . . My teacher's *voice* is so *raspy* that I wish I had *earplugs*."

(Thirteen-year-old Michelle)

And still another:

(Kinesthetic) ". . . . I like to *wind up* my toy and *play* with it."

(Five-year-old Billy)

". . . . I *feel good* when I *hug* my doggie."

(Seven-year-old Tina)

Sensory language preferences are easily recognized by the predicates or action words (verbs, adverbs and adjectives) a person uses to express himself. Predicates tend to reflect one of the three major sensory experiences of *seeing* (visual), *hearing* (auditory), and *feeling* (kinesthetic). (See "List of Predicates" Chart on p. 108.) Noting the types of sensory predicates a person uses reveals the communication system that is most familiar to him. Although each of us uses visual, auditory, and kinesthetic words when speaking, we tend to rely on one system more than the others. This one system could be identified as the conscious communication system.

How does making such an identification help us in creating effective metaphors? It would seem natural that using a child's sensory language preferences would enhance the metaphor's effectiveness by increasing its degree of *relational familiarity*. The child is more likely to relate and respond to something familiar than unfamiliar. In fact, one recent study confirmed that matching a person's predicates actually increased relaxation and "appeared to enhance rapport and influence" (Yapko, 1981). While more research in this area is certainly needed, therapists can discover for themselves the positive therapeutic benefits and common-sense practicality of using the child's own preferred sensory predicates to establish rapport and expand the relevance of the metaphor.

LIST OF PREDICATES

Visual

see
observe
focus (focus in on)
clear (clarity)
sparkle
shine
glisten
gleam
glow
colors (colorful)
bright (dark)
get the picture
hues
visualize the
    problem
flash
watch
looks
visualize
reflect
dim
blur
foggy
illuminate
kaleidoscope of
    colors
appears to be
looks like
paint a picture
photographic
hazy

Auditory

giggle
voice an opinion
speaking up
hearing
listening
sound
click
tune in/tune out
roar
rumble
whistle
cracking/
    crackling
snap, crackle & pop
volume, loud, quiet
chirping
barking
sipping
yelling/shouting
static.
wordy
harmony
scream
dialog
tone ("I like
    his tone")

Kinesthetic

grasp
hold
pet, petting
touch
feel comfortable
uncomfortable
painful
hurt
heavy (light)
smooth (rough)
cold (warm)
texture (velvety,
    coarse)
sensitive
blocked
stuck
move closer
turn around
walking (running,
    crawling)
letting go (holding
    on)
relaxed
excited
electric
angry, mad
falling
tight (tense)
in touch with (out
    of touch with)
solid

Eye Movement Cues: An Unconscious Communication System?

While Grandma completed each part of her cloth, I continued practicing each step of my own creation. Remembering back, I could see it was a unique experience of learning that took place over many days and weeks.

In addition to the nonverbal minimal cues previously discussed, eye movement patterns can also be utilized as indicators of unconscious communication processes. The significance of eye movement patterns as reflections of internal states has long been sought. In the field of hypnosis, eye behavior (eye blinking, eye roll, and pupillary dilation) has traditionally been utilized as a behavioral index of hypnotizability and trance depth (Spiegel & Spiegel, 1978; Tebecis & Provins, 1975). With the advent of research in brain specialization triggered by the Sperry-Bogen discovery (Sperry, 1968), scientists have been investigating the relationship between particular types of eye movement patterns and variations in brain functioning. There is agreement among some researchers that eye movements do indicate differences in cognitive involvement and hemispheric dominance: There is a contralateral relationship between hemispheric dominance and lateral direction of eye movements; there is a further relationship between types of cognitive task (verbal-analytic vs. spatial-holistic) and hemispheric dominance (Galin & Ornstein, 1973; Kinsbourne, 1972; Kocel, Galin, Ornstein, & Merrin, 1972).

In the NLP approach (Bandler & Grinder, 1975; Beck & Beck, 1984; Dilts, 1983; Owens, 1977), eye movement patterns are believed to provide a kind of external graphing of internal, sensory-system accessing activity. For a typical, righthanded person, the NLP graph reads as follows: (1) Eye movements to the upper left indicate that *past visual memories* are being stimulated; (2) eye movements to the upper right indicate a visual construction of *new or future images;* (3) eyes defocused reflect *imagery;* (4) eye movements in a lower-left direction indicate the accessing of an *internal auditory process;* (5) eyes moving horizontally to the left or right indicate an auditory *process;* and (6) lower-right eye movements indicate the accessing of *kinesthetic (sensory-feeling) experiences.** (See Figure 1.)

This eye movement system rang intuitively true for us as clinicians, and so we have utilized it in much of our work. However, we also recognize and respect the need for scientific validation of it. We conducted a recent on-line computer search of the Psychological Abstracts data base covering the time period from 1967 through May 1984 for all papers dealing with the subject of eye movement patterns and brain functioning. We found 101 references, but none in relation to the specific NLP model mentioned above. The overall direction of the research was inconclusive at best, with a significant number of researchers failing to correlate eye movement patterns with specific or consistent types of brain functions. One investigator (Ehrlichman & Weinberger, 1978) concluded that further research would be required before inferences about brain functioning could be drawn reliably from eye movement patterns. In an unpublished response to this issue, Rossi (1984) wrote:

> The possibility remains, however, that these large-scale statistical studies may be obscuring highly individualized but reliable relations between eye movement patterns and brain functioning that could be valuable for clinical study. If such relations exist, they need to be published in the form of individual case studies that can be assessed and replicated by other clinicians.

We hope to provide clinical examples that will be useful in the ways suggested by Rossi.

The relationship between language preferences and the sensory systems they reflect is straightforward and easy to learn. What is to be gained from attempting to use a child's eye movement patterns? Learning to observe something as complex and exploratory as eye movement patterns might seem unnecessary or confusing to some readers. However, we will describe our application of it because it has proven consistently fruitful and exciting for us.

---

* Additional eye movement patterns are delineated in the NLP system. See Lankton, 1980.

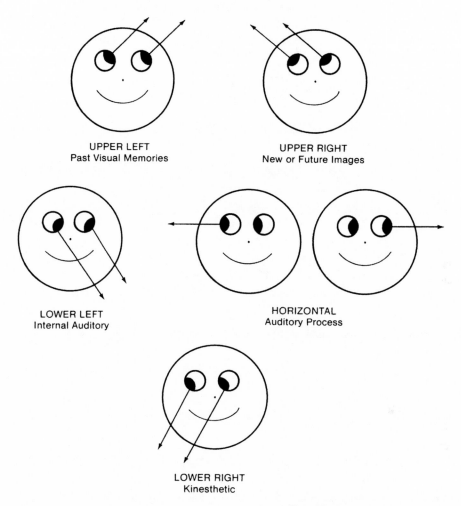

UPPER LEFT
Past Visual Memories

UPPER RIGHT
New or Future Images

LOWER LEFT
Internal Auditory

HORIZONTAL
Auditory Process

LOWER RIGHT
Kinesthetic

Figure 1: *Eye Movement Patterns*

Illustrations as you are
looking at the person.

Eye movement patterns provide another dimension of minimal cues that can be woven into the therapeutic metaphor. In addition to matching the child's *conscious sensory experiences* with appropriate predicates, the therapist can make use of eye movement patterns to more accurately reflect the child's *unconscious sensory experience*. For example, a child might use predominantly visual predicates to describe an experience while gazing consistently to the lower right (kinesthetic channel). The therapist could then use this information to interweave kinesthetic predicates, in addition to visual predicates, into the metaphor in a special way. Eye movement patterns can also be utilized spontaneously in the therapy session to guide the therapist's remarks, as is demonstrated in the following case example.

Annie's Eyes

Annie is an attractive, dark-haired preteen girl who was brought to my office by her parents because she was failing in school. They claimed that before she began "running around with a bad crowd who's into drugs," she had been a straight–A student and very mature for her age. "She was the perfect child until she met them!"

I began by asking Annie to describe how *she* experienced the problem. As she spoke her eyes moved to an upper left position.

Annie: Like I *felt* like I was *bored* and wanted to have fun. Then I met these new kids. *[Annie's eyes return to the therapist.]*

Therapist: Annie, how did you just get the memory of that experience?

A: Huh?

T: Did you have a picture in your mind?

A: [Pause; her eyes dart upper left] Kind of like I just remembered *seeing* these kids when I first met them.

Questioning in this way provides a means of verifying the internal sensory process being mirrored by the eye movement pattern. In this case, questioning confirmed that Annie's unconscious communication system was visual and could be accessed into conscious awareness upon request. If Annie had not been able to respond to the question—if she "drew a blank" and had no idea how she was processing the memory—then her visual system would be considered her "out of conscious" sensory system—the system that was blocked, out of the range of her conscious awareness, and thus generating or contributing to the problem. (The "out-of-consciousness" sensory system will be discussed in the next section.)

Annie's session continues:

T: And then what happened?

A: These kids *liked* me, but said I was a Miss Goody and they wanted me to do what they did . . . like *get loaded* and *skip* school with them.

T: So what did you end up doing?

A: *[Her eyes dart upper left again]* Well, I was *angry* about a lot of things—like I just didn't want to have to be so perfect all the time. So I *cut* a lot of classes and took uppers and smoked pot. *[Eyes return to therapist]* But now I've really got myself in a big problem and I'm *scared.* Like I'm *stuck* and there's no way out.

T: *[I lean forward a bit, and look directly into her eyes]* That must *feel awful* being so *stuck.* I'd like to *give you a hand* to help *pull* you out of that place. *[I paused for a moment while I slightly touched her hand.]* Together we're going to find a way out of this so you can begin to *feel* a whole lot *better* and. . . .

so you can begin to *see* yourself looking *happy* again, the way you used to *look.*

In the above dialogue, rapport was first established on the conscious level by using kinesthetic predicates, as Annie had done. In order to process those predicates, she remains in a "here and now" level of consciousness. Next, presenting visual predicates helps to shift her focus inward as she engages in an unconscious and absorbing search: Since the use of her internal visual system is unconscious, she has to alter her present conscious state in order to retrieve the images that are connoted by the visual predicates. Matching the unconscious sensory system with appropriate predicates thus intensifies rapport and facilitates a state of altered consciousness (trance, absorption). Now the conscious and unconscious communication doors are open to the blocked, "out-of-conscious" sensory system, wherein lies the therapeutic key.

We realize that the sentences used as illustrations of matching Annie's sensory systems can sound somewhat contrived or artificial when read in print. Indeed, in the early learning stages it can also feel contrived to the therapist to speak in this carefully chosen manner. However, we found that with practice it became a very natural and genuine means of entering the child's world. Rather than being a mechanistic process, it is really an approach based on a spontaneous and immediate utilization of what is being presented.

QUESTIONING FOR EYE MOVEMENTS

Annie's case illustrates how questioning was used to verify the internal sensory process being mirrored by her eye movement patterns. Notice that these questions were either *open-ended* or *leading:*

Open-ended: "How did you just get that memory of that experience?"
Leading: "Did you have a picture in your head?"

In general, we begin with the open-ended question. Then, if the child looks puzzled or does not respond, we will follow through with the leading question. Often a leading question is necessary simply because this type of *questioning for internal experience* is uncommon and unfamiliar. We are not used to it, and in order to answer the question we must retrieve information that is unconscious and unfamiliar. The leading question quickly clarifies what the therapist wants to know.

It has been suggested that the use of leading questions amounts to "leading the witness." Is the therapist, in effect, telling the child how to answer by providing the possibility of a picture (or a sound, or feeling) as an answer? In our experience, no. If the sensory information is ongoing and available, as it was in Annie's case, it will be retrieved upon questioning. If it is blocked, the child will be unable to grasp the question or will answer literally.

Take the example of the child whose eyes dart to a kinesthetic position as he is describing an argument with his mother. The therapist asks at that moment, "What are you aware of experiencing right now?" The child looks at the therapist blankly and answers, "Nothing." The therapist may even tell the child to "look back where you were just looking and continue to tell me about that fight."

The child continues talking for a few minutes and then the therapist asks, "Are you aware of feeling something as you talk about that argument?"

The child answers, "No." *[Eyes dart to kinesthetic channel]*

"Well, what are you aware of?" the therapist asks.

"The snag in the carpet *[in his external line of vision]*."

This type of literal response to a leading question is common when the sensory system mentioned in the question is blocked ("out-of-conscious"). When it is not blocked, the child responds with an answer reflecting some facet of his inner experience: "the knot in my stomach," "my mom's face all red and angry," or "the awful yelling," for example. When the sensory information is retrievable upon questioning, the therapist then knows that it is a viable resource. When that information is not available the therapist then knows it is part of the problem. In the next section we will discuss this "part of the problem" as being an "out-of-conscious" sensory system.

It is important to stress at this point that eye movements are not a fixed or straightforward phenomenon in the way suggested by the above example. In the clinical setting, children's eyes often do not simply move to one position and then return to the therapist, although this does occur. Depending on the subject matter, the child will more often move her eyes to many positions. To the keen observer, however, eye movement *patterns* will become evident. These *patterns* may be viewed as representing unconscious sensory strategies the child has developed as a means of processing the world around her. These patterns or strategies will often vary in relation to the child's strengths and weaknesses. In the problem area, for example, the child might engage her kinesthetic system most frequently, while in a positive area of her life, she relies more dominantly on the visual system.

For teaching purposes in our examples we usually discuss only one eye movement pattern as revealing one unconscious communication system. However, some children may have two unconscious communication systems. That is, their eye movements may consistently demonstrate that they process experiences in, for example, a highly visual *and* a highly kinesthetic modality.

The "Out-of-Conscious" Sensory System: A New Theoretical Perspective?

We would work each day. Grandma would show me how to do something new and send me home to practice. When we met the next day I would show her what I had accomplished. Each part of the cloth was unfolding with delicate beauty. I was learning.

Before presenting the theoretical concepts in this section, we would first like you to take a moment and think in personal terms. How many of you, your friends, or clients have tried in vain to quit smoking or lose weight? We know all the pros and cons about cigarettes and overeating, yet something inevitably intervenes to block our resolve. We feel stuck in the habit and no matter what we do as therapists, either for ourselves or for our clients, this one area of inner work never seems to improve in any permanent way. In this section we are going to suggest that what is interfering with our positive processes of change is what may be termed an "out-of-conscious" sensory system (Heller & Steele, 1986). The following exchange is excerpted from a presentation made on this topic.* We are including it here because it provides a casual and personal introduction to an otherwise abstract and theoretical concept.

Joyce Mills (JM): "I'd like to give a personal example. I used to have a fear of flying and went through many hours of traditional hypnotherapy for it, but to no avail. I then met a therapist, Dr. Steven Heller, who introduced me to the concept of an "out-of-conscious" sensory system. In this framework we each use our primary sensory channels (visual, auditory, kinesthetic) to varying degrees and *at* varying levels of consciousness. I was aware of being a very visual person, and I was certainly aware of being highly kinesthetic—my anxiety reactions to flying left no doubt in that area. The missing element was, therefore, my auditory system. What was it "doing" while I was panicking?

I soon discovered that I had been carrying on internal dialogues with myself, of which I was completely unaware, concerning all manner of terrifying possibilities. In response to these dialogues which were perpetuated by my out-of-conscious auditory system, I generated frightening images (visual) which in turn led to frightening feelings (kinesthetic). These feelings then perpetuated more fearful auditory dialogues, and in this way the proverbial vicious circle became established. Clearly, a solution would have to involve some way of interrupting my negative utilization of my own, internal auditory process. Richard then worked with me hypnotically and metaphorically toward this goal and my phobic reaction soon disappeared."

Richard Crowley (RC): "The problem with the other approaches Joyce had tried was that they involved visual and kinesthetic retraining—*seeing* herself *feeling* comfortable on a plane—but no auditory retraining. Therefore, she continued to generate scary pictures from an out-of-

---

* Paper presented at the Annual Scientific Meeting of The American Society of Clinical Hypnosis, Dallas, Texas, 1983.

conscious dialoguing process, despite her valiant attempts to visualize comfort. My approach was to integrate pleasant auditory experiences from other parts of her life into the airplane experience. In questioning Joyce, I discovered that she liked baseball for many reasons, including the excitement of the yelling and screaming that typically occurred throughout a game. Certainly, such outer hubbub would provide a positive override to the negative inner hubbub she often generated unknowingly for herself. Yelling and screaming at a baseball game was one way she could engage her auditory channel in a positive and exciting direction.

"While she was in trance, I presented a baseball metaphor to her containing interspersed suggestions and utilizing all the positive auditory associations she already had—the sounds of her own excitement at the game, the sound of the bat connecting with the ball, the sounds of the crowd cheering, the sounds of the vendor. I then integrated multisensory aspects of *flying in a plane* with a *fly ball:*

> And the higher and further a fly goes, it becomes more and more exciting, way up there in the air. And the *pleasant sounds connected with the flight* of that fly ball . . . up there . . . *going comfortably to its destination* . . . lets you see all that beauty up there. Even imagine being that *nice fly in the air* . . . so *happy hearing those thunderous cheers* egging you on further and further in your *smooth flight in the air.* And knowing the sound of a home run being hit lets the runner leave home plate and go all the way out there to all those comfortable bases until *you can arrive safely back at home plate,* proud of your abilities.

"On her next airplane experience, Joyce unconsciously drew upon the baseball metaphor to generate pleasant auditory messages for herself, which in turn generated pleasant visual and kinesthetic responses. All of her sensory systems were now in full cooperation in the activity of creating comfortable, fearless airplane experiences. A positive domino effect followed whereby other areas previously associated with fear were now opened to Joyce! She added snow skiing, ocean swimming, and even river rafting to her side of the scoreboard."

It is important to note that conscious recall of the metaphor will not necessarily generate the needed changes. If the conscious mind had the solutions, there would not have been a problem in the first place.

Rarely will a person even consciously think about the story in the situation for which it was intended. Rather, it functions as a positive, unconscious, posthypnotic suggestion that offsets or supercedes the negative programming that was fueling the problem.

The concept of an out-of-conscious system has emerged because of a need to differentiate among levels or degrees of unconscious processes. Different levels of unconscious processes would naturally have different clinical implications. For example, the type of unconscious process involved in a person being unaware of the glasses on his face is probably qualitatively (and neurologically) different from the unconscious process involved in being unaware of negative internal dialogues. This points to the need for a concept of unconscious processes that more adequately reflects the rich complexity actually present.

The concept of differentiating among *degrees* of unconscious processes has precedents in the writings of both Freud and Jung. Freud (1936) clearly described two levels of unconscious processes with the formulation of his unconscious-preconscious "agencies of the psychical apparatus." Jung, in his book *Psyche and Symbol* (1958), also alluded to three levels of unconscious processes (p. 3):

> The sum total of unconscious contents . . . fall into three groups: first, temporarily subliminal contents that can be reproduced voluntarily (memory); second, unconscious contents that cannot be reproduced voluntarily; third, *contents that are not capable of becoming conscious at all. [Italics added]*

Another interesting parallel can be found in Jung's theory of "psychological types" (1921/1971) in which he discusses how personality is shaped by the strengths and weaknesses of four functions of consciousness: thinking, feeling, sensation, and intuition. These four functions interact in ways Jung described as *primary, auxiliary,* and *inferior* or repressed. The *conscious primary function* is usually supported by an *unconscious auxiliary function,* and both are counterpointed by the least developed, least used, *inferior function.*

Two aspects of Jung's theory of psychological types are of particular pertinence to our presentation of an out-of-conscious level of sensory functioning. One is that Jung stressed how unrecognized differences in personality types were often responsible for the serious gaps in communication that occur on all levels of society (including the therapy session). The second aspect involves his description of the psychodynamic relationship among the three levels of functioning which he terms primary, auxiliary, and inferior or repressed, and which is strikingly similar to our model of conscious, unconscious and out-of-conscious levels of functioning (Jung, 1921/1971, pp. 406–407):

> For all types met with in practice, the rule holds good that besides the conscious, primary function there is a relatively unconscious, auxiliary function which is in every respect different from the nature of the primary function. . . . I have frequently observed how an analyst, confronted with a terrific thinking type, for instance, will do his utmost to develop the [inferior or repressed] feeling function directly out of the unconscious. Such an attempt is foredoomed to failure, because it involves too great a violation of the conscious standpoint. . . . The approach to the unconscious and to the most repressed function is disclosed, as it were, of its own accord, and with adequate protection of the conscious stand-point, when the way of development proceeds via the auxiliary function. . . . This gives the patient a broader view of what is happening, and of what is possible, so that his consciousness is sufficiently protected against the inroads of the unconscious.

Jung's description of reaching the "repressed function" by bridging it into conscious awareness via the unconscious auxiliary function is similar to our utilization of language predicates (conscious) and eye movement patterns and minimal cues (unconscious) as a means of retrieving the out-of-conscious system. By implication, Jung is referring to two different levels of unconscious processes here. The auxiliary function, though unconscious in relation to the primary, conscious function, is familiar and identifiable. The inferior function, however, is deeply repressed and should not be approached directly but only through the mediation of the auxiliary function.

In another book, *Memories, Dreams and Reflections,* Jung (1961) described a personal experience which could be viewed as his spontaneous discovery of a way to integrate his own out-of-conscious system. In a moving chapter entitled, "Confrontation with the Unconscious," Jung related the frightening experiences he underwent in his desire to directly experience his own unconscious (Jung, 1961, pp. 176–177):

An incessant stream of fantasies had been released, and I did my best not to lose my head but to find some way to understand these strange things. I stood helpless before an alien world; everything in it seemed difficult and incomprehensible. I was living in a constant state of tension; often I felt as if gigantic blocks of stone were tumbling down upon me. One thunderstorm followed another. My enduring was a question of brute strength. . . . To the extent that I managed to translate the emotions into images— that is to say, to find the images which were concealed in the emotions—I was inwardly calmed and reassured. Had I left those images hidden in the emotions, I might have been torn to pieces by them.

If we were to view Jung's experience from a sensory systems perspective, we could rephrase his description to suggest that the more he tried to comprehend and understand (thinking/auditory), the more tumultuous he felt (kinesthetically overloaded). Only when he was able to translate his emotions (kinesthetic) into images (visual)—that is, only when he was able to bring his out-of-conscious visual system into the experience—was he able to regain his inner calm and reassurance. Indeed, he would have been "torn to pieces" without this vital connection.

Table 1 provides a historical overview of how the unconscious has been viewed by the major schools of psychology. The concept of the unconscious (or of unconscious processes) has played a central role in most schools either from an offensive position (there is an unconscious and this is how to deal with it), or from a defensive position (there is no such thing as an unconscious). Among the three major schools for which the unconscious is a central concept, we see an interesting distribution of valuation: For Freud the unconscious was primarily negative; for Jung it was primarily positive although it contained both positive and negative aspects (The Self and the Shadow); and for Erickson it was primarily positive. All three viewed pathology as a result of negative functioning in one area of the psyche or the other: For Freud it was in the unalterable, primitive Id; for Jung it was an unintegrated Shadow; and for Erickson it was the learned limitations of the conscious mind.

Both the Freudian Id and the Jungian Shadow are suggesting implicit, unobservable psychodynamic processes. As such, the concepts are several levels removed from the "raw material" they are describing. The Ericksonian framework of learned limitations comes closer to describing a primary process, but even it is a generalization of an abstract concept (learned limitations). The theory of an out-of-conscious *sensory system,* however, attempts to tie both conscious and unconscious processes to *specific, ongoing, observable sensory patterns.* As such, it is a step toward "materializing" what has been psychology's most elusive area: the unconscious.

The specific term "out-of-conscious" was coined by Heller (Heller & Steele, 1986), but the concept has also been described by Cameron-Bandler (1978) as a sensory system that is "outside of consciousness." She explained (p. 53):

> Another important distinction to be made [concerning sensory systems] is whether . . . a person can see his own internally-generated pictures, feel internally-generated feelings, hear internally-generated sounds or words. Often, with people who come into therapy, one system will lie outside of consciousness. . . . When the system outside of consciousness is the one that typically generates their experience . . . it becomes impossible for the individual to have choices concerning what kinds of experiences are internally-generated.

For Heller, and in our approach, the "out-of-conscious" sensory system plays a pivotal role in both the creation and the therapy of any psychogenic (and sometimes organic) problem. Through a process of "Unconscious Restructuring" (Heller & Steele, 1986), resources can be identified and bridged into the problem area. Metaphor, according to Heller, is the primary vehicle of this type of change because its message is communicated indirectly. Through metaphor, the out-of-conscious sensory system is opened up and activated in relation to the problem.

In our opening example of Joyce's fear of flying, her positive auditory resource of enjoying the clamor of baseball games was restructured on an unconscious level: In her inner "map" of associations, the auditory resource which was formally attached solely to the context of baseball games, was now also associated with flying in airplanes. Because her fear of flying was being mediated by her auditory system, identifying it and restructuring its use in a positive direction triggered two

TABLE 1

HISTORICAL OVERVIEW: THE UNCONSCIOUS IN PSYCHOLOGY

School	Key Concept		Nature of Key Concept	Function of Key Concept	Means of Thera-peutic Change
	Unconscious	Other			
Analytical (Depth) Freudian	Central		Innate; biological; primitive; animalistic; survivalistic; in-cestuous; murderous; egoistic Intrinsically Negative	*The unconscious as:* –source of organismic energy (li-bido); –receptacle for repressed impulses; –generator of symptomatic re-sponses	Bring unconscious contents into consciousness to modify and social-ize amoral "Id" forces Ego Orientation
Jungian	Central		Innate; psychological; collec-tive; transpersonal; tran-scendent; archetypal; numi-nous Intrinsically Positive	*The unconscious as:* –the directive principle of the psy-che; –receptacle of personal memories & experiences; –receptacle of collective imagistic structures—"archetypes"	Individuation process whereby un-conscious contents are made con-scious toward unification of the "Self"—the total personality Transpersonal Orientation
Behaviorism	Denied	Behavior	"Prima Facie" (independent of biology & neurophysiol-ogy; physiological (condi-tioned response); objectively measureable; determined mainly by environmental contingencies Intrinsically Neutral	*Behavior as:* –the primary element of personal experience; –source of prediction & control of human activities; –"prima facie" indicator of envi-ronmental reinforcers	Learning new behavioral/emotional response patterns (reconditioning) toward more appropriate or de-sired functioning Ego Orientation

Humanistic	Neutral	Self-actualization	Innate; experiential; holistic/unitary Intrinsically Positive	*Self-actualization as:* —motivational principle of human life; —primary means of personality (mind/body) integration; —primary source of personal meaning & growth	Removing mental, emotional & physical blocks so that potentials can manifest; facilitating & enhancing intrinsic resources Total Personality Orientation
Cognitive	Neutral or denied	Cognition	Neurological; learned; alterable Intrinsically Neutral	*Cognition as:* —primary mediator of belief systems which— —are the primary determinants of experience	Examining existing beliefs; altering or discarding beliefs generating problem or symptom Ego Orientation
Ericksonian	Central		Innate; learned; experiential; autonomous Intrinsically Positive	*The unconscious as:* —storehouse of all experience, memory, & learning; —primary source of highest potentials; —primary source of problem/symptom resolution	Indirectly activating unconscious resources and potentials to resolve problem/symptom and enhance functioning Total Personality Orientation

simultaneous benefits: It harnessed the major source of the problem and opened up a whole new pathway of possible internal resources.

The child who grows up in a home where yelling is a daily reality may find it necessary to "turn off" his internal auditory channel in order to deal with the overload. Of course, he does not make a conscious decision to involve one of his sensory systems as a defense mechanism. The system simply *gets implicated* by virtue of the nature of the outer stimuli threatening the child. Since the solution for the child appears to be pulling the plug on his own auditory channel, he does so—but in the process he is also disconnecting a significant part of his sensory resources. This is similar on a psychological level to what occurs on a physical level in cases of organically-based learning disabilities. For teaching purposes, we are likening the out-of-conscious sensory system to a *non-organic learning disability* whereby a "mental block" is created out of the disuse or misuse of one or another sensory system. A sensory systems approach to the diagnosis of a child's problem is a nonintrusive, observational one that can enhance the ease with which the therapist is able to perceive and treat the presenting problem.

Although Erickson himself never discussed a level of the unconscious as being "out-of-conscious" as we are referring to it here, he does suggest it with his concept of a "mental block" (Rossi & Ryan, 1985). Erickson was presented with a fifth grader, Tommy, who was unable to read even a first-grade book. To begin with, Erickson entered the child's world by stating it to be a waste of time to try to teach him to read, so instead they should just have a good time. He then cleverly shifted the boy's negative experience of *reading* toward a more positive and less threatening experience of *looking* and *examining* road maps to determine where Tommy would like to go on his vacation. Erickson commented (Rossi & Ryan, 1985, p. 183):

> We were *looking* at a map—we weren't *reading* a map. That is an important distinction. The boy and I examined this map and that map. Whereabouts in the Western United States should he go on his vacation? Now, let's see . . . Where is Yellowstone Park? . . . Where is Yosemite Park? . . . Where is Olympic Park? . . . What city is it near? . . . Which highway goes from Yellowstone Park down to Grand Canyon? And so on. We never did *read* the maps; we *examined* the maps.

By the time school opened in September, Tommy was reading at his appropriate age level. Erickson explained (Rossi & Ryan, 1985, pp. 183–184):

> You enlist the aid of the child; you meet the child instead of trying to force him to recognize that c-a-t spells *cat,* or that d-o-g spells *dog.* The child already knows that, but he has a mental block. Your task is to make it easier for the child to circumvent his own blocks.

Thus, Erickson made it easier for the child to overcome his "mental block" associated with reading by reframing it into a pleasurable, fun activity.

From a sensory systems point of view, Erickson recognized that reading *per se* was not the problem—there was no organic basis for the learning disability. Rather, a "mental block" was preventing the boy from demonstrating a skill he had indeed acquired but could not manifest. This was confirmed by Tommy's easy adaptation to "looking at" and "examining" maps. It could be speculated that Tommy's "mental block" was an out-of-conscious auditory system that generated negative internal dialogues and thus interrupted his natural ability to read. When Erickson reframed the focus from reading to "looking up places," he stimulated positive associations—positive auditory dialogues—that helped rather than hindered Tommy in his task of examining the maps.

To demonstrate how an out-of-conscious sensory system might operate, we will present three hypothetical cases of test-taking anxiety (which are composites of our clinical cases) in which the inaccessibility of a particular sensory system can be viewed as generating the problem.

AUDITORY

With an out-of-conscious auditory system, the child is not aware of his own internal voice that is saying negative, critical, or frightening things. The child has a kind of amnesia for this internal dialogue which gives it free rein to perpetuate the ongoing problem. It is similar to being in a deep hypnotic state and very receptive to posthypnotic suggestions. The child whose presenting problem is test-taking anxiety is unaware that he, himself, is both hypnotist and subject. *As hypnotist* he says such things as, "When you take that test, you'll freeze up and forget everything," or, "You'll never pass the test—you're too dumb!" *As subject* he automatically and unconsciously responds to these negative suggestions when he is in the actual test situation. Even though he has learned all the necessary material to pass the test with flying colors, his out-of-conscious internal dialogue blocks the information with its prophecies of failure.

KINESTHETIC

The anxiety associated with test-taking can also be found in the example of a child whose out-of-conscious sensory system is kinesthetic. This child may be so out-of-touch with his feelings about the exam that when questioned, "How do you feel about taking that test?", he responds by shrugging his shoulders and saying, "I don't know," or "Nothing." Yet as the test draws near, the child begins to develop psychogenic symptoms such as diarrhea, stomachaches, and headaches— all of which indicate a strong kinesthetic reaction. The child simply does not associate his physical symptoms with his anxieties about taking the test.

VISUAL

With an out-of-conscious visual system, the child is unaware of the negative internal pictures she is generating which trigger her disturbing feelings of anxiety. She may wait until the last moment to develop this anxiety and then, despite having studied diligently, she appears to develop a mental block while taking the test and either scores far below her potential or cannot even finish. When questioned about what happened "inside" as she was taking the test, the child can only respond with, "I don't know—I just got so scared I went blank." In actuality she was flashing mental pictures—internal visual memories— of a time months ago when she was humiliated by scoring the lowest grade on a test. She *sees* herself failing again and again. In her current situation she takes this past mental picture and projects it onto all test-taking situations.

Thus far we have discussed the child who has one sensory system blocked, such as in the test-taking examples. Sometimes, however, a child may have two or even three symptoms in an out-of-conscious condition. An example of this is the anorexic teenage girl who does not hear her internal dialogue criticizing her weight and appearance (out-of-conscious auditory); who sees herself as fat even when she looks in the mirror at her 86-pound body (out-of-conscious visual); and who feels fat on her body even when the bones are protruding (out-of-conscious kinesthetic).

Why one child develops an out-of-conscious visual system in relation to test-taking while another experiences an out-of-conscious auditory or kinesthetic cannot be known with any certainty. How and why sensory differences emerge is still a matter of speculation. It would seem that both nature (biogenetic make-up) and nurture (early life experience) interact to produce unique sensory constellations in each of us. Why else would two children reared in essentially the same home environment develop different sensory responses? The child mentioned earlier who turned off his internal auditory process in response to the yelling in his home may have a sister who, in response to the same environment, develops a blocked kinesthetic system. She has incipient ulcers as a result of her sensory "choice," while her brother has learning disabilities as a result of his. The why of it remains unanswerable. Ultimately, such questions of etiology are unimportant in relation to current functioning, which simply *is* the child's reality.

Ascertaining the Out-of-Conscious Sensory System

There are several ways by which the out-of-conscious system(s) can be ascertained in the clinical setting:

1. Literal cues
2. Presenting problem or symptom
3. Omission of information
4. Eye movements
5. Drawings

LITERAL CUES

Previously we spoke about language predicates as indicating the conscious communication system. When a *negative* is added to the descriptive word or phrase, it can often amount to the child's own literal description of his out-of-conscious sensory system:

A teenage boy: "I just *can't see* myself asking a girl out." (Out-of-Conscious Visual)

A nine-year-old girl: "I *never hear* the things the teacher asks me to do." (Out-of-Conscious Auditory)

A teenage girl: "*I can't feel* anything since my boyfriend left me." (Out-of-Conscious Kinesthetic)

This kind of information gives the therapist a direct target area to aim for in opening up the child's blocked sensory system(s).

PRESENTING PROBLEM OR SYMPTOM

The child's presenting problem or symptom can also serve as a literal communication about which sensory system is out-of-conscious.

A. *Out-of-Conscious-Visual:*
  1. Sometimes a child's presenting problem appears to be a lack of coordination so that he is frequently banging into things. The complaint is that he "doesn't pay attention," or "never watches where he's going." Rather than being a problem in muscular functioning or proprioceptive cuing, it is actually an out-of-conscious visual system that interferes with his external vision.
  2. Frequent physiological or psychosomatic complaints such as exaggerated blinking, eye tics, eye infections or sties, etc.
B. *Out-of-Conscious-Auditory:*
  1. An example of this situation is the child who daydreams in school and cannot answer the teacher's questions because she simply did not hear what was said. Or a common complaint of parents is that their teenager has a vacant look on his face and doesn't hear anything that is said: "It's like talking to the wall."
  2. Frequent physiological or psychosomatic problems such as tinnitus, laryngitis, and infections of the ears, nose and mouth.
C. *Out-of-Conscious-Kinesthetic*
  1. In the case of enuresis, the child has no awareness of the

sensations in his own bladder. Similarly, in the case of obesity, the child has no awareness of feeling full, or is able to deny it to an extreme degree.

2. Frequent physiological or psychosomatic complaints such as headaches, stomachaches, body rashes or extreme sensitivity to heat or cold.

OMISSION OF INFORMATION

Another way to ascertain an out-of-conscious system is to notice which sensory system the child *least* uses in his life. For example, when working with a teenage boy who tells me he loves *listening* to music, that he *taps out* the beat, that he *sings* around the house and *loves to dance,* I would note the omission of visual processes. This information would help guide me in formulating a treatment approach that would include opening up the visual sensory system he is not using in a positive way. (See "Living Metaphors" in Chapter 6.)

EYE MOVEMENTS

In the previous section we discussed eye movements as a means of identifying an unconscious communication system. Observing eye movements in combination with questioning for subjective experience can also be used as a means of pinpointing the out-of-conscious system. For example, in the case of Annie whose eye movements suggested a visual process, our questioning confirmed that she was accessing visual memories. This told us that her unconscious communication system was visual and available upon request. If she had not been able to bring her visual memories from unconscious to conscious awareness, then her visual system would have been identified as her out-of-conscious system based on the fact that she *could not* retrieve the pictures.

It is especially helpful to observe the child's eye movements while he is talking about his problem, or while the parent discusses it. A consistent eye movement pattern in response to a discussion of the problem can pinpoint the child's out-of-conscious sensory system. While the child is talking, his eyes typically will dart to various directions representing the different sensory channels as described in the NLP graph. When the child's eyes move to a particular position, the therapist can ask a direct question to learn if the child is aware of an auditory, visual, or kinesthetic experience. If the child does indeed see an inner picture in the visual eye movement channel, or hear an inner voice or sound in the auditory eye movement channel, or is aware of feelings or sensations in the kinesthetic eye movement channel, then this is the child's unconscious sensory system. If, on the other hand, the child cannot respond to the questioning and reports experiencing nothing, then that specific sensory system is blocked and out-of-conscious. It is the sensory system that is contributing to the child's problem and needs to be activated and brought into positive use.

DRAWINGS

The use of drawings provides valuable information about a child's sensory functioning. At times a literal picture of the out-of-conscious sensory system may even result from the drawing process. Techniques and case examples involving a variety of drawing strategies are discussed in Chapter 7.

The following case illustrates an extreme example of sensory dysfunction in which identification of the child's out-of-conscious systems presented a kaleidoscopic rather than fixed pattern of functioning.

Sean's Rainbow Puppy

Seven-year-old Sean was a boy with normal to above average intelligence, yet his classroom behavior was so uncontrollable that he had been asked to leave two schools. He would call out answers inappropriately during class and get up out of his seat and walk around at will. His records showed an absence of learning problems in the areas of reading, writing, spelling, and math. However when behavioral aspects of Sean's profile were explored, it was discovered that he was described as being a "space cadet." In one report it was stated that Sean's affect was "flattened, as if the lights are on, but no one is at home." Yet he would also have aggressive outbursts in which he hit and knocked into the other children. He was observed to be extremely uncoordinated both at work and at play. His parents and teachers described how he continually bumped into things such as desks, doors, chairs and other large objects, and how he would fall down unexpectedly in a "Raggedy Ann" manner. At first they thought he was only "clowning around" but then realized there was something more significant taking place within him. No one, however, had a clue as to the source of the problem.

A neurological examination was recommended and the results were normal. Because Sean's profile indicated many characteristics of a minimally brain-damaged child, Ritalin was suggested by Sean's physician as a possible treatment approach. In discussing this recommendation with the physician and parents, it was agreed that "metaphorical therapy" be attempted first as an experimental alternative to medication at that time.

When Sean first walked into my office, his shoulders were slumped and his movements were limp and inert. He plopped down on the couch and waited listlessly; he did not look around the room to check out his surroundings as most children did. I introduced myself and talked casually to him for a few minutes. He did not make any eye contact with me, but instead began an eye movement pattern I had never seen before (or since). Periodically his eyes rolled around in a rapid and defocused way, creating quite a strange impression.

Therapist: Sean, do you know why you're here today?
Sean: [Shrugging his shoulders and mumbling] I dunno.
Therapist: I was wondering if your mom or teacher had told you anything?
Sean: Uh-uh. *[Shaking his head no].*

In a straightforward manner I told him, "I am aware that you need some help because you are having problems at school. Is that true?" Sean did not respond; he sat inertly on the chair with a blank expression on his face. Our interactions continued in this uninformative manner. Sean's monosyllabic, grunt-like responses yielded no language cues, and his eye movements were too atypical and erratic to be of any help in the ways in which I had learned to ascertain sensory system functioning. Still, I received the blatant communication that Sean was literally unaware of himself as a physical body. He would sit on a chair and uncontrollably slide off it, as if his body were unable to produce the proprioceptive cues necessary for locating the parameters of the seat. He seemed to have no perception of his body in relation to his environment, and no sense of connection to his own responses and emotions. Both physically and emotionally, Sean was a child without personal boundaries. Yet he was very bright: He was able to do his math and his reading; he could comprehend and carry out both verbal and written instructions; he could complete his assignments, memorize well, and recite well in class.

In short, my overall impression from this first meeting was one of Sean as a living, three-dimensional paradox—there, and yet not there.

When I questioned Sean about the things he enjoyed, he seemed to perk up slightly.

"Animals," he replied flatly. "I have a turtle, a cat, and a new puppy."

"Really," I said. "I love animals, too. What do you like about them?"

"I dunno—I just like 'em."

I noted Sean's comment about liking animals and his new puppy. This information would later be utilized in formulating a storytelling metaphor.

I made a school visit to observe Sean on the playground. I wanted to verify the little he had told me and, hopefully, piece together a more comprehensive picture for myself. What I saw simply confirmed my original impression.

When it came to interacting with the other children, Sean was clumsy and somewhat bizarre. His movements were erratic and sometimes he would hit or knock into someone accidentally. The other children assumed it was intentional and would disregard Sean's repeated apology, "But I didn't mean it—I didn't mean it."

As I worked with Sean over a period of time, I noted that his case illustrated a very complex shifting of sensory-system dynamics. Sometimes one system was blocked, sometimes two, and once in a while, all three. This reminded me of the importance of staying *present in the moment* for each child: I could not fixate or label Sean's out-of-conscious system once and for all; instead, I had to remain open to cues that mirrored the flux of inner change in Sean's life.

When Sean's functioning was at its most problematic, all three of his sensory systems were seriously blocked at the same time. Overall:

Visually: He did not see where he was going and bumped into things such as desks, doors, and objects, as well as other children on the playground.

Kinesthetically: At times he appeared listless, "spacey," and inert, inexplicably falling down and sliding off chairs. At other times he would burst into spurts of inappropriate or aggressive behavior, particularly at school. His range of emotional responsivity was polarized between no visible affect whatsoever and uncontrollable outbreaks.

Auditorially: At times he spoke in monotones and monosyllables. His repeated use of the word "Huh?" indicated he did not hear the therapists's questions. Moreover, his erratic and bizarre eye movements led us to speculate that he may have been engaged in a painful and "hyper" internal auditory dialogue.

With Sean's earlier comment about his new puppy in mind, I developed a metaphor about "Rainbow the Puppy." This therapeutic story was the first of many created for Sean over the next two years. Although there were times when all three sensory systems were seriously blocked in Sean, as noted above, his kinesthetic and proprioceptive abilities were the most consistently out-of-conscious. Therefore, there was a purposeful interweaving of the major sensory systems within the metaphor, with an emphasis on his kinesthetic system. It is our experience that in such cases involving comprehensive sensory blockage, focusing on and opening up any one system will have a kind of circular domino effect of opening up the others.

> Rainbow was a little puppy with many colors on him, a very special little dog. He belonged to a family who loved him very much. They got him when he was a puppy, and, like most puppies, Rainbow was mischievous and needed to be taught many things. He chewed old shoes, got into the food in the pantry, and knocked things over with his tail.
>
> Rainbow's family didn't quite know how to teach him, so first they had to learn all about Rainbow and his special qualities. They tried all kinds of things month after month, but Rainbow kept doing what he wanted to do. He kept chewing shoes, knocking things over, and sometimes he was even confused about where he was. For example, sometimes he would think he was in the bedroom when he was in the den, or in the kitchen when he was in the bedroom. It was so confusing at times. Lots of

things are confusing at times. *[At this point there was a long pause. Sean was directed to continue taking nice deep breaths and getting that sense of feeling so good inside, as he continued listening to the story with his eyes closed.]*

Rainbow liked to do many things. He liked to play, to bury bones, and to look for other friends to play with. But it was hard for him to find friends. He used to look out the window and watch the other dogs playing, and he thought that he could just run out and play with them. But he had forgotten something very important; he had forgotten that it takes time to make friends. Well, at first he sat on his step on the top of the porch and watched the other little dogs playing together. He watched them as they ran around the grassy fields, around the grass in the yards, and over the pavement. He watched and waited, watched and waited, until one day one of the other dogs came bounding up to him playfully, nudging him to come join him and his friends. Rainbow was so happy! At last he had learned how to make friends!

Now the children who owned Rainbow loved him. They petted him at night and tried to get him to be still. But, as with most puppies, Rainbow had a difficult time being trained in the beginning. He was so active and busy all day that it was difficult for him to just lie down at the end of the day.

One day as he was running about, his owners called him in and said it was time to go to dog training school. The next thing he knew, Rainbow found himself in the park on a very long chain. Every time he broke into a run he felt a stop. He didn't know what that stop was, except that it was like a yank or a pull. A definite stop. Well, he tried to run again. He tried to run here and there, and wham-o, he was stopped.

Interested, he looked around to see where the STOP was coming from. Somehow he knew that something was stopping him from dashing about. Well, the class lasted about an hour, maybe two. It seemed like forever to Rainbow. It's hard when you're a puppy. After all, he was seven months old. And at seven months old there is a lot of running around to do. Well, he watched the other dogs as they learned, and little by little they learned how to sit. That's right, little by little they learned how to lie down and roll over. And they learned how to walk closely to their owners. Then, of course, there was the time when the leashes were taken off and the dogs could play freely—freely and comfortably—flopping their ears and tails in the park and barking with laughter.

Day after day this class took place with the instructions. And this little dog, this Rainbow, would run about. And then suddenly, surprisingly, without anyone being aware of when or how, Rainbow surprised himself! And it's nice to be surprised. Rainbow experienced something different. All he did was hear those words that got his attention easily—Heel, Stop—and he stopped right then and there! When he did, he got a delicious reward of a dog biscuit. Like a special cookie, a favorite cookie. It's nice to hear the crunchy sound of a favorite cookie or a biscuit—something Rainbow enjoyed so deeply. And Rainbow, in his own special way, was able to do all kinds of wonderful things with that biscuit. He chewed it, he threw it around, he tossed it in the air. He did all kinds of things. But most of all he learned that you may get a reward for simply paying attention. And, it's nice to have rewards.

We can look at Rainbow and think of how enjoyable it is to see all his colors blend together, each one separately and together. That's right. You might be wondering about many, many things right now. A part of you knows that it is nice to imagine that little dog, Rainbow, and to hear about his adventures: about how he learned to do many things; how he learned to sit; how he learned to stay; how he learned to roll over and laugh at himself again; how he enjoyed playing totally.

Now this story may have many, many meanings for you, and you might enjoy one part particularly. A favorite part. That's right. And as you look back, you can just begin to get a sense of how special it would be to be able to see that little dog, Rainbow, to remind you how easy it is to STOP, to take a look about, and to enjoy what you're doing. That's right.

Now in a moment you can allow yourself to have a special dream. And enjoy totally whatever part of that story you want to. And when you're finished, you can just take a nice big stretch, take a nice deep breath, feeling really good for the rest of the day. Knowing that there is lots for you to learn and enjoy and have fun with while you continue to play. That's right. Giggles of laughter and rainbows of color that make you aware of feeling good inside.

In addition to storytelling metaphors, other aspects of Sean's therapy included his participation in the "Blue Sparkle" group mentioned previously; the use of artistic metaphors (discussed in Chapter 7); and the assignment of carefully chosen living metaphors. For example, Sean learned how to use a camera to open his visual system; he gathered rocks of different weights to help engage his kinesthetic senses; and he recorded the sounds of nature for his auditory enrichment. I also worked closely with his teachers and parents to ensure that the approaches and theories being used to help Sean were understood and supported.

Over the course of a two-year period, the flattened affect Sean had presented initially began to slowly, slowly brighten—as if a blank canvas were being filled in, day by day, with the richness of color and form. He joined a scouting group and enjoyed many camping experiences with other children. His teacher reported an enhanced participation in classroom projects and a "remarkable improvement" in his personal sense of awareness. Sean's parents and his two sisters summarized Sean's changes with the statement, "Now we really know he's here."

Recently I saw Sean at a carnival. He ran up to me and gave me a big hug. With a twinkle in his eyes he excitedly exclaimed, "Hi! Wanna see me go on that big roller coaster?"

With a smile on my face and a delightfully warm feeling inside, I replied, "You bet I do!"

6

Three-Level
Communication: Bringing
It All Together

*Many weeks later Grandma told me that she had
completed each section of the cloth and was ready to
join all of them together. I watched with curiosity
and wonderment as she showed me how to connect the
different sections so that each blended into the other.
She again saw a look of apprehension on my face.
With reassurance and encouragement she explained
that as I practiced and learned each step, I would
discover how to interweave all the sections into a
whole in my own unique way.*

In Chapter 1 we discussed Erickson's use of what Rossi termed
"two-level communication" (Erickson & Rossi, 1976/1980) as a means
of communicating simultaneously with a patient's conscious and unconscious minds: While the conscious mind was occupied with the
literal content of a story, joke, pun, or analogy, the unconscious mind
was receiving carefully chosen suggestions that had been "interspersed"
throughout the verbalization. We would like to expand upon this
model by proposing a type of *three-level communication* that adds a
powerful therapeutic dimension to the storytelling metaphor via a process
of sensory interweaving. In presenting a therapeutic metaphor to the

137

child, the *storyline* communicates the first (conscious) level of meaning; the *interspersed suggestions* communicate the second (unconscious) level of meaning; and a *process of sensory interweaving* communicates a third, out-of-conscious level of meaning. This model of three-level communication within the context of a therapeutic metaphor could be depicted as follows:

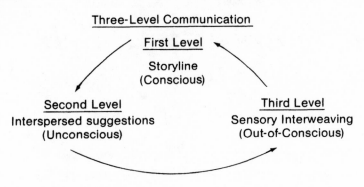

Three-Level Communication

First Level
Storyline
(Conscious)

Second Level
Interspersed suggestions
(Unconscious)

Third Level
Sensory Interweaving
(Out-of-Conscious)

Storyline: First Level

As the first level of communication, the *storyline* occupies the child's conscious mind by presenting an interesting plot. We have already presented various ways of generating a storyline as the basis of a therapeutic metaphor. In Chapter 3 we discussed the six basic ingredients of storywriting that can be used as milestones in the development of a metaphorical storyline: presenting a metaphorical conflict that matches the child's problem, personifying unconscious processes via various characters, integrating parallel learning situations of previous success, presenting a metaphorical crisis that serves as a turning point of resolution, developing a new sense of identification, and culminating with a celebration. We also summarized several different sources of material for the storyline: preordained themes, fairy tale motifs, the child's own imagination, the therapist's own real-life experiences, and the therapist's functional/imaginative associations.

In Chapters 4 and 5 we presented several ways of personalizing the storyline in accordance with each child's unique personality and life learnings by eliciting positive memories and experiences, and by observing and utilizing minimal cues in the form of sensory and language preferences. Once the storyline has been crafted out of all these elements, the therapist can then begin the process of interspersing whatever therapeutic suggestions are needed by the child.

For teaching purposes, we are presenting this material in a linear, step-by-step fashion. In reality, of course, no such fixed process occurs. As the therapist grows increasingly familiar with the metaphorical framework, all three levels of communication—the storyline, the interspersed suggestions, and the sensory interweaving—unfold together in an integrated and unified manner.

Interspersed Suggestions: Second Level

While the child's conscious mind is absorbed in the literal aspects of the story, important therapeutic suggestions that deal with the presenting problem can be interspersed throughout the storytelling process. These suggestions are assimilated into the context of the story so that they do not appear to be directed at the child. The child consciously hears the suggestions in relation to the storyline rather than as injunctions to himself. On an unconscious level, however, the suggestions are "heard" in a personally meaningful way. In our earlier example of the story Erickson told to Joe for pain control, many interspersed suggestions of *comfort* and *feeling good* were introduced within the context of how a tomato plant grows and functions. Joe would not have been receptive to these suggestions if they had been given directly to him, but he was able to receive them cushioned by the distance of metaphor and familiarized by his own resource area of flowers, planting seeds, and growing vegetables. In discussing the interspersal technique exemplified in Joe's case, Erickson wrote (Erickson, 1966/1980, pp. 262–263):

It is a technique employing ideas that are clear and comprehensible, but which by their patent irrelevance to the patient-physician relation and situation distract the patient. Thereby the patients are prevented from intruding unhelpfully into a situation which they cannot understand and for which they are seeking help. At the same time a readiness to understand and respond is created within the patient. Thus, a favorable setting is evolved for the elicitation of needful and helpful behavioral potentialities not previously used, not fully used, or perhaps misused by the patient.

Interspersed therapeutic suggestions are subtly defined or underscored during the storytelling process by way of *vocal dynamics*. The therapist simply shifts the tonal quality of his voice to a slightly softer or slightly lower timbre. In this way, the interspersed suggestions gain a "voice all their own." Much has been written about the subtle and complex use of vocal dynamics in the giving of suggestions (Erickson, 1944/ 1980; Erickson, 1980c; Erickson & Rossi, 1976/1980; Erickson, Rossi & Rossi, 1976; Lankton & Lankton, 1983)—so much so that one could easily become intimidated or overwhelmed, shying away from attempting it in the clinical setting. In reality, though, most of us have had a great deal of past and present experience in having stories read to us or in reading stories to others. One's own life experience can serve as an easy teacher in learning how to modulate vocal tones to subtly emphasize the interspersed suggestions.

To illustrate how interspersed therapeutic suggestions can be sprinkled safely throughout a story, we will reproduce a portion of our "In the Pink" metaphor and italicize the interspersed suggestions:

At that moment a twinkle appeared in the little elephant's eyes. He realized there was a time, there is a time, when *it is so important to be different—* when *being different can even be wonderful.*

The older, wiser elephant nudged him gently and said, "That's right. There are many, many times when *being different is such a wonderful ability, like all the abilities you have now.* And I wonder if you are able to *teach some of those abilities, to share some of those abilities with the other ones* who may not understand."

The little pink elephant thought and thought and thought with that same twinkle and said, "Yes, I certainly could!"

He went back to where the other little elephants played and he began to *show them three other abilities* that he had. He wanted to *share those three abilities* so that they could *experience them in a new and different way.* He showed them how many things he could do by being pink. And they were amazed. They realized that being pink could be quite exciting and different, and they really tried hard themselves to become pink.

Interweaving: Third Level

We now turn our attention to the third level of communication which takes place as the metaphor unfolds. Through a careful use of sensory-rich language, a simultaneous process of *sensory interweaving* is initiated. The purpose of sensory interweaving is twofold. One, it helps bring integration and balance to the child's overall sensory functioning; and, two, it is specifically focused on unblocking and opening up the out-of-conscious system. Sometimes this is accomplished by stressing the out-of-conscious system via a preponderance of appropriate predicates. More often, a consistent flowing back and forth among visual, auditory, and kinesthetic predicates will succeed in retrieving the out-of-conscious system. Heller (Heller & Steele, 1986) suggests that whatever is blocking the out-of-conscious system may eventually "crumble" with the experience of sensory interweaving.* In our framework, the interweaving process allows the child to reexperience a whole cluster of inner resources that can now be diffused into the problem area. In this way, the child resolves the problem by drawing upon healthy coping strategies from areas in which all three sensory systems are functioning well.

For example, in working with a child who has provided the beach as her favorite experience, the therapist could begin as follows:

> As you are *sitting* there, making yourself *comfortable,* I am going to *tell* you a story and *talk* to you in a way that may help you *see* some pleasant *images* and *memories* from your past.
>
> I remember a child *playing* in the sand at a beach and *digging* a hole near the water's edge. She built a sand wall out of wet sand and then *designed it by looking* for seashells, seaweed, old wooden pieces and even stray feathers. I *enjoyed watching* it coming together. As the *sound of the waves* continued, she would *look up* every so often to *watch* them *crash.* Then she would even forget the *rhythm* of the *sounds of the waves* in the background, because she enjoyed *seeing* all her work *developing* into such a beautiful castle.

When interweaving is successful, a kind of *process confluence* is experienced within the child: she is now "in touch," "in tune," "in

---

* Lankton (1980) and Cameron-Bandler (1978) refer to this process as "overlapping"; Heller & Steele (1986) use the term "overlaying."

focus," in *balance*. This is because an entire channel of experience which had been blocked is now opened and linked into the other systems in a positive and enriching manner.

The process of interspersing therapeutic suggestions and interweaving sensory systems occurs simultaneously with the unfolding of the storyline. We have presented them here as separate, discrete phenomenon for the sake of simplicity. In reality, it would be more accurate to view interspersing suggestions and sensory interweaving as two pathways that sometimes run parallel, sometimes intersect, and sometimes join as one. There will be points in the story when you will focus on interspersing a suggestion without particular regard to the sensory language used; and at other times, sensory interweaving will be integrated into the therapeutic suggestions.

As with any multilevel skill, a time comes when you stop thinking about it in a laborious, step-by-step way. It is somewhat like the apprentice juggler who must learn how to . . . throw up the first ball . . . then throw up the second ball while catching the first . . . then throw up the third ball while catching and throwing the first two. Each movement is measured and conscious. Eventually, though, his skill increases so that he produces an apparently effortless and smooth pinwheel of flying balls.

We will now reproduce the same portion of our "In the Pink" metaphor a second time, showing *interspersed suggestions* in italic type and **interwoven sensory predicates** in bold face type.

At that moment a **twinkle** appeared in the little elephant's eyes. He realized there was a time, there is a time, when *it is so important to be different—*when *being different can even be wonderful.*

The older, wiser elephant **nudged** him **gently** and said, "That's right. There are many, many times when *being different is such a wonderful ability, like all the abilities you have now.* And I wonder if you are able to *teach some of those abilities, to share some of those abilities with the other ones* who may not understand."

The little pink elephant **thought** and **thought** and **thought** with that same twinkle and said, "Yes, I certainly could!"

He went back to where the other little elephants **played** and he began to *show them three other abilities* that he had. He wanted to *share those three abilities* so that they could *experience them in a new and different way.* He **showed** them how many things he could do by being pink. And they were **amazed.** They realized that being pink could be quite **exciting** and different, and they really tried **hard** themselves to become pink.

Living Metaphors

During the course of a child's treatment we will often present a number of *living metaphors* as out-of-the-office assignments. As the name suggests, a living metaphor is an activity that can be incorporated into the child's daily life and which somehow metaphorizes a process in the child that is needed to resolve the problem area. It also helps to reintroduce pleasant sensory experiences which are associated with the sensory system in the child's life that has been blocked. The living metaphor is an excellent complement to the storytelling metaphor because it helps to "anchor" or "ground" the therapeutic message into an actual physical experience. The unconscious abilities activated on an internal level during the storytelling metaphor are then given a focused opportunity to become actualized through the carrying out of various metaphorical assignments.

For example, the child who painfully bites his nails might be told a metaphor involving a garden and the care and growth of various plants. In addition, a living metaphor could be assigned in which the child is told to plant ten tiny plants and watch over them each day, cultivating them so that they grow tall and sturdy. The child could even be sent to the local nursery to learn what measures are taken to protect growing plants from being eaten by snails and other garden pests.

Living metaphors can be generated in direct relation to the presenting problem, or as a more global sensory assignment aimed at opening up and integrating the three major systems. In both cases, retrieval of inner resources (past positive memories and associations) and the out-of-conscious sensory system(s) is the primary goal. In the following case example, a teenager's presenting problem was used as a basis for the living metaphor.

The "Hot Sauce" Cake

Fifteen-year-old Elaina was the oldest of five children. Her mother had died when Elaina was eleven and the responsibility of the other children had fallen to her. Over the past few years, Elaina had become rigid, overly responsible, and continually felt compelled to be perfect. One of her issues in therapy was her fear of dating a boy she liked very much. After working on this problem, we learned that she kept imagining herself saying the wrong thing; the boy then would laugh at her and she would be humiliated and lose him. Elaina had composed an entire scenario for herself, orchestrated in detail by an out-of-conscious auditory system.

In addition to artistic and storytelling metaphors, a living metaphor was assigned in which Elaina was told to go home and bake two cakes—one by following the recipe "perfectly," the other by adding one ingredient which she believed would completely ruin the cake. The next week she was to bring in a piece from each cake. She was perplexed by the assignment, but agreed.

The next week Elaina returned with her two pieces of cake, proudly stating that she had added *hot sauce* to the second. She was asked what she had learned from the experience. She replied that "with a good recipe, it would take a lot to really mess it up." We both tasted the hot sauce cake and again confirmed that "it really wasn't that bad." She then went on to make a spontaneous conscious connection between her discovery with the imperfect cake and her feelings about dating the boy she liked: She realized it would take more than one

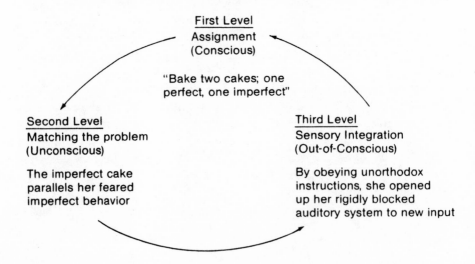

First Level
Assignment
(Conscious)

"Bake two cakes; one perfect, one imperfect"

Second Level
Matching the problem
(Unconscious)

The imperfect cake parallels her feared imperfect behavior

Third Level
Sensory Integration
(Out-of-Conscious)

By obeying unorthodox instructions, she opened up her rigidly blocked auditory system to new input

imperfect comment to ruin the whole experience.

This process of creating a living metaphor involves the same three-level dynamics of conscious, unconscious, and out-of-conscious interaction as depicted for the storytelling metaphor (see diagram on p. 144).

Following is a supplemental list of sensory assignments that can be used as a springboard in generating living metaphors that are tailor-made for each child. These assignments are designed to help the child develop an awareness of the sensory system that has been blocked in the problem area.

SENSORY ASSIGNMENTS

Visual

1. *Photo Album:* Have the child get a camera and take pictures of things she enjoys seeing. Next, have her assemble the photos in an album and label each picture with one word representing how she feels when she looks at it. A variation of this assignment is to have the child select a color or shape (circle, square, triangle; blue, pink, yellow) that symbolizes the desired therapeutic goal (being happy, feeling confident, getting better grades), and then photograph the color or shape wherever it is spotted (out in the yard, in a park, or in the neighborhood).

2. *Notebook:* Have the child cut out pictures from magazines of things she would like to do and glue them on the pages of a blank notebook. The pictures can also be assembled on a large poster board to create a collage of favorite experiences.

3. *Different Perspective:* Have the child take pictures of a favorite object from six different angles—six different points of view—so that she can develop new ways of seeing the same thing.

Kinesthetic

1. *Weights:* Have the child go to the supermarket (with a parent if he is a younger child) and select various fruits and vegetables. The child holds one in each hand to determine which feels heavier or lighter. Each piece is then weighed on the scale to verify the child's estimate.

2. *Textures:* Each day have the child find three objects that feel hard, smooth, rough, and soft, in order to learn tactile discrimination.

3. *Balance:* Have the child learn to balance a book on his head; or, get a long, narrow piece of wood and practice walking from end to end; or go to a playground and learn how to balance on the seesaw.

Auditory

1. *Favorite Music:* Have the child arrange her records or tape cassettes, beginning with the ones she likes to listen to the most; or have her write down the lyrics to her favorite songs.

2. *Favorite Sounds:* Have the child go to the beach, the zoo, on a nature hike, or simply outside in the neighborhood, and tape record the different sounds he likes to hear. Later, he can listen to the recording when alone.

3. *Favorite Associations:* Have the child select five favorite activities and then tape record the favorite sounds associated with each activity (such as a baseball game, a trip to the zoo, etc.).

To illustrate how the major concepts discussed thus far can be applied in child therapy, the following case will be presented in detail. The ingredients of storywriting, the observation and utilization of minimal cues including language preferences and eye movement patterns, and the application of the three-level communication model of interspersed suggestions and sensory interweaving to the creation of therapeutic metaphors will be highlighted.

*A Teaching Metaphor: Sammy The Elephant and Mr. Camel**

Eight-year-old John was a willowy, brown-haired boy who was referred for therapy by his pediatrician for secondary functional enuresis. According to his mother who was a single parent, John had been dry from the time he was three-and-a-half until five years of age, with only occasional accidents. This had changed dramatically after she received a job promotion requiring them to move to another city rather abruptly. John had begun wetting the bed almost immediately after the move. His mother was reassured by her doctor that John's bedwetting was just a reaction to the move and should subside within a short period of time. However, three years later the problem still remained

* This case was presented in a paper entitled, "Therapeutic Metaphors for Children" at the 25th Anniversary Meeting of The American Society of Clinical Hypnosis, Denver, Colorado, October, 1982.

unresolved. John's chronic bedwetting was inconsistent in pattern: He would have symptom-free periods lasting almost two weeks, followed by unrelenting nightly occurrences for weeks on end.

After John had enthusiastically explored the office with its games, puppets, and varied art supplies, he was asked if he knew why he was here. Suddenly the vibrancy in John's facial expression disappeared. Sheepishly he responded, using primarily auditory predicates, with such statements as:

"Mom *told* me you'd *listen* to me about my problem."
"She *said* you'd *tell* me stories to make it go away."

At this point his conscious sensory system in relation to his problem area was identified as auditory. It was then noted that John's eye movements favored the upper left direction as he spoke, suggesting an unconscious visual system. This was confirmed when John was asked what he was experiencing when his eyes were in an upper left position. John readily described visual memories of his mother and himself from the past.

John was then asked directly, "How do you feel about your bedwetting?"

His eyes moved to a lower right (kinesthetic) channel, his breathing changed, and his left leg began to vibrate uncontrollably. In a confused and hesitant manner, he answered, "I don't know."

Further direct inquiry was made regarding sensations and feelings being experienced, yet John had no answers. Even when his eyes were directed back to the kinesthetic position, he remained out-of-touch with any feeling whatsoever. We therefore felt that John's out-of-conscious sensory system was kinesthetic.

John's presenting problem of enuresis—of *not feeling* the signals of his bladder and thus *losing control* of it—was another indicator of a blocked kinesthetic channel. In addition, it appeared that John did not have an accessible *feeling* response in the problematic areas we had been discussing. However, once we began to explore John's hobbies, he switched to using kinesthetic predicates. He particularly liked baseball and mentioned "running the bases," "hitting the ball," "diving for it," and so forth. There were also a number of other hobbies he actively pursued, and again kinesthetic predicates were used in discussing them. In other words, some aspects of John's life involved positive kinesthetic experiences over which he had mastery. He had had concrete experiences of being *comfortable and in control* in kinesthetically-dominated situations. These concrete experiences constituted resources which could be mobilized in dealing with his problem area.

At this point, John looked around the office, noticing all the toys, puppets, and stuffed animals. As he reached for the cuddly elephant on the shelf, his eyes widened. As if a picture were brought suddenly into focus, John cheerfully began to tell us about a recent visit to the circus. He specifically described his excitement when he watched the elephants parade into the ring, each holding another's tail with his trunk, and how cute the baby elephant was at the end.

At this point, the therapeutic goal was to evoke the resources of comfort and control which John had established in other areas and reattach them to the out-of-control area of bedwetting. A treatment plan utilizing the therapeutic metaphor as a means of unconsciously restructuring the enuretic problem was implemented.

A circus motif involving a young elephant was selected as the background structure. An edited transcription of the metaphor with commentaries follows. Interspersed suggestions are italicized, sensory interweaving is in boldface type, and the ingredients of storywriting are pointed out in sidebars. Please be aware that we are boldfacing only the more obvious, descriptive sensory words. In addition, we did not boldface sensory words that occurred within the interspersed suggestions in order to avoid an overload of factors. The primary purpose of presenting the metaphor in this way is to provide an overall view of the blending of the various elements involved.

INTERWEAVING CONSCIOUS, UNCONSCIOUS, AND OUT-OF-CONSCIOUS SENSORY COMMUNICATION SYSTEMS

(Auditory)	John, since you **mentioned** you like to **hear** stories about animals, I'm going to **tell** you a story about a favorite animal of mine *[pause]* a little elephant. A little elephant that actually lived in a circus. And as I'm **talking,** John, I'd like you to begin
(Visual)	to **see** the story unfold, just like when you're **watching** television, and you can **imagine** your favorite cartoon

show or **see** your favorite characters.
[pause]

(Kinesthetic)

And as you begin to get very **comfortable,** *[pause, as John shifts his body]* that's right, taking all the time you need to just **breathe easily** and **comfortably.** And as you're **sitting** there, John, take a nice, **deep, satisfying** breath in through your nose and out through your mouth, as if you were **blowing** a feather in front of you. *[pause]* That's right. Just **slowly** and **comfortably.**

In this opening communication with John, we began a process of sensory interweaving by matching his most accessible and conscious auditory system with the appropriate predicates *hear, tell* and *talking.* In this way the familiarity of the language would act as a bridge to his problem area. We then activated his unconscious visual system by matching visual predicates such as *see, watching,* and *imagine* with the intent of reinforcing and extending our "bridge of familiarity." Next his out-of-conscious system was introduced through the use of kinesthetic phrases such as *get very comfortable, breathe easily, comfortably, blowing a feather,* and so forth. Here we are associating kinesthetic inevitabilities* such as sitting and breathing with the pleasant experiential state of comfort. The further implication is that *all* inevitable kinesthetic functions can be comfortable.

EVOKING UNCONSCIOUS RESOURCES AND ESTABLISHING THE
METAPHORICAL CONFLICT

*Unconscious
Resources*

John, the story takes place at the Barnum and Bailey Circus, out in the middle of an unknown place *[pause]*, a small town with fields *big enough to hold* the big tents and all the circus equipment. **Imagine hearing** the excitement of the people and the animals as you **watch** everyone doing their job, putting everything exactly where it needs to be placed in order to **pull**

---

* See Erickson & Rossi, 1979, for a discussion of the association of posthypnotic suggestion with behavioral inevitabilities.

up the *big tent that's going to hold everything within it [pause]*—all the people, the animals, the acts, the trainers, the jugglers, the tightrope walkers, and much, much more. And as *you already know, John,* the animals help *put it all together.* The animals are a very important part of the circus. The elephants are often used to **carry** the **heavy** buckets of water and the great big **heavy** beams that **hold up** all the tents and the different displays. The elephants move these beams and buckets around by **carrying** them in their trunk. And it's amazing when you **look** at a large elephant and **watch** him carry a large beam. *[pause]* He does it with such ease. **Imagine hearing** that elephant. **Imagine the sound** that an elephant makes as he's **reaching over** to **see** the next beam he's going to *carry comfortably.*

Metaphorical Conflict

All of the elephants are doing their work so well *[pause]* except for one little elephant named Sammy. Little Sammy **went over** just like everyone else and took his trunk, **wrapped** it around the handle of a large bucket of water, and began to **lift** it and *hold it.* Within a short period of time . . . **BOOM** . . . you **heard** it land and **saw** it begin to **roll.** Sammy hoped that nobody had **noticed** what he had done *[pause]* but the others started **yelling** *[pause].* "What did you do that for—it almost **rolled over** my paw!" **roared** the lion. "Can't you **grab** hold of it; can't you *hold onto it longer* the way everyone else does?" the older elephant **bellowed.**

Sammy got **scared.** He decided that maybe he hadn't paid enough attention, so he began to **watch** the other elephants **carry** the water and the beams. He **watched** them very closely, and then he went back and tried again. *Using all those muscles within* that trunk of his, *John,* he **wrapped** it around the handle of the bucket of water, **saw** himself **picking** it up, and *felt really good inside* as he **walked** along, **swaying** from side to side, just about **bringing** it over to where they needed it . . . and **BOOM** . . . down again! This time the beam **rolled** and **rolled** so far that it **knocked** over the soda machine and the soda **spilled** everywhere. Everyone was very **angry** and **upset** with Sammy now. "Can't you *control that water yet!*" they **yelled.** *"You can control that water [pause], all the elephants do. They control it very well. [pause]* Just **watch** what they do to control their trunk **carrying** whatever they **carry** within their trunk."

Well, Sammy was quite **frustrated** at this point. He tried and tried, day after day, but **BOOM** . . . down went the buckets of water every time he tried. All he **felt** was the animals and circus people **looking** at him so **meanly.** He could **tell** by the **look** in their eyes that they were very **upset** with him. Sammy didn't know what to do to **please** them. He felt really **ashamed** of himself, and **sad.** At times, he would even go off by himself and **cry.** "No one understands," he **mumbled,** "no one really cares."

In the preceding paragraphs we are acknowledging that John's unconscious mind has the resources to resolve his dilemma of bedwetting through the interspersed phrases, "the big tent that's going to hold everything within it," "you already know," "put it all together," "he does it with such ease," "carry comfortably," and "you can control that water." Sammy the elephant is introduced and symbolically presents the same difficulty that John is experiencing. The following paragraphs continue to match the child's sadness, frustration, confusion, and parent-child conflicts. Interspersed suggestions are continued regarding control over the urine in his bladder.

PERSONIFYING UNCONSCIOUS PROCESSES AND REITERATING PAST LEARNINGS AS THE BASIS OF CURRENT CHANGE

Personifying *unconscious* *processes*

Time passed. *[pause]* One day when Sammy was **very sad,** the circus camel **heard** him **crying** and said: "You don't **look** very **happy.** Is there anything I can do to **help** you **feel better** now?" Sammy answered: "I don't know. I keep trying and trying to **hold onto** that bucket, to do my part, but I keep **spilling** it. I keep **letting** it **go** too soon."

Reiterating past learnings

The camel thought for a moment and then began reminding Sammy of all the things that Sammy had learned to do since he'd been in the circus. The camel said: "When you were born, you couldn't **walk** right away. You had a time when your legs were **shaky**. *You had to learn* to take each step, one after the other. At first you had a difficult time, yet you continued to *practice and learn*. After a while, you *learned* to **walk** successfully. *You* also *learned* how to **pick up** grass and **eat** it with your trunk. *You learned* how to **eat** all by yourself. Now your trunk can **carry** just the right amount of food to **totally satisfy** you, so that *you can feel good*. You learned to **recognize** when you are *full and comfortable*. You **feel** so **good** inside, and you can be **surprised** at how long *you can hold onto that good feeling for a long, long time*, Sammy." *[pause]*

Sammy thought for a few minutes and then answered, "Yes, I do remember that."

The camel is introduced to personify the part of John which contains the abilities, learnings, and resources necessary to overcome his problem. Additional suggestions associating past learnings with success and comfort are interspersed. This serves two purposes: (1) it satisfies the logical thinking patterns of the conscious mind ("Oh, that's right, I did learn how to do all those things successfully; that must mean I can learn to do other things successfully"), while (2) stimulating *unconscious search* (Erickson & Rossi, 1979) for ways to apply those past successes to the current problem.

PERSONIFYING PARALLEL LEARNING SITUATIONS: IMPLICATION AS AN INDIRECT SUGGESTION FOR THERAPEUTIC CHANGE

The camel continued: "It's just like the bicyclist here at the big top. I remember years ago when he couldn't

Personifying parallel learning situations

even **ride** the bicycle. He would **get up** on his bike and **fall down.** As a matter of fact, someone had to teach him how to *hold on* to the handle bars correctly. He had to *practice holding on for a long time.* And after he learned to *hold on,* he was able to *relax and enjoy the feeling of letting go.* When you **watch** him later today, Sammy, pay attention to that **look** on his face and the fun he is having *being in control* of that bike. **Telling** you about the bicyclist," mused the camel, "also reminds me of the juggler here at the circus. I remember when he first came here all he could **juggle** were two little bowling pins. Now he can **juggle** big bowling pins and dishes, and he can **mix** all those things together. *[pause]* He can **juggle** balls, pins, and dishes all at the same time while **riding** a bicycle. His

Implication for change

balance is perfect. He *knows exactly when to let go and hold on* to each of those items. You just have to *trust you can do it.* [pause] Some things take a little more time to learn than others and you have all the time in the world you need to *learn that now."* *[long pause]*

In the preceding paragraphs, the camel presents parallel learning situations in the bicyclist and the juggler which model positive outcomes for John. Possibly the most potent element of the therapeutic metaphor is demonstrated here in the implication that quietly surrounds the story. *Implication* allows John's unconscious mind to (1) identify the positive outcomes and (2) marshall the processes and resources needed to actualize them. At no time is any overt connection made between John and Sammy, yet the implication that *John can learn just as Sammy is learning* is a curiously inherent element of the storytelling process itself.

STRUCTURING A METAPHORICAL CRISIS WITHIN A CONTEXT OF INEVITABLE RESOLUTION: VISUALIZING THE RESOLUTION

Metaphorical crisis

Suddenly Sammy and the camel **heard** sirens. They **looked up** and **saw** flames in the distance. "It **looks** like there's a fire at the farmhouse way over there," the camel said. "But those fire engines won't be able to get through the pass, because the bridge was **washed** out. The only other way to **put out** that fire is for the other elephants to **carry** water in their trunks and **spray** it on the fire. But they are busy with the trainer way across town getting ready for the parade later today."

Little Sammy **looked** at the camel rather **curiously** and said, "Well, what are we to do?" The camel replied, "It's up to you now." "What do you mean?" asked Sammy. The camel said, "I'm going to teach you something important. As you know, camels *carry water for a long, long time.* I'm going to teach you how to do that, so *you can carry water for a long period of time too.* And once *you can learn to do that,* you will be able to go over to the lake, **put** your trunk in, **see** yourself **hearing** all that water going in past your trunk, and *hold on to it for a long period of time successfully.* Then you can **see** yourself **walking** along over there to where the fire is and **putting out** that fire by *letting go* of the water *just at the right time.* Not a mile before, not a half mile before, not even twenty feet before—but only when you are at exactly the right spot. Then you can **aim** your trunk and **let go** of all the water." *[long pause]*

Inevitable resolution

Rehearsal

"Simply remember [pause] when you held onto a special happy feeling for a long time [pause]. Or maybe you **carried** the **excitement** for a long time of wondering what gift you'd be getting on your birthday. Since everyone knows elephants have good memories and always remember everything that is important *[pause], remember something important you learned a long time ago and still carry happily with you now."* *[long pause]*

Utilizing past pleasant memories

A crisis situation is now presented to Sammy. The fact that all of the other elephants are busy is meant to emphasize the message that "it's up to you now." He really cannot look to anybody else (parents, siblings, teachers, friends) to resolve this crisis (bedwetting). The camel continues his teaching function by describing the learning process that

Sammy needs to experience. This is done within the framework of the camel's natural water-carrying abilities, which acts as a personification of John's natural (physiological) water-carrying abilities. Here the camel conveys the inevitability of Sammy's successful learning by visualizing in detail the actions that Sammy will then go through to resolve the crisis. This depiction also acts as a *rehearsal technique* (Erickson, 1980f) for future real-life action.

Memories of past pleasant experiences are then associated with the current learning process in phrasing that is pertinent to John's bedwetting problem. Throughout, emphasis is placed on the concept of John's unconscious resources and abilities.

ESTABLISHING A SECONDARY LEVEL OF AWARENESS THROUGH THE "HERO'S JOURNEY": RECOGNITION, CELEBRATION, A NEW IDENTITY: THE DOMINO EFFECT

Secondary level of awareness	"After **listening** to you Mr. Camel," said Sammy, *"I feel I can see myself doing all of that. [pause]* I feel I can do it now." *[long pause]* So the camel and Sammy went over to the lake and Sammy **took in** as much water as he could *hold comfortably. [pause]* Then he began the long walk over to the fire. Sammy got all the way over to the fire and just like the camel had **told** him, Sammy **let go** of all the water at exactly the right time and place. Just the **sound** of that water **hitting** the fire at the right time gave him such a **happy, joyful feeling** inside. His face **lit up** as he **heard** everybody **clapping** and **cheering.** "Hurray, Sammy, you did it!", they all exclaimed. Sammy **felt** very **special** for the first time in a very long time. He was written up in the local newspaper for his special ability and talent—*[pause]—being able to hold on to the water for such a long time and knowing exactly when and where it was time to let go of it all successfully.*
The hero's journey	
Celebration	
New Identity	
Parallel Learnings: The Domino Effect	As the days went by, Sammy was *able to discover other abilities* that he had forgotten about. He thought to himself, "Once *you know how to hold onto the water, [pause] you can hold onto anything successfully.* Just at

New
Identity

that moment, the camel was **walking** by. Sammy **saw** him and **shouted, "Watch** this!" He went over to the main tent, **picked up** a **heavy** wooden beam, and brought the beam all the way over to the center of the tent where it belonged. As he **gently** let it down, Sammy **felt** so **good** inside. He **saw** himself **letting go** of the beam so **securely** and **hearing** it **land** so **gently.** The camel **smiled** at Sammy and said, *"You have learned that and much, much more. And as you continue to be a part of this circus, an important part, you will continue to learn more and more each day."*

Parallel
Learnings in
the future:
The Domino
Effect

Weeks later, as Sammy was **playing,** he **saw** the camel again. The camel reminded Sammy, "Anytime you want to *see yourself doing anything in the future,* just *remember all the important things you've learned. [pause] You can learn anything else you need,* just by taking your time and **holding on** to those **happy** memories." Sammy **looked** at the camel, **nodded** his head and said, "Thank you, Mr. Camel, for reminding me of something I knew all along."

Sammy now can *see himself* accomplishing the critical task of putting out the fire. The use of this type of phrasing—"I can see myself doing that" and (later when the camel says) "Anytime you want to see yourself doing anything in the future"—is twofold: (1) it activates the visualization process of rehearsal mentioned previously, and (2) it activates a *secondary level of awareness* (Rossi, 1972/1985) which acts as a bridge between the conception of the new realization ("I can *see myself* doing that") and its actualization in real life ("I *can do it* now").

Finally Sammy does actualize his new conception that he can learn how to hold on to water. He saves the day, and is appropriately rewarded by the community via joyous celebration. This part of the metaphor exemplifies the unconscious and archetypal experience of the *hero's journey* (Campbell, 1956) whereby the individual comes into his birthright as the controlling force in his life through the transcendence of his personal problem (Rossi, 1972/1985).

The victory achieved is then used as the springboard for the ex-trapolation of many other abilities and potentials. It is important to give time to this culminating phase of the metaphor. While it may be tempting to end on the high note of victory with the crowds cheering Sammy, it is just as important to "ground" the abilities and potentials marshalled to achieve the victory into continuing, everyday realities. Thus the victory initiates a domino effect by which Sammy "can hold onto anything successfully."

UTILIZING "LIVING METAPHORS" TO INITIATE THE
ACTUALIZATION PHASE OF THE METAPHORICAL PROCESS

In the course of his treatment, John was given a number of *living metaphor* assignments. In one assignment, he was told to purchase a hamster and take responsibility for it as his own pet. This idea was first discussed with his mother and she readily agreed. The hamster was chosen as a means of directly accessing John's out-of-conscious kinesthetic system: He would be holding and touching the animal frequently, and he would be totally *in control* of the hamster's care, including its food and *water*. Moreover, since hamster cages must be *kept dry*, it was hoped that John would unconsciously generalize this care to himself. (At no time was the problem of bedwetting ever directly mentioned in relation to the assignment.)

In another living metaphor, John was put in charge of watering the family's garden in the early evening. He was to wear a watch and time himself carefully: He was to water for three minutes, stop for one minute; water for four minutes, stop for two minutes; water for eight minutes, and stop altogether. This procedure was explained to John in terms of the differing absorption rates of the various plants. It was hoped that this exercise would give him a kinesthetic sense of *having complete control over the turning on and off of water*. Still another living metaphor involved kite flying whereby John would experience a third variation of control in the kinesthetic sensation of holding on and letting go at just the right moment.

John was seen weekly for a total of three sessions, with two follow-up telephone conversations with his mother. The first session consisted of a presentation of the elephant metaphor, followed by the homework assignment of obtaining and caring for the pet hamster. In the second session, only one bedwetting incident was reported, and John was noticeably more relaxed. In this session, a number of brief metaphors integrating the themes of *being in control, holding on,* and *letting go* were presented. This was followed by the living metaphor of watering the lawn.

In the third session, John eagerly reported that he had not wet the bed for an entire week, and his mother reported an overall happier child. The therapist continued to reinforce the progress by presenting additional brief vignettes of success. The living metaphor of kite flying was introduced to continue the unconscious work of successfully *holding on* and *letting go.* In a one-month follow-up, John's mother reported only one bedwetting incident, which represented the most control he had experienced with this problem since its inception. A six-month follow-up revealed that John's enuretic behavior had ceased entirely, and there were no indications of symptom substitution.

It has been many years since the crocheting experience with my grandmother, yet I still have the beautiful tablecloth. Each time I begin learning something new and feel doubtful of my abilities to accomplish it, a simple glance at the tablecloth reminds me that the abilities are all there. . . . . It just takes time.

PART THREE

Multidimensional Applications

7

The Artistic Metaphor

With gentle brush strokes the artist begins to transpose a reflective experience onto canvas. Blendings of colors and shapes emerge, soon mirroring the expanse of a deeply private masterpiece.

In addition to utilizing metaphors in a storytelling fashion to integrate sensory systems and evoke unconscious change, another therapeutic application of metaphor can occur through the use of what we term the *artistic metaphor*. The artistic metaphor utilizes drawing strategies, board games, and healing books, all originally conceived and created by the child, to provide another dimension of therapeutic experience.

Both the storytelling metaphor and the artistic metaphor have the special focus of integrating left- and right-brain functions on conscious and unconscious levels via multisensory approaches. Because the artistic metaphor involves the use of objects in space, it is both multisensory *and* three-dimensional. This helps to further expand the metaphorical message into tangible, physical terms. It has now given an external expression to the internal realm of feeling and sensation. It has opened still another door through which the unconscious mind can express and resolve the child's problem by way of conscious representation. The child dips into an inner bank of creativity, retrieves unconscious images and feelings, and then translates them into movements of colors and shapes in a shared experience with the therapist.

Terri's Tears

Twenty-three-year-old Terri had a reported mental age of ten. She was brought in for therapy because she was having great difficulty controlling tearful outbursts. Her schooling focused on occupational rehabilitation, with little emphasis on emotional growth and development.

When Terri entered the office with her parents, she was immediately enamored with all the toys, materials, and new things she saw. She definitely appeared to enjoy the atmosphere. When asked what her own room looked like, Terri started talking about a grandmother, now deceased, who used to share her bedroom. She then went on to talk about other areas of her life, such as her friends, hobbies, and experiences at work. When asked if she would like to go to dances on her own or with friends, Terri answered yes, but then curled up on the couch saying that she was afraid.

At this point Terri was provided with paper and markers and was gently asked to draw what the "afraid" looked like to her. As she drew she repeatedly said, "I don't know what this is . . . I don't know what this is." The therapist wrote those words on her drawing (*Drawing 1*).

DRAWING 1
Terri's Afraid Feeling

Terri was then asked to draw what the "afraid" looked like "all better." She agreed and turned the paper over *(Drawing 2)*. Notice that implicit in her willingness to draw this next version was her unconscious agreement that "I can make it better." She began drawing and when she came to the rectangle design she pointed and said, "My grandma is in there." She kept putting her finger over the dots on the first picture saying, "I don't know what that is." Her mother asked if those could be the people at the funeral or the pallbearers carrying the coffin. Terri said, "People? No." I then told her a story about a little boy who once drew a picture for me with lots of dots on it which he said were tears. At this point I remained silent. Terri took her index finger and pointed to her cheeks, nodded her head yes, and said, "Tears," acknowledging the new awareness.

DRAWING 2
Terri's "All Better" Feeling

After looking at both pictures and hearing the conversation, Terri's father said in a soft voice, "Terri, I don't think you understand. Joyce would like you to draw how it looks *all better*." With deep emotion Terri exclaimed, "IT *IS* ALL BETTER! It's not in *here* anymore [pointing to her heart], it's *here* [pointing to the drawing]!"

Each of us shared in a momentary recognition of the deeply profound emotion evoked by Terri's enlightening experience. No art therapy textbook or training manual could more clearly or more poignantly describe the purpose of artistic expression in therapy than Terri's spontaneous grasp of what she was experiencing. This once again confirmed for me the ease with which children can resolve for themselves such major life issues as death and loss when they are given a way to express their feelings.

Since research has indicated that the right brain plays a dominant role in mediating imagistic, emotional, and kinesthetic processes (Galin, 1974; Gazzaniga, 1967; Sperry, 1968), use of a therapeutic tool such as the artistic metaphor that engages all three areas would have particular advantages. *Imagistic aspects* of the artistic metaphor involve conceiving and visualizing the new creation. *Emotional aspects* involve drawing upon the problem area of painful feelings as well as evoking a resource area of past pleasant feelings. *Kinesthetic aspects* are comprised of the physical tasks and activities needed to construct or draw the final rendition.

In addition, the artistic metaphor employs tools (crayons, markers, paint brushes, construction paper, etc.) and activities (drawing, building, game playing) that are common positive experiences for most children. This helps to buffer the metaphorical message within an environment of receptive familiarity, which in turn helps to release a rich field of symbols, background structures, and themes that can aid the therapist in generating future storytelling metaphors.

Theoretical Perspectives

Art therapy as a credentialed treatment approach in its own right is still in its early stages of development. However art as a vehicle of expression has been used in a naturalistic manner throughout history. In terms of twentieth-century psychology, art therapy has been viewed from three broad perspectives.

In the first perspective, art is viewed as a vehicle for uncovering and interpreting unconscious conflicts. Freud, for example, considered art to be "closer" to unconscious processes because the visual perceptions underlying it were more archaic than those involved in either cognition or verbal expression (Freud, 1923). He viewed the unconscious as a primary motivating force in creativity and therefore considered art to be a form of sublimation whereby unconscious conflicts were expressed symbolically. More contemporary psychoanalytic viewpoints support Freud's position by describing art therapy as "a discipline that seeks to uncover insights in the conflictual sphere of the patient's psyche or to reinforce existing suitable defenses against the emergence of painful memories or feelings" (Lakovics *et al.,* 1978).

In the second perspective, art is viewed as a transpersonal and transcendent process. As noted previously, Jung had personally discovered the therapeutic value of expressing himself artistically. With the addition of his concept of the archetypes, a wider, grander significance that far surpassed the personal, conflictual realm emphasized by Freud was accorded to the role of art. For Jung, artistic expression was a means by which man expressed the sacred and the mysterious. It therefore became another way of expressing the psyche's "transcendent function" (Jung, 1916/1960) and constituted an important element in the therapeutic process of "individuation" (Jung 1934/1959). His systematic description of the significance and meaning of mandalas (circular patterns or images) throughout history and as they appear spontaneously in a person's artwork remains as a valuable resource for art-oriented psychotherapists.

The third perspective reflects a more here-and-now approach appropriate to the emergence of art therapy as a primary or secondary treatment modality. Edith Kramer, one of the pioneers in modern-day art therapy, described its function as one of "supporting the ego, fostering the development of a sense of identity, and promoting maturation in general" (1971, p. xiii).

An overview of art therapy literature demonstrated how it is currently viewed as both a diagnostic and a curative tool (Naumberg, 1958; Rubin, 1981) that can achieve a wide range of therapeutic objectives:

— Enhance and expand the self-concept (Poore, 1977; Remotique-Ano, 1980);
— Enhance interpersonal skills (Neyer, 1976);
— Enrich sensory experience (Oaklander, 1978);
— Extend cognitive orientation in inner and outer realities (Kreitler & Kreitler, 1978);
— Provide a demonstrable value to community mental health programs (Whitney, 1983);
— Provide "sublimation" via artistic expression (Kramer, 1971);
— Provide a therapeutic play medium for the classroom (Nickerson, 1973);
— Reinforce defenses (Lakovics et al., 1978);
— Reflect personality structure (Lakovics et al., 1978);
— Reflect unconscious conflicts (Lakovics et al., 1978; Bassin, Wolfe & Thier, 1983);

— Strengthen ego skills (Naumberg, 1958; Neyer, 1976);

— Transform thoughts and feelings (Capacchione, 1979).

Thus the spectrum of views about art and art therapy flows from Freud's emphasis on it as an expression of unconscious conflicts, to Jung's emphasis on its transcendent qualities, to today's art therapists who focus on its ability to mirror and strengthen the ego (personality, self, etc.).

In our view, artwork can achieve any of the therapeutic objectives espoused along this spectrum. However we have found it most helpful to simply stress what we term its "living benefits." These living benefits include the ongoing experience of releasing pent-up feelings *as well as* the simultaneous activation of inner resources and strengths. From a metaphorical viewpoint, the most salient function of artwork is to depict the child's problem *and* unconscious solutions *as they exist in the present moment.* We have found that analyzing or interpreting the artwork is not nearly as fruitful as emphasizing the child's multisensory experience of allowing unconscious processes a time and space to create and express.

The following excerpt from *The Little Prince* (de Saint-Exupery, 1943)* best conveys our philosophy in this area (pp. 7–8):

Once when I was six years old I saw a magnificent picture in a book, called "True Stories from Nature," about the primeval forest. It was a picture of a boa constrictor in the act of swallowing an animal. Here is a copy of the drawing.

---

* Reprinted by permission of William Heinemann, Ltd.

In the book it said: "Boa constrictors swallow their prey whole, without chewing it. After that they are not able to move, and they sleep through the six months that they need for digestion."

I pondered deeply, then, over the adventures of the jungle. And after some work with a colored pencil I succeeded in making my first drawing. My Drawing Number One. It looked like this:

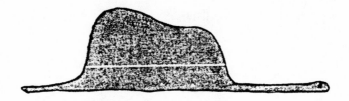

I showed my masterpiece to the grown-ups, and asked them whether the drawing frightened them.

But they answered: "Frighten? Why should any one be frightened by a hat?"

My drawing was not a picture of a hat. It was a picture of a boa constrictor digesting an elephant. But since the grown-ups were not able to understand it, I made another drawing: I drew the inside of the boa constrictor, so that the grown-ups could see it clearly. They always need to have things explained. My Drawing Number Two looked like this:

The grown-ups' response, this time, was to advise me to lay aside my drawings of boa constrictors, whether from the inside or the outside, and devote myself instead to geography, history, arithmetic and grammar. This is why, at the age of six, I gave up what might have been a magnificent career as a painter. I had been disheartened by the failure of my Drawing Number One and my Drawing Number Two. Grown-ups never understand anything but themselves, and it is tiresome for children to be always and forever explaining things to them.

We have taken some of the concepts common to the field of art therapy and developed our own techniques for metaphorical intervention (Crowley & Mills, 1984a, c). These techniques include: (1) Inner Resource Drawings, (2) The Pain Getting Better Book, (3) The Resource Board Game, and (4) the Magic Puppet Theater. For teaching purposes we will provide a detailed description of each technique. However, we encourage readers to view these descriptions not as literal instructions but as frameworks within which your own creativity can emerge.

Inner Resource Drawings

In Chapter 4 we discussed the value of eliciting favorite experiences and observing minimal cues as ways of gathering information for the therapeutic metaphor. The *Inner Resource Drawing* is another primary source of information as well as a healing vehicle in its own right.

The use of drawing as a form of therapy for both adults and children has become increasingly common. The notion of "right-brain drawing" that emerged in the last decade has emphasized the special capacity inherent in artwork for evoking unconscious processes (Edward, 1979). Traditional uses of drawing in the clinical setting have been analytical in focus: Drawings are viewed as a means of depicting personal and family dynamics for greater insight, analysis, and under- standing. Our use of the Inner Resource Drawing is not so much to shed light on past familial and interpersonal dynamics as it is to mediate current vital therapeutic elements for the child in therapy.

As a means of therapeutic intervention, the Inner Resource Drawing serves several important purposes. For one, it helps the therapist identify the child's out-of-conscious sensory system; for another, it can provide an experience of catharsis and emotional release. It can also act as a feedback system for families that helps to clarify each member's view of solutions, and it acts as an immediate feedback system for the child who can now see solutions and resources take tangible shape and color. For the therapist, the Inner Resource Drawing provides a map of resources and background structures that can be incorporated into later storytelling metaphors. It can also provide an alternative means of communicating with the excessively verbal or nonverbal child.

For both child and adult, drawing tends to evoke a range of unconscious processes not normally available to one's everyday consciousness. Our reliance on language as our primary means of communication necessitates a reliance on the specific, the literal, and the linear (Lamb, 1980). Drawing, on the other hand, is a global process which, like the linguistic metaphor, conveys contexts, nonrational associations, intuitions, and impressions. A host of internal feelings and sensations can come together in the course of a five-minute drawing that might otherwise never be verbalized.

The Sound of Music

Fourteen-year-old Luke, who was a member of the family mentioned earlier in the Storm Metaphor (page 46), had been suspended from school for possession of various drugs. With this development, Luke's father and stepmother requested that I work with him in individual therapy on a short-term basis.

In demeanor, Luke appeared easygoing and "cool." He laughed a lot but spoke little and had a sheepish peripheral smile. Despite the laughter and the smiling, it was obvious that he was masking most of what he really felt.

During our initial session, I asked him to draw a picture of some things he enjoyed in his life. There was a threefold purpose for this request: 1) to lessen his anxiety by shifting the focus away from the problem area to an area of enjoyment; 2) to elicit favorite experiences to serve as a background structure in a storytelling metaphor; and 3) to look for possible clues about how Luke's sensory systems were functioning.

Luke's drawing clearly expressed his enjoyment of stereos and music (Drawing 3). This positive auditory resource was further validated in his comment, "Just having music on makes me feel good." From a sensory system viewpoint, Luke's kinesthetic expression of feeling good was generated by his auditory experience of music. This information was later integrated into a storytelling metaphor that described the emotional conflicts within a rock group on tour. Luke's lack of self-worth and his need to "get high" were matched throughout the metaphor by various characters and events. His "solutions"—his positive auditory resources—were integrated with enjoyable kinesthetic experiences from his past such as bicycle riding and skateboarding, which he had all but forgotten. In addition, I gave him a "living metaphor" assignment to go home and rearrange all his music to fit his moods

so that he would become consciously aware of what made him feel
better. Rather than focusing on the drug problem, or even mentioning
it again, I sought instead to simply help him feel better about himself
by utilizing the things he really liked to do.

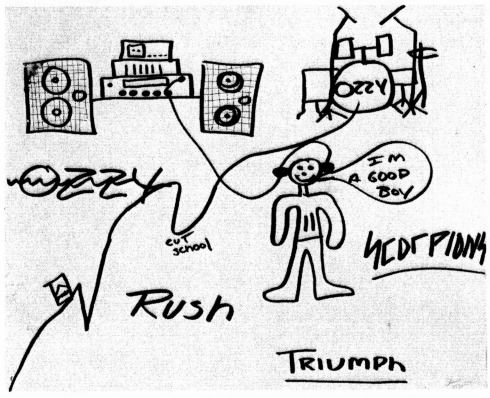

DRAWING 3
Luke's Positive Auditory Resource

After a number of sessions, individual therapy was terminated with
Luke. By this time the father and stepmother had decided to keep
Luke and Carolyn in their family because of the marked improvements
in behavior. Luke was attending school regularly and reported no use
of drugs; both Luke and Carolyn were more cooperative at home.
Ironically, despite all the successful work on the part of the father and
stepmother, the cotherapists, and the teenagers themselves, within a
year Luke and Carolyn decided for unknown reasons to return to their
natural mother and her abusive boyfriend.

The Boy Who Was All Ears

Craig was seen initially when he was five years old for short-term therapy with his family. At that time the parents were having difficulties dealing with his constant tantrums, phobias, and aggressive behavior. Craig's problems had begun at the age of 18 months and were attributed to his father's absence from the home, which had lasted some two years.

Family relations had improved greatly after the initial twelve sessions. The parents reported that they felt more comfortable with Craig, both at home and in public. Although Craig's level of fearfulness and aggression had diminished significantly, the problem was not yet ameliorated entirely. He was seen periodically over the next two years to help him further develop appropriate coping skills for dealing with daily frustrations, especially as they related to his peers.

This case occurred when I was first beginning my study of Ericksonian approaches. Out of habit, I was still viewing Craig from a traditional family therapy point of view: looking for what role he played in the family as the identified patient, helping him find ways to reintegrate into the family structure, working with the family and his school, and so forth. Yet obviously something was missing because his behavior problem was continuing. Even though the family had been willing to make tremendous changes, and the school had been willing to work with me and also make the needed changes, still Craig struggled with behavior he could not control.

In previous sessions I typically asked Craig to draw his painful feelings by saying, "Draw a picture of how you *feel*." He would usually respond by drawing himself looking "sad" and "mad." He would draw the picture quickly and then spend the rest of the time covering it with descriptive words. The drawing itself (*and* his entire visual system) was thus quickly overshadowed by his more dominant verbal (auditory) process.

One day during an office visit with Craig, who was now seven, we were sitting at the art table. He was talking very fast, randomly jumping from one topic to another. At one point he started crying about a hurtful school experience that had occurred earlier that day. I noticed that his eyes were in a left (auditory) position as he described how mean the children at school had been. I suddenly realized how I could apply what I was currently learning *right then*. I asked Craig how he was recalling the incident. Was he hearing it again as he described it to me? He looked at me blankly and said he didn't know. I now perceived his overall behavior as expressive of an out-of-conscious auditory system: his tendency to talk incessantly; his excessive reliance on words rather than shapes when drawing; and his consistent eye-movement patterns in an auditory position as he described past events.

I quickly reviewed in my mind the two questions we had been taught to use as springboards to ascertaining the child's sensory profile: Which sensory system is generating Craig's problem? Which sensory system is not being utilized to help Craig generate solutions? Since Craig was already overloaded kinesthetically from the incident at school and was expressing it in a highly anxious, out-of-conscious, auditory manner (the problem), my new approach suggested that he needed to shift to his little-used visual system (the solution). My instructions to him changed from:

> Draw a picture of how *you feel*
> > to
> Draw a picture of what your problem *looks like* without using any words *(Drawing 4)*.

Even with this change in instructions, I realized that Craig was still left anchored into the problem. Again spurred on by my new Ericksonian perspective of emphasizing the positive, I asked Craig to:

> Draw a second picture of what the problem *looks like all better (Drawing 5)*.

DRAWING 4
Craig's Problem

DRAWING 5
Craig's Problem Looking "All Better"

Drawing 4 is Craig's response to the instruction to draw what his problem looked like. Note that the eyes in this drawing are in a parallel left auditory position, which amazingly matched Craig's own eye movements as he described his upset at school. Also notice the multiplicity of ears surrounding the face, and the sharp, biting teeth sticking out of a wide-open, devouring mouth. From a sensory systems perspective, Craig had drawn an almost unbelievably literal depiction of his out-of-conscious auditory system—the system which appeared to be perpetuating his behavior problems at school.

Drawing 5 is Craig's response to draw what his problem at school would look like "all better." Several important changes appear in the second picture. First, he used very different colors (in the first picture he used red as the only color; in the second picture he used soft brown tones). Second, the ears on the left side are fewer in number. Third, the mouth and teeth now form a wide smile. Most significantly, the eyes have shifted from a painful left auditory position to a here-and-now visual position of looking straight ahead.

Inner Resource Drawings continued to be utilized throughout Craig's therapy. In addition, it was suggested that he enroll in a sculpting class to further expand his sensory awareness into pleasant kinesthetic and visual areas.

What is fascinating about this case is that I learned only after Craig's treatment had ended that his father was an alcoholic. In an emotionally intense conversation I had with Craig's mother, she told me how she had not been able to reveal the facts about their painful family life at the time of her son's therapy. She now explained how Craig's problems were perpetuated by the intense denial and anger she had struggled with in relation to her husband's drinking problems. In public she would act as the "perfect wife and mother" in order to control and conceal her true emotions. However, at home her "perfect front" would crumble and she would take out all her anger and fear on her son. She went on to say how she would yell at him at home but never in public.

This information was particularly interesting to me in relation to Craig's unconscious drawings of his out-of-conscious auditory system. With the intense denial taking place in both his mother and father, Craig had been trapped in his own pain which was clearly depicted in his pictures long before the true situation was openly discussed.

The importance of the drawing process for Craig became even

more meaningful with this new information about his family. How clearly his drawings had demonstrated the availability and potency of his inner resources: Despite the blanket of denial and anger the child lived under, he still knew what "all better" looked like on an unconscious level. Equally impressive, his drawings illustrate how the therapist can work effectively with only the presenting symptom and despite the withholding of what is traditionally considered to be vital psychodynamic information.

In our conversation, Craig's mother proudly went on to describe how the entire family is involved in Alcoholics Anonymous, Al-Anon, and Alateen—and how the once closed windows to happiness in their lives are now opened. She also mentioned that Craig, who is now in the sixth grade, had become the top student in his school and has won many important accolades. She stressed that the most important "winning," however, was their family's newfound happiness and sense of well-being.

The "Pain Getting Better Book"

The "Pain Getting Better Book" was created as a metaphorical tool to help children cope with physical pain. Its purpose is to provide an artistic implement by which (1) painful sensations can be objectified, and (2) at the same time, untapped inner resources can be accessed. The visual and kinesthetic aspects of drawing are focused in a way that helps promote greater comfort via the dissociation that naturally occurs as a result of the drawing process. This dissociation, which is viewed as a key to pain management (Barber, 1982; Erickson & Rossi, 1979), may also alter the actual physiology of the pain by its positive effects on the child's endorphin system.*

It is extremely important to note that the "Pain Getting Better Book" is meant to function as an adjunctive treatment approach to medical diagnosis and treatment. Naturally, it is recommended that all pain symptoms be evaluated medically to determine the etiology. This technique is not used to mask the pain but rather to control, dilute, or dissociate it.

---

* See Rossi (1986b) for a fascinating explication of the latest research in mind/body connections.

Suzie's "All Better" Sounds*

Blonde-haired, eight-year-old Suzie was hospitalized for tests to determine the cause of pain being experienced in her kidney area. (The tests later proved negative, indicating that her symptoms were psychogenic in origin.) Since Suzie was my friend Rita's daughter, I naturally went to visit her. When I entered the room, Suzie was lying in bed talking to her mother in a low voice.

Suzie told me, "It hurts real bad right here," pointing to the area of her kidneys. I asked her if she had any drawing paper and crayons or markers. She said yes and handed me a plain, spiraled notebook. I then asked her to close her eyes, take a slow, deep breath and imagine what the pain looked like. When she had the picture in her mind, she was to open her eyes and draw it on paper *(Drawing 6)*. While she drew, Suzie's attention was completely absorbed in her task. It was as if none of us were in the room with her.

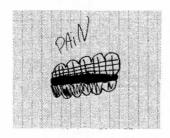

DRAWING 6
Suzie's Pain

DRAWING 7
Suzie's Pain Looking "All Better"

I then asked Suzie to draw what the pain would look like "all better." She again began drawing almost immediately *(Drawing 7)*. The expression on her face was markedly more relaxed than before we started the drawing process. Finally, she was instructed to "make one more drawing of what would help picture one change into picture two" *(Drawing 8)*.

After completing the third drawing, Suzie said that she felt much better and that "the pain doesn't hurt so much." She then took her

* This case was first described in a paper presented at the Annual Scientific Meeting of The American Society of Clinical Hypnosis, San Francisco (Crowley & Mills, 1984c).

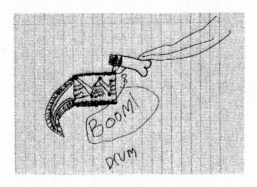

DRAWING 8
Suzie's Positive Auditory Resource (Drum)

pen and spontaneously wrote on the front of the notebook, "My Pain Getting Better Book." During her hospital stay, she replaced the pain medication by drawing more pictures in her book. In addition, her mother said that she used her book to help her through various hospital procedures.

Some months later when Suzie was home with a minor illness, her mother reported that she again asked for her "Pain Getting Better Book" to help her feel better. It now appeared Suzie had indeed discovered a very powerful pain medication—the healing abilities of her own unconscious mind.

I was very intrigued by the sequence of Suzie's drawings. Her first two pictures were abstract and nonspecific—doodle-like—while her third illustration was concrete and very specific in depicting a drum with the word, *Boom!* This pattern of two abstract pictures followed by a third illustration depicting some kind of auditory stimulus continued throughout her hospital stay *(Drawings 9–14)*.

After Suzie's release from the hospital, I learned from Rita that Suzie had spent the day previous to her hospitalization at her best friend's home, and had been fidgety and "out of sorts" upon her return to her own home. Rita had asked Suzie what was wrong and her dejected reply had been, "Oh, you know how Katy's mother is." Suzie did not want to discuss it further because her favorite TV program was on, yet even that did not seem to help her feel better. Rita added that Suzie had complained of headaches and stomachaches on other occasions after returning from Katy's home.

Katy's mother, Rita continued, was an extremely critical and ar-

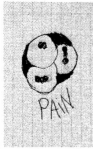

DRAWING 9	DRAWING 10	DRAWING 11
Suzie's Pain	Suzie's Pain Looking "All Better"	Suzie's Positive Auditory Resource (Cymbals)

gumentative person. Throughout the course of an ordinary day, she would routinely find fault with everything and everyone she encountered. Katy was "used to it," according to Suzie, but Suzie herself was very affected by the woman's vocalizations.

As I looked at Suzie's drawings in her "Pain Getting Better Book," I was amazed at the consistency with which an auditory stimulus was depicted as the means by which the problem would be resolved. For Suzie, her auditory process was clearly a valuable resource that had particular significance in light of her unresolved problem about her best friend's mother, whose vocal criticalness (an auditory process) had become overwhelming. The eruption of her psychosomatic symptomatology indicated, however, that Suzie's resource was not being used— indeed it had become out-of-conscious. My guess was that in tuning out the negative auditory stimulus of Katy's mother, Suzie's positive use of her own auditory system had become an unwitting casualty. Once Suzie got back in touch with these positive uses via her drawings, she was able to eliminate her own pain.

Another interesting aspect of Suzie's drawings was that what the real problem *appeared to be* and what the solution was clearly *depicted to be* both involved the auditory sensory system. The *sounds* in the third picture let us know which sensory system could change Picture One, the problem, into Picture Two, the solution. In this specific example, the painful out-of-conscious *auditory system* generating Suzie's pain would thus be neutralized and disarmed by the utilization of those other *pleasant sounds* in her auditory channel that were associated with her positive feelings. This case beautifully demonstrates how the problem and its solution are often different sides of the same sensory coin.

To recapitulate, the "Pain Getting Better Book" involves three simple steps in which the child is asked to draw:

1. How the pain looks right now;
2. How the pain looks "all better";
3. What will help Picture One change into Picture Two.

These drawings serve several purposes. First they help the child *dissociate* from the pain by transforming it into an image on paper. The very act of seeking to give a *visual image* to the pain activates a "secondary level of awareness" (Rossi, 1972/1985) which helps the child disconnect from the *feeling of pain*. The child gains some distance

DRAWING 12
Suzie's Pain

DRAWING 13
Suzie's Pain Looking "All Better"

DRAWING 14
Suzie's Positive Auditory Resource (Piano)

from the pain for the first time, which opens the possibility of seeing it in a new form.

Second, giving the pain a tangible image gives the child a sense of knowing what she is dealing with—of moving from the unknown to the known. This is an important step in helping the child gain a sense of control over the pain. It is similar to the experience of finding a puddle of water on the kitchen floor. At first, before the location of the leak is identified, all manner of plumbing catastrophes are envisioned. Once the actual leak is located, however, it comes back under control. In much the same way, giving shape and color to something so amorphous as pain helps to control and "de-catastrophize" it.

A third purpose of the drawings is to help facilitate a switchover in sensory systems not unlike switching a television channel from a scary movie to a pleasant one. The sick child is stuck in a painful kinesthetic channel. All the child's attention is usually focused on the *feeling of being sick.* Drawing what the pain looks like helps activate other parts of the brain which diffuse attention and provide a wealth of helpful resources.

The fourth purpose of the drawings is a powerful one of *implication.* By asking the child to draw how the pain would look *"all better,"* the therapist is implying that "all better" does exist. When the child agrees and begins to draw the picture, her actions signify that "all better" is now also a potential reality. She now begins to build a metaphorical bridge from discomfort to comfort, using her own "unconscious medicine." This bridge is brought into existence with the second drawing, and then made real and concrete with the third drawing which symbolically depicts the child's abilities and resources to actualize it.

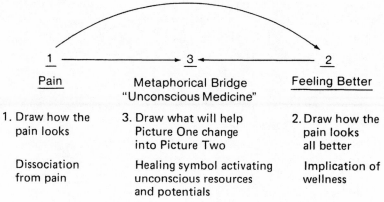

1	3	2
Pain	Metaphorical Bridge "Unconscious Medicine"	Feeling Better
1. Draw how the pain looks	3. Draw what will help Picture One change into Picture Two	2. Draw how the pain looks all better
Dissociation from pain	Healing symbol activating unconscious resources and potentials	Implication of wellness

Family Drawings

The strategies of the Inner Resource Drawings we have discussed thus far have been used primarily with the child working alone with the therapist. We would now like to present additional applications of the drawings to include more than one family member within the session. This use of drawings allows the therapist to gather an abundance of information in the form of background structures and inner resources that can be used later for creating storytelling metaphors. Drawing with family members can also help to establish an internal homeostasis within the family as each member is unconsciously linked to the other in the shared activity of drawing.

The Family That Drew Together

Little six-year-old David was having problems with his peers in school. At home his parents reported he was "just impossible." He had an older brother of 14, Paul, who was always telling David to get out of his room and leave him alone. The situation had escalated to such a point that the father wanted to stay at the office to avoid the fights at home. The mother, also a working parent (part-time), tried to create a pleasant atmosphere when she was home, but inevitably failed.

The whole family was asked to come in to the initial session. My office is set up very much like a family room, with a play area, L-shaped couch, and movable tables so that the family can interact on many familiar levels.

The session began in the usual manner with the family members finding their own places to sit. After an initial greeting to all present, I began by talking to David first. This is something I do frequently in order to initiate an equalizing process as soon as possible: Since David (the identified patient) is inevitably feeling badly about himself, the scale of family self-worth is already out of balance.

At this point, David and the other family members did not need to hear about the problem one more time. Their perception needed a shift towards positive and restorative abilities. Therefore, I asked David about the things he liked to do. He pointed to the drawing paper on the play table and said he liked to draw. I commented, "Learning to draw can be a very interesting experience." I then went into verbiage at some length about the way a child delights in learning new things. The purpose was twofold: One was to indirectly shift the parents' focus away from their child, David, and onto an inner focus of their own child within, thereby unconsciously activating an openness to receive new learnings; and secondly, to reinforce the equalizing process between each family member.

Three sheets of drawing paper were given to each of the four family members, along with markers and a masonite board to lean on while they drew. They were given instructions to draw the three pictures depicting what the problem looked like, how it would look "all better," and what would help Picture One change into Picture Two.

After the verbal assignment was given, I added, "And as you do that, enjoy discovering something important for you." There was a momentary pause at that point to emphasize the suggestion to discover something important.

Each family member now became involved in a privately absorbing experience while at the same time sharing unconsciously in a unified family activity. There was no interaction or exchange during the drawing process. At the end of each exercise, the family members shared their pictures.

The differences among family members were immediately apparent in their drawings, particularly in the third drawing. The mother and her younger son, David, depicted their solutions as occurring in activities for the family as a whole; the father and Paul, on the other hand, drew individual sporting activities. The family members readily recognized the paired differences in their drawings and acknowledged that these unspoken alliances did exist: Mother and David tended to side with one another, as did Father and Paul. They all expressed puzzlement and amazement that something no one ever talked about openly was suddenly made visible in their drawings.

I then pointed out that in addition to the differences, the drawings also depicted a very important similarity: all of their third drawings were *outdoors* and *involved activity*. When family members are at odds, as these were, it is equally important to look for similarities that can bridge an experience of agreement between the opposing forces. When I pointed out the similarities to this family, each face brightened with relief. Once the problem was clearly depicted in their initial drawings, I then moved on to reframe their subsequent three-step drawings in terms of similarities.

The Attention Getters

One day a pregnant mother and her two children arrived in my office. The mother was feeling very out of control because of the demands for attention by her two children. Their behavior appeared to be connected with the "intrusion" of the forthcoming birth. Brian, age nine, was being "forced" to move into his younger sister's smaller bedroom so that she, Patty, age five, and the new baby could share the larger bedroom. While neither child was pleased with the upset in their living styles, Brian was most vehement about it, frequently expressing his anger at his mother and at Patty. The age-old wail of "It's not fair" was the soapbox from which Brian refused to move.

After ten minutes or so of discussion, both children agreed with me that the problem with their mother was one of "not getting enough attention." I then gave them crayons and drawing paper with instructions to draw what "not getting enough attention" would look like *(Drawings 15 and 16)*. Once completed, they were asked to draw how that feeling would look "all better." This drawing helped to reawaken an important "all better" feeling that had been all but forgotten *(Drawings 17 and 18)*. Their last drawing was to depict an experience they had had in the past which was connected in some way to the "all better" feeling they had just drawn *(Drawings 19 and 20)*.

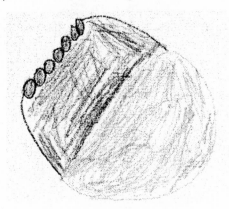

DRAWING 15
Brian's "Not Getting Enough Attention"

DRAWING 16
Patty's "Not Getting Enough Attention"

DRAWING 17
Brian's "All Better" Feeling

DRAWING 18
Patty's "All Better" Feeling

Brian's third picture *(Drawing 19)* consisted of a baseball batting cage; he commented that he liked being taken there by his father. At this point he also asked to draw a soccer game, as he was an avid player. His mother commented that Brian's high and low moods were especially obvious after he played in a soccer game because he was such a "perfectionist." Speaking for the father who wasn't at our meeting, the mother agreed that the father would be willing to take Brian to the batting cage this coming weekend.

Patty's third picture *(Drawing 20)* portrayed a picnic scene and ways were agreed upon in which the mother and Patty could enjoy one of their meals together in picnic fashion in the backyard or local park.

DRAWING 19
Brian's Positive Resource (Baseball)

For Brian and Patty, the baseball batting and the picnic scene symbolically represented their own unique experience of the "all better" feeling of attention. No analysis is needed here—just simple utilization of the information in a storytelling metaphor, or an active implementation of it as a homework assignment or living metaphor.

In the following session both children happily reported experiencing the events depicted in their drawings. To say the least, they were quite pleased with the much-needed attention. Even the mother reported great relief from their constant demands on her time. However, now Brian began to show his true colors of underlying discontent by making snide remarks at Patty such as, "Look at her. Her feet are always moving. She can never keep them still." The mother retorted as always,

DRAWING 20
Patty's Positive Resource (Picnic)

"Now cut that out. Stop picking on your sister so much. Doctor, this kind of stuff goes on all the time!" Brian resounded with, "But it's *true*. She wiggles her feet all the time!" Poor Patty was looking like a dented ping-pong ball in a never-ending match. At this point, a spontaneous idea popped into my mind and I interrupted the ping-pong game by reframing a number of behaviors.

"You're right, Brian. You're perfectly correct in your observation about your sister." Brian beamed with delight because he was being acknowledged.

"Patty does move her feet a lot."

Patty and the mother now looked somewhat confused at my apparently taking sides with Brian.

"And foot movement in young children is a good indicator of natural, underlying talents—like a ballerina or dancer of some kind. You know, all the studies that I've read about wiggling feet say the same thing: That kid will grow up to be famous, using the ability of those feet."

Looking directly at Patty, whose eyes had already defocused, I asked, "Could you show me again what is obviously a wonderful natural talent to continue moving and wiggling your feet as I speak?" She nodded and acquiesced with a big smile of surprise.

Brian, who now was in his own trance with his mouth slightly open, was asked to tell me if his feet moved a little or a lot when he was playing in a soccer game.

"A lot," he admitted.

"That's right. And if your feet hadn't learned how to move a lot when you were younger [implying Patty's age as I glanced quickly in her direction], would you be the good soccer player you are today?"

"No," he replied.

Before Brian could resume his ping-pong match with his sister, I quickly acknowledged his abilities as an excellent drawer, handed him crayons and paper, and asked him to draw something fun.

The Battleship Boy

A pleasant eight-year-old boy named Matt entered the office accompanied by his mother. I had conversed with her previously on the telephone and knew that she viewed her son's problem as being "his poor attitude about school." Matt had become "unhappy and withdrawn," and communicating with him had become increasingly difficult since the family had moved from Washington to California a year ago. In this initial session, I decided not to let the mother reiterate her concerns about Matt's behavior but instead sought to enlist his help nonverbally. I knew he did not want to be in my office, and I was even more certain that he did not want to hear about his problems again. I therefore attempted to establish an unconscious alliance with him by entering his world of fantasy and focusing on his strengths.

"Matt, I don't want you to tell me, but just remember a pleasant or happy time in your life, or something you enjoy doing a lot." His eyes went to an upper left position (visual) as he smiled and nodded his head affirmatively.

"Great!" I acknowledged. "Is it easy for you to *hold onto that pleasant experience?*"

Matt nodded yes.

"That's nice to know. Now I'd like you to remember a time when you weren't so happy—or something you didn't like to do much."

Again Matt went on an internal search (as his eyes darted in an upper left movement) and quickly nodded his head, but there was no smile this time.

"That's quite a creative ability you have to see those experiences, and I imagine you're in control of *holding onto that pleasant one* and letting go of that other one, aren't you?"

Again a smile and a bigger nod appeared.

"Now, I'm really curious, Matt, as to what that pleasant memory was." Matt eagerly told me that he loved to draw, especially battleships, planes, and tanks.

"Oh, all those things are very powerful," I said. "I imagine if we were both inside one of those powerful tanks on the beach now we would really be protected, huh?"

Matt agreed. I proceeded to make noises like a tank and he joined in. As we continued acting out this fantasy together, Matt commented that battleships were even more powerful than tanks. I asked him to show me just how powerful they were by drawing one. He readily agreed to do so and his mother interjected that "he's *always* drawing battleships." At the end of our meeting, Matt said that he would bring in some of his battleship models for the next session.

In a subsequent session, the father accompanied Matt. The father described his own problem of communicating with his son regarding school activities and chores at home, especially emptying the trash container in the kitchen "that piles up so high it falls all over the floor."

I looked at Matt and said, "It's time to inspect the battleship. We want to be prepared and protected at all times in case of enemy attack. Oh! Look over here. There are a lot of empty shells piled up and scattered over the deck in front of our battle stations. Something needs to be done or there could be a problem later on. I'd like you, Matt, to get some of the sailors on deck to clean up that mess and remind them how important it is to keep the decks clean of all that used-up stuff."

Matt agreed and gave the commands to the men. "Just in time," I exclaimed, looking toward the sky. "Matt, it's enemy fighter planes!" We continued making noises and fighting off the enemy together.

The following week the father returned with Matt and reported that he had used the battleship metaphor to deal successfully with the issue of emptying the trash. By reframing the trash into empty shells, Matt was more than eager to protect the battleship!

Remembering the father's second concern regarding communicating with Matt about what occurs in school each day, I handed Matt some drawing paper and implements, asking the simple and direct question, "Can you show me something that happened at school today on this paper?" Without hesitating, Matt went into his world of drawing and produced a picture filled with multicolored communications. I pointed out to the father that Matt is creative visually and that he finds it easier to communicate using his strong visual system. Later, I suggested, Matt could be encouraged to communicate verbally about the content of his pictures.

I gave both father and son an assignment to be carried out first in the office and then whenever the father was having difficulty communicating with Matt. A large piece of drawing paper was presented, with Matt sitting on one side and his father on the other. They were to select a theme to draw, and each one was to contribute in the creation of an entire picture, an entire story. Needless to say, the theme they drew together for the first time was battleships. As they jointly drew their interacting sketches, I noticed four-digit numbers on each battleship and asked Matt to total them. After simply glancing at the numbers 2691, Matt immediately calculated the correct total. Since math had become one of Matt's "bad attitudinal problems" in school, I now suggested that he and his father create a "new math" of adding and subtracting enemy planes as a part of their "mission."

As an aside, I also pointed out to the father how Matt's ability in math obviously depended upon which sensory system was activated. When math was presented as a primarily auditory-thinking process, as it typically is in school, then Matt performed poorly; however, when it was presented in a strong visual context to which he could relate, he suddenly became quick and accurate.

Since I enjoy playing off words, I suggested that much more could be learned as they continued drawing and interacting. "Sometimes a *plane* is not necessarily something that flies, as in a *plain* sandwich," I commented. The father smiled, thought for a moment and then said, "Or like the prairie and the *plains* are very open." From Matt came a smirk and the comment, "Or when a carpenter *planes* the wood." Laughing, we both yielded to the creative mind of an eight-year-old boy.

The Resource Board Game

Playing board games has long supplied pleasurable ways to spend hours with friends or family. Those of us who work with children have put these games to another therapeutic use. Strategic games such as chess and checkers can provide a nonthreatening means of establishing rapport and at the same time provide valuable information into the source of resistance, fear, and character problems (Loomis, 1957). Board games such as the Talking, Feeling, Doing Game (Gardner, 1973), the Ungame (Ungame, 1975) and Imagine (Arden Press, 1978), to name but a few, have enhanced our repertoire of child therapy techniques.

Through our therapeutic work with children and their families, we have expanded the concept of the pre-printed board game. Using the "Treasure Map" exercise by Capacchione (1979, p. 172) as a springboard, we have integrated carefully chosen elements of metaphorical construction into the "Resource Board Game," a game which is individually created by the child. Each time the game is played, it is recreated anew. Information from the child about her world is transformed by the child herself into symbols (metaphors) which unknowingly represent her problem, her conscious and unconscious blocks, and her inner resources. In this way, the "Resource Board Game" becomes another vehicle for the original creation of therapeutic, multisensory metaphors. First we will describe how the game is created and played, and then we will present a case illustration.

CREATING THE RESOURCE BOARD GAME

First the child is provided with a large piece of drawing paper or poster paper along with drawing implements such as crayons or markers. The child is asked to draw "something you want to have in your life—something important for you," in one corner of the paper. In the opposite diagonal corner the child is told to draw a favorite character or object that could help him get to the goal.

Second, the child is asked to close his eyes and imagine a map that would lead the character or object to the goal. When the map is very clear in his mind, he is told to open his eyes and begin drawing it.

Third, the child is asked to draw three obstacles on the board that could impede the character or object from achieving its goal. The instruction could be stated something as follows: "Now put in three things that might get in the way of Mickey Mouse (or whoever) reaching the treasure chest (or whatever)."

Fourth, the child is asked to create a specific resource as a counterpart to each obstacle. These three resources (which are, of course, symbols of the child's own inner resources) are drawn on paper (approximately 3" x 5") and cut out with scissors, to be used later as the game is played. These are called the "resource cards."

Fifth, the child is asked to draw as many connecting spaces as she wishes along the mapline from the starting point to the end of the game. In this fashion, the obstacles also become spaces on which to land.

Sixth, the child now creates the symbolic pieces to move along the map's spaces. These symbolic pieces can be drawn on paper and cut out, made out of clay, or borrowed from among the child's favorite things. (One little girl suggested using her ring and the therapist's ring as the pieces.)

Finally, the therapist or child draws a circle approximately six inches in diameter on a piece of paper and divides it into equal, pie-shaped pieces. The child then draws each of the original pictures from the smaller resource cards onto each of the pie-shaped pieces and numbers them with any number from one to six. These numbers correspond to the die used in the game. An option is to have the child choose two numbers for each pie-shaped space. This doubles the child's chances of achieving success in overcoming the obstacles as the game is played.

Pictorially, the first alternative would appear as follows:

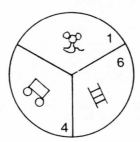

The second alternative:

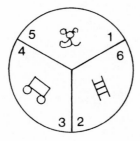

The purpose of drawing the larger resource pictures is to further anchor the resources into the child's unconscious mind. This larger resource card is placed next to the board game while playing.

PLAYING THE RESOURCE BOARD GAME

The players (therapist and child) begin by placing their symbolic pieces on the favorite character/object and throwing a die. The player moves the piece according to the number shown on the die. If she lands on an obstacle, she throws the die until she gets the number corresponding to the matching resource on the larger resource card. She is then handed a corresponding smaller resource card which is turned in as a ticket to "go ahead," and she now moves forward according to the number on the die. This process continues back and forth until the child reaches the goal. If the therapist reaches the goal first, she can either return to the beginning and continue playing, or simply stay on the goal and allow the child to play until she also reaches the goal. Some children will spontaneously add new symbols of obstacles and resources as they play. The case illustrations that follow will demonstrate how each child's temperament must dictate the unfoldment of the game.

It is important to note that the game is over *only when the child reaches the goal.* At that point the child receives a token for winning, such as a sticker, a marker, or a balloon to take home as a positive reminder of the accomplishment. In general, young children are content to play the game for the sheer pleasure of the experience and do not need the incentive of reward. The older ones, however, engage in the activity with the edge of competitiveness; they really want to win. If the therapist lands on the goal first, some ingenuity is usually required to reframe the child's "loss" into an opportunity for greater gain in the end.

As the game is played, the therapist can intersperse simple, helpful suggestions. For example, as the child begins creating the resource cards the therapist might say, "It's nice to know *you now have all those things that can help you* over those obstacles." Or as the child moves off an obstacle by obtaining a resource card, the casual statement can be made, "It's nice to know *you can have fun and learn many new things.*"

The child is especially receptive to suggestions given during this time because of the intense absorption that occurs as the board game is created and played. The condition of intense absorption is a natural trance state in which suggestions can pass unimpeded by conscious censorship on their way to the unconscious mind (Erickson & Rossi, 1979, 1981; Erickson, Rossi & Rossi, 1976). The physical tasks involved in assembling and playing the board game occupy the conscious mind while the deeper issues are processed unconsciously. The following case describes how the Resource Board Game came into being.

Erica's Rainbow

Erica was a lovely, bright-eyed girl of eight who was seen every other week for several months for the adjustment problems she was experiencing with her new foster family. Her mother had died when she was four and her father had been unable to care for her.

After returning from a recent visit with her father, who lived back East, Erica was described as experiencing "emotional upset" by her foster mother who had accompanied her. Erica had looked forward to the trip for many months, thinking that she would see her father every day. When she got there, however, her father was able to see her only minimally because of a recent auto accident which had resulted in a revoked license. The foster mother did her best to get Erica over to the father, but transportation remained a problem throughout the visit.

As the foster mother relayed the story, I decided to use an indirect method for helping Erica regain a sense of strength while dealing with her feelings of rejection and anger. Knowing how much Erica enjoyed artwork and playing games, I asked her to create her own game as an experimental therapeutic intervention. With Erica as the stimulus, we both set about creating what I spontaneously named "The Resource Board Game."

A large piece of paper was given to Erica, and the steps in creating the Resource Board Game described in the previous section were created. Erica began by drawing one of her favorite cartoon characters, Mickey Mouse, as the goal in one corner, with Minnie Mouse as her helper in the opposite diagonal corner (Drawing 21). She then easily filled in the map and drew in her three obstacles: a swamp, an alone cave, and an alligator. Then she spontaneously and without instruction returned to the Mickey Mouse corner and added a rainbow. Her resource cards were the next step. As illustrated, she drew a ladder to help her out of the swamp, a car to take her out of the alone cave, and a horse that could help her jump over the alligator to the rainbow and Mickey Mouse. Erica then redrew the resource pictures onto the larger resource card and numbered them accordingly. She then drew a heart and a balloon as her symbolic pieces (Drawing 22) and cut them out so that they would stand, tent-like, on the board.

Finally, spaces were drawn in between the obstacles on the board. Erica also spontaneously drew in a little house with rain outside saying, "It's raining outside but inside it's safe."

It is important to note that no interpretation occurs during this process or at any other time. Whatever inner qualities were symbolized by the various parts of the game remained Erica's private, unconscious knowledge. Analyzing the symbols was superfluous to Erica's personal, living connection to them as strengths and resources.

As we began playing the game, Erica's emotional state clearly changed

DRAWING 21
Erica's Resource Board Map with Goal (Mickey Mouse),
Helper (Minnie Mouse), Obstacles (Swamp, Alone Cave, Alligator), and Rainbow.

DRAWING 22
Erica's Smaller Resource Cards (Ladder, Car, Horse),
Larger Resource Card, and Two Symbolic Pieces (Heart and Balloon)

from one of guardedness and detachment to one of lively enthusiasm. The resource cards, her favorite cartoon character, and her helper seemed to manifest a visible retrieval of her own inner resources which had been blocked by the disappointingly sad experience with her father.

In subsequent sessions, Erica came into the office gleefully asking to play with her Resource Board Game. Storytelling metaphors naturally emerged from the rich supply of background symbols Erica created during the game itself. Helping a delightful child such as Erica recapture her coping abilities and natural sense of self through her own Resource Board Game became a truly engaging and therapeutic encounter for both of us.

Jana's Blossoming

This second Resource Board Game was also created by an eight-year-old girl, Jana, who was brought in by her recently divorced mother for problems of weight-gain and self-criticalness.

I quickly ascertained that Jana's kinesthetic system was out-of-conscious because of her obvious problem with overeating. I also suspected that her auditory system was out-of-conscious because of her mother's report of her incessant, self-critical ramblings. Her out-of-conscious auditory and her seriously blocked visual system became even more evident as we began creating the board game. Like a malfunctioning computer, Jana's major sensory systems were "down." She was in a world all her own on a level of consciousness that was painfully uncomfortable.

At this point I felt it would be helpful to introduce the process of drawing the parts of the Resource Board Game as a twofold means of interrupting her constant talking and at the same time contacting her overridden feelings and emotions. In order to shift her focus off literal verbiage and onto symbolic representations, she would have to access another realm of experience, another "part" of her brain.

What is particularly interesting about this case is the contrast between Erica and Jana's response to the drawing. Erica had leapt at the idea; she had responded easily and creatively, even initiating drawings beyond my instructions. For Jana the process was slow and halting; her drawings were extremely simple, lacking the visual flair so evident in Erica's. As she drew, Jana would mutter criticisms to herself such as, "This is no good. . . . I want to start over. . . . What is this supposed to look like. . . . This isn't right." Moreover, every time she was asked to draw a symbol, she said she needed to *write the words* first because she *couldn't picture* it. For example, when asked to draw a symbol of what she wanted in one corner, she wrote in words "living in a house." I then asked her to *draw* a symbol of those words, and she did *(Drawing 23)*.

DRAWING 23

Jana's Resource Board Map with Goal (House) and Obstacles (Person, Block, Train)

Following the next step in creating the game, I asked her to imagine a helper that would help her get to her goal. She thought for a long time and then said, "I can't."

I then asked her to imagine a map leading to her goal. Again she thought for a long time and said, "I can't."

I said, "Let's try this. Close your eyes and give me your pointer finger." I took her finger in my hand and began moving it on the paper in a zig-zag fashion talking softly about how "it's nice to discover the path from your mind to your fingers that can help show you the way to find what you want." Jana opened her eyes, smiled, and began her map. Notice that she did not choose to draw a helper in the corner opposite to the goal (*Drawing 23*).

The obstacles were created next. Again, this step required guidance from the therapist but *never* direct suggestion about what to draw. After some time, Jana drew a person, a block, and a train. Until this point Jana had used only one color, dark blue, in her drawing.

Next Jana was asked to draw her resources, "things that could help her get past those things in the way." Again it was difficult for her to create the symbols. However, Jana did draw a wagon to help push the person out of the way, a ladder to climb over the block, and a bridge to go over the train. These cards were all drawn with a black marker and with very simple lines (*Drawing 24*).

DRAWING 24
Jana's Smaller Resource Cards (Wagon, Ladder, Bridge)

The next step presented to Jana was the larger resource card which I had already drawn and sectioned into threes (*Drawing 25*). At this point a dramatic change was noted. Jana's auditory monologue and preoccupation with writing words lessened considerably. In addition, she shifted from using one dark color to selecting many bright colors. Not only did she recreate the resource symbols, but she added new symbols around them as she became totally absorbed in her new expression.

As Jana finished drawing the bridge, she picked up all the markers and began letting her hand create a design. As she did this, I again talked softly to her about "how colors can begin to blend together to form new and different designs, and how much fun it can be to simply watch as that happens." She was noticeably more relaxed as she continued with her designs, so I chose this moment to add "and as

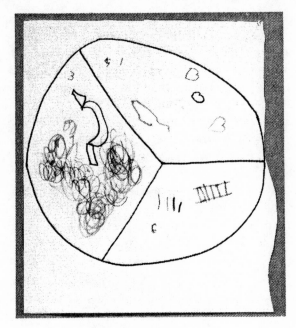

DRAWING 25
Jana's Larger Resource Card

you are enjoying that, I can almost hear the color turquoise begin to laugh with the orange and the yellow and the red. I wonder, as you begin to listen, when you'll hear them too!" Jana was delighted with imagining *hearing* the *colors* communicate.

The child coming for therapy is often vividly aware of how *others* see the problem, yet completely unaware of how she sees it or what she herself can do about it. The Resource Board Game gives the child an opportunity to get in touch with *her* view of both the problem and her own resources, within the familiar and nonthreatening context of a board game. Identifying and making visible the goal, the helpers, and the resources automatically imply that these things do exist and are in reach. The child creates her own *total picture* of the situation which provides a new, unconscious perspective that *in itself* can positively alter the nature of the problem.

Furthermore, the Resource Board Game is a three-dimensional activity and in that sense may be a "fuller" experience for some children than creating only two-dimensiional drawings. The added kinesthetic and movement aspects of throwing the die, making and moving the symbolic pieces, and manipulating the resource cards help to make the Resource Board Game a richly evocative sensory and therapeutic experience.

The Magic Puppet Theater

Historically, puppets and puppet theaters have enjoyed a long-standing, worldwide prominence in the celebration of rituals, holidays, and holy days. In contemporary times, the work of Jim Henson, creator of the Muppets and Sesame Street, has brought puppets into the daily lives of millions of children. Set against lively backgrounds and sporting irresistible personalities, these puppets teach their viewing audience a wide array of academic as well as social and humanitarian concepts.

Not surprisingly, puppets have also found their way into the repertoire of child psychotherapy materials, joining ranks with the more familiar sandtrays, paints, and magic markers. As with these other artistic materials, puppets have been found to serve both diagnostic and therapeutic purposes (Hawkey, 1951). Typically, ready-made puppets are provided to the child, who then partly or entirely sets the scene and creates the action and dialogue, either freely or with guidance from the therapist.

Erica's Magic Puppet Theater

Another alternative to this format arose spontaneously during my work with Erica, the child discussed in the previous section (*Erica's Rainbow*). In this session it appeared that Erica was hiding her fears of being moved again behind an extremely pleasing "good-girl" front. Since Erica's fears were realistic—she had lost her mother, been unable to live with her father, and had experienced temporary placement in various foster homes—it became apparent that my current focus would be on providing a way for Erica to solidify her own strengths so that she would be better able to deal with these and future situations.

While Erica and I were playing with the ready-made puppets in my office, I became aware of feeling somehow limited or restricted in my own creativity. Erica also began to show signs of distraction and kept glancing at the art table. She asked if we could draw now. Knowing that the puppets were a favorite of Erica's, I wondered how these two variables of *drawing* and *puppets* could be bridged together.

Since puppets act as symbols of the child's inner world, it suddenly occurred to me that Erica could become the creator of her own puppet symbol instead of being the recipient of an already created one—and she could do it in a way that combined drawing with puppets.

I asked Erica if she would like to create her own puppet theater. With great excitement, she responded, "Could we? Oh, yes!" And so the Magic Puppet Theater began its therapeutic birth.

I asked Erica to draw her own theater on a large sheet of plain white paper *(Drawing 26)*. She drew the curtains, stage, and backdrop design. Using a scissors, we then cut a slit across the stage.

The next step was to create the characters. Erica drew seven different princesses, a witch, a king, and finally asked if I would help her with

DRAWING 26
Erica's Puppet Theater

DRAWING 27
Erica's Paper Puppets

the wizard. Each character was the size of an adult finger *(Drawing 27)*. We then cut out each drawing and clipped the characters into the slit on the paper stage. Erica began the story with two of the characters playing with each other. As their interaction continued, Erica added the element of a terrible storm which was gathering on the horizon. At this point I asked her to create another backdrop depicting

DRAWING 28
Erica's Storm Backdrop

the storm *(Drawing 28)*. She was quite vivid in her description and included thunderous clouds and lightning bolts.

Meanwhile, all her characters were busy dealing with the story. After some time had passed, Erica had the wizard ask one of the princesses what would help clear up the storm. The princess said, "A rainbow." Again Erica was asked to make a backdrop, this time of the rainbow *(Drawing 29)*.

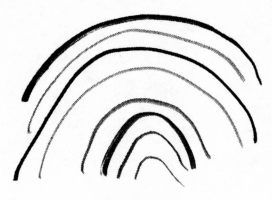

DRAWING 29
Erica's Rainbow

Erica now had the wizard ask the princess what would help bring the rainbow out when it was needed. Erica's eyes opened wide and she began to smile as she responded, "I know, a *rainbow machine!* Let's make one!" *(Drawing 30)*. Erica delighted in creating this final step in her Puppet Theater.

As I watched Erica's puppet story unfold I was struck by two aspects in particular. One was her creation of a storm which seemed to act as such a natural counterbalance to her "good girl" facade by symbolically (and safely) representing the very real turmoil she was feeling. The second striking aspect was her creation of the rainbow as the all-important helping agent. In the initial session with Erica, "rainbows" had been her immediate response when asked what things she liked. Here again her unconscious resource reappears spontaneously, as it did in The Resource Board Game, to help her solve the problem of the storm—her own internal turmoil.

A wonderful bonus of the "Magic Puppet Theater" technique is its double-decker effect of interlocking a metaphor within a metaphor.

DRAWING 30
Erica's Rainbow Machine

The puppets created by the child are themselves a metaphor of the child's environment and perceptions, and at the same time they function as a vehicle through which a metaphorical, therapeutic message can be delivered.

Kenneth's Laughing Ghosts

This second puppet theater was created by a bright, creative, and highly energetic six-year-old named Kenneth. I had been working with Kenneth and his parents periodically for a year, helping them with appropriate limit-setting in relation to Kenneth's aggressive behavior, and helping Kenneth become more comfortable with separating from his mother. When he was a toddler, Kenneth's mother had been seriously ill and then had become pregnant with his baby sister, Mindy. The mother was emotionally torn between gaining her own strengths back and caring for her children. Though her husband was supportive, he was immersed in trying to establish a new career. During this time, the mother of one of Kenneth's friends died suddenly, exacerbating Kenneth's fears of losing his own mother.

Not surprisingly, Kenneth's behavior began to reflect his fears. He increasingly clung to his mother and would scream and cry when she went out with friends. His aggressiveness towards other children and his baby sister increased. His mother reported that Kenneth had also been a difficult baby, which she recognized was due in large part to their preemptive separation caused by her own health problems.

Knowing how much Kenneth enjoyed drawing and cutting with scissors, I asked him if he would like to make a Magic Puppet Theater with me. His eyes lit up and with a broad smile he answered affirmatively. I felt the Magic Puppet Theater would be a particularly good tool to use in Kenneth's case because he always talked about how everyone else felt—his friends, his mother, his father, his sisters—but rarely spoke in the first person about how *he* was feeling. The Puppet Theater would offer a natural and nonthreatening way of entering Kenneth's world.

DRAWING 31
Kenneth's Puppet Theater

First Kenneth drew the stage *(Drawing 31)* and then a number of characters he called ghosts *(Drawing 32)*. He told me they were quiet ghosts who didn't talk. He then drew a backdrop *(Drawing 33)* and told me it was the night with a big star and moon. He began to cut out all the ghosts and asked if I would help. Of course, I agreed.

As the session continued, Kenneth told me that although the ghosts were quiet, they knew a lot. He then said he wanted to draw more characters, so he did. He drew so many ghosts that there wasn't time

DRAWING 32
Kenneth's Ghost Puppets

left in the session to cut them all out. I told Kenneth that it was perfectly all right to take them home and bring them back next week.

When Kenneth's mother came in at that point, he happily showed her his project and asked if she could make some puppets, too, so that we could all play next week. I recognized there were two possible ways to proceed: one, deny the request in light of the separation issue (the request could be viewed as a manipulation on Kenneth's part to get his mother into the session), or, two, recognize a positive facet in Kenneth's request and utilize it toward further therapeutic value. Since utilization is the main philosophy underlying my therapeutic strategies, I chose the second alternative.

I told the mother she could participate next week and that she would have to create her own puppets as an assignment and bring them in with her.

The following week, Kenneth and his mother came in and promptly went over to the drawing table to show me their new puppets. Mom's were rather specific (Drawing 34): a mother, father, son, and daughter. Kenneth, however, had more ghosts and also brought in a King and a Queen (Drawing 35).

As we placed the puppets on the board, Kenneth told his mother to go first. She spoke of the specifics of their family; Mom in the kitchen, Dad coming home from work, children playing in the den, and so forth. As I glanced at Kenneth, I noticed he was quickly losing interest. I interceded at this point by shifting my attention to the colors of Kenneth's ghosts, and, since Mom was describing dinnertime, I spoke about things that ghosts might like to eat. I then brought the King and Queen into the story. Kenneth's eyes widened and he spontaneously blurted out, "They have to have a place to live! Let's make a castle for the King and Queen and ghosts" (Drawing 36). Kenneth then became the director, carefully describing to us how he wanted his castle to look. It appeared his aggressiveness was now being channeled into a more positive direction, as he gained a sense of being in control in a fair and effective way.

The experience of interacting and creating as we went along became the metaphor itself—not only for Kenneth, but also for his mother. As she entered the playful, imaginative world of her son, her demeanor relaxed, her creativity began to blossom, and a beautiful interchange between mother and son emerged. Now the quiet ghosts began to laugh and make silly sounds. Kenneth said the ghosts liked the castle.

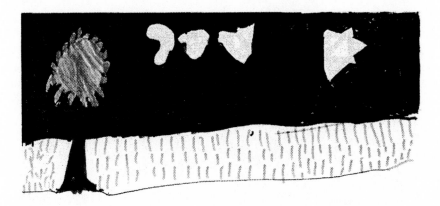

DRAWING 33
Kenneth's Night Backdrop

DRAWING 34
Puppets Made by Kenneth's Mother

DRAWING 35
Kenneth's King and Queen

As Mom interacted with the ghosts, Kenneth went over to the King and Queen and said they were going out to play for a while. He returned to the laughing ghosts and continued his fantasy kingdom.

In the next few sessions, Kenneth's ghosts continued to take on more life and substance, with each ghost developing a perceptibly distinct personality. The Magic Puppet Theater truly became a safe stage for the emergence of Kenneth's own diversified personality. Indeed, from my perspective, the change in behavior of Kenneth's ghosts was mirroring a reflective image of his own unconscious change as it was occurring.

DRAWING 36
Kenneth's Castle

8

Cartoon Therapy

While walking on a path through a garden, I noticed the many varieties of plants and flowers . . . how some grew strong, some grew wild, and some grew in unusual ways. It was as if I were surrounded by a whirlpool of colorful fragrances, whispering sounds, and soft images. Pausing for a moment, I gathered this bouquet of experiences and placed them in the memories of my heart . . . memories later to be recalled as my unseen imaginary friends.

Therapeutic Dynamics of Cartoons

Going as far back in time to the first Mickey Mouse Steamboat Willie cartoons, children throughout the world have enjoyed the fantasy creations provided by the art of animation. Little did Walt Disney realize the fantastic therapeutic tool he was creating for so many to appreciate and learn from in the years to come. In recent years, certain cartoons have come under criticism for portraying what some adults consider to be negatively aggressive behavior. Regardless of what the critics say, the fact remains that children love cartoons and will sit watching them in long periods of rapt attention.

Because cartoon characters and their adventures are, *ipso facto,* powerful symbols for many children, we readily utilize them as fully developed living metaphors that can act as a symbolic alternative for

209

working through fears, anxieties, and conflicts (Mills & Crowley, 1983). Cartoon therapy can be used in conjunction with any of the metaphorical interventions we have described thus far: The child's favorite cartoon character can be incorporated into Storytelling Metaphors, drawn and cut out as goals or helpers in the Resource Board Game, made into puppets for the Magic Puppet Theater, or drawn as part of an Inner Resource Drawing experience. Indeed, we have even used the Flintstone characters as the basis for the creation of an original comic book dealing with child abuse, which we designed for Childhelp USA. A summary of *"Gardenstones: Fred Protects the Vegetables"* is presented at the end of this chapter.

On a conscious level, cartoon characters can become important imaginary friends accompanying the child to the doctor's office (Gardner & Olness, 1981), or giving the child emotional support to deal with the school bully, or helping him cope with nightmares, and so forth. On an unconscious level, the cartoon helper symbolizes the child's inner strengths and resources, which is why he feels a resonance with the character in the first place. Of course, the child is completely unaware of this fact; he simply enters a "world all his own" in which his favorite cartoon character is experienced as possessing wonderful abilities.

In the Snoopy and Charlie Brown cartoons, for example, children strongly identify with Snoopy's delightful and imaginative qualities that help him solve the problems that come his way. Snoopy's resourceful and lighthearted approach to life matches the child's own similar qualities, and the child automatically (but unconsciously) makes this connection. At the same time, Charlie Brown's endless insecurities may also parallel the child's pocket of fears, and so another level of connection is made. While children are empathizing with Charlie Brown's latest catastrophe, they are also relating to Snoopy's cheerful attempts to teach Charlie Brown how to feel more confident and look on the bright side. Thus, their insecurities are validated in Charlie Brown's endearing flub-ups *and* their strengths are activated by Snoopy's positive qualities.

Casey's Amazing Cube

One afternoon, my eleven-year-old son, Casey, came home from school very worried about the new math concepts being taught. Although he had been a good student in the past, he was now fearful that he would not be able to learn the new material. In a matter-of-fact way,

I asked Casey to select a cartoon character he knew would enjoy the challenge of the new concepts and who would also help him stop worrying so much. After reflecting for a moment, Casey responded that he liked Rubik the Amazing Cube because Rubik knew how to help Carlos and the other kids in the cartoon whenever they were in trouble. I then asked Casey to draw a picture of Rubik *(Drawing 37)*. After the drawing was completed, I asked him to imagine this new friend helping him whenever he was worried about learning something new. Casey smiled and said he liked that idea.

DRAWING 37
Casey's Cartoon Helper,
Rubik The Amazing Cube

In this example, as in the example of Snoopy and Charlie Brown, both the problem and its solution are personified in the cartoon characters. Carlos and his friends matched Casey's worry, while Rubik the Amazing Cube matched Casey's abilities and potentials.

Mr. T to the Rescue

Ten-year-old Timmy initially came to my office because of the terrifying nightmares he had been experiencing for several years. In the middle of the night, he often could be heard crying uncontrollably in his room. Soon after, he would be at his parents' bedroom door requesting refuge for the night. The concerned yet disgruntled parents would acquiesce after reassuring Timmy that he was safe from harm.

Because Timmy's relationship with his father had become progressively more distant due to this problem, the father was given the assignment of being at Timmy's bedside as soon as he heard crying. Timmy was to remain in his own bed, with the father instructing his son to draw (1) what the nightmare looked like, (2) what cartoon character would make him feel safe and secure, and (3) how the problem would look all better. The father was told to talk about the third picture slowly and in synch with the rhythm of Timmy's breathing until he fell asleep. The parents later decided on their own to "wallpaper" Timmy's room with the "all better" pictures. Within three weeks the nightmares had disappeared, with Timmy having spent only two nights in his parents' bedroom. Moreover, the father-son relationship was rekindled as a result of the nightly interactions.

At the end of that summer, Timmy's return to school triggered undue anxiety. The problem came to the attention of the school counselor who suggested that the school phobia be treated professionally. Soon thereafter, Timmy was seen again in the office. Since Timmy obviously enjoyed drawing, he was given a box of crayons and asked to draw how the fear associated with going to school looked *(Drawing 38)*.

DRAWING 38
Timmy's School Fear

Timmy was then instructed to select and draw the cartoon character he knew would confront his fear and protect him. As mentioned previously, implicit in this request is the belief that resolution is possible. By carrying out the request and drawing the picture, Timmy acknowledged, at least on an unconscious level, that help did exist for this seemingly helpless predicament. With ease, Timmy immediately sketched Mr. T as his protector *(Drawing 39)*.

DRAWING 39
Timmy's Cartoon Helper, Mr. T

DRAWING 40
Timmy's Gift (A One–Million Dollar Bill)

Next, Timmy was asked to select and draw a gift, in consultation with Mr. T, which would turn the fear into what he wanted it to be. "Timmy, what would be the most powerful gift you and Mr. T could give to that scary feeling so that you could become friends?" Timmy took the crayon and drew a picture representing money. At first it was only a twenty-dollar bill; then he thought about it for a few moments and made it into a million dollar bill *(Drawing 40)!*

Finally, Timmy was asked to draw how his fear now looked after receiving the $1,000,000 gift from himself and Mr. T *(Drawing 41)*. I now gave Timmy a gift of a one-dollar bill in monopoly money. The suggestion was made that he use a crayon to change it into a one-million-dollar bill, and that he take it to school and look at it whenever he felt the need to do so. Timmy continued his sessions for another month, during which time storytelling and artistic metaphors were frequently utilized to further reinforce his growing feelings of adjustment to his new class.

DRAWING 41
Timmy's Fear Looking "All Better"

A Research Interlude

Timmy's selection of Mr. T brings up the controversial issue of the value and impact of cartoon viewing on children. Do aggressive cartoon heroes adversely affect children's behavior? In our clinical experience, Mr. T, The Incredible Hulk, Spider Man, and all their counterparts can have a positive and therapeutic value for children when used wisely by the therapist. We have yet to see a case in which the therapeutic utilization of a powerful cartoon character exacerbated a behavior or acting-out problem. In Timmy's case, he needed someone big and strong to match the terror he felt about school; Mr. T served that purpose. We received no reports of Timmy imitating Mr. T in any behavior. Rather, Mr. T seemed to activate Timmy's own self-confidence by functioning as a secret friend rather than as a flaunted behavior.

To discover if and how cartoons were being tested experimentally, we ran an on-line computer search of the Psychological Abstract Data Base covering the time period between 1967 and October of 1984. Of the 21 papers listed as involving the use of cartoons in a therapeutic setting, two were completely unrelated to our subject matter, while seven used cartoons in an ancillary capacity—that is, the cartoon format was not evaluated in itself but served as part of the research methodology. Thus cartoons were used to illustrate projective and evaluative tests (Copp, 1972; Manoly, 1980; Perlowski & Reisman, 1974; Scott, 1978); to illustrate model behaviors (LaFleur & Johnson, 1972); as "funniness ratings" (Schienberg, 1979); and as an attentional tool with severely retarded adolescents (Nathanson, 1977).

Of the eight studies reported in which cartoons functioned as primary research variables, three dealt directly with the subject of aggression. Hapkiewicz and Roden (1971) randomly assigned 60 second-graders to three different treatment viewing groups: aggressive cartoon, non-aggressive cartoon, and no cartoon. Their results indicated "no difference among the groups on measures of interpersonal aggression." In other words, aggressive cartoons did not affect behavior in a negative way.

Ellis and Sekyra (1972), on the other hand, obtained opposite results. Using a similar research paradigm, the investigators found that children who had just viewed a five-minute aggressive cartoon emitted a greater number of aggressive behaviors than children who had viewed a five-minute neutral cartoon.

Finally, Hapkiewicz and Stone (1974) conducted a study of 180 six-to-ten-year-olds to ascertain the effect of real-life versus imaginary aggressive models on children's interpersonal play. Children were shown three different types of film: real-life aggressive film, imaginary cartoon aggressive film, and a nonaggressive film. Results indicated that the real-life aggressive film significantly increased the aggressive play among the boys (but not among the girls), while "no significant difference between the aggressive cartoon and nonaggressive film" was found.

The six remaining studies found various positive applications of cartoons: as a successful means of reducing pain in young burn victims (Kelley, Jarvie, Middlebrook, McNeer & Drabman, 1984); as an effective behavioral conditioner in reducing acting-out behavior (Greelis & Kazaoka, 1979) and thumbsucking behavior (Bishop & Stumphauzer, 1973); and as a "positive social influence" (Brody, 1976).

The last study, by Fung and Lazar (1983), comes the closest to our use of cartoons. In treating a highly anxious nine-and-a-half-year-old boy with von Williebrand's Disease (a bleeding disorder caused by capillary defects), the therapist asked the child to play an "imagination game" in which he could select a favorite figure who would give him something special. In the first session, the boy chose Santa Claus; in the second session, The Incredible Hulk. The therapist reinforced the child's selection of the Hulk by reminding him that the Hulk was a powerful ally who would protect him from harm.

We can see from the above overview that research studies on the effects of cartoon viewing are too few to be conclusive in any way. It is noteworthy, however, that only one study (Hapkiewicz & Stone, 1974) correlated aggressive behavior with cartoon viewing. All the remaining studies reported positive and valuable effects of the cartoon.

We would add that research conducted in school classrooms where cartoons are shown along with other types of film (such as in the aggression studies cited above) is not entirely relevant to our application of cartoons in a one-on-one clinical setting. In the classroom situation, children watch a cartoon and then go out to play in an undirected manner. The impact of the cartoon remains amorphous and unconscious, and their play may or may not reflect a modeling influence of what was viewed. In a clinical environment, however, a cartoon character that is already experienced as a "favorite friend" is carefully brought into the child's conscious awareness and given a specific role in relation to the problem area. To our knowledge, no large-scale research of this particular use of cartoons exists—only the few case reports of the clinicians cited above.

Scooby Doo to the Rescue

Five-year-old Davey was having violently fearful nightmares. His parents reported how he would awaken each night screaming uncontrollably that "The monsters are getting me!" They had tried every approach they could think of, but to no avail, and now felt frustrated and helpless in their inability to comfort their little boy.

While the parents were present in the session, I asked Davey if he could draw a picture of the monster. He eagerly picked up the markers and began his drawing (Drawing 42). I then asked him to draw a picture of his favorite cartoon friend, one that he knew could help

DRAWING 42
Davey's Monster

DRAWING 43
Davey's Cartoon Helper, Scooby Doo

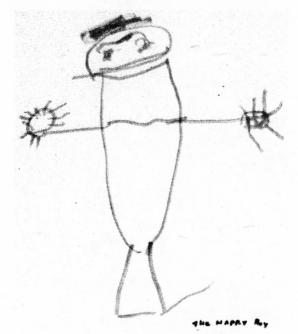

DRAWING 44

Davey's Problem
Looking "All Better"

The HAPPY Boy

DRAWING 45

Davey's Nightmare

him with the monster. His eyes widened as he exclaimed, "It's Scooby Doo!" His parents were puzzled by this; they thought that Scooby scared Davey because of the ghosts in the stories. At that point Davey blurted out, "Oh no! Scooby makes the ghosts go away!" I commented to the parents how sometimes we as adults need to remember how to see things through a child's eyes. Davey picked up an orange marker and painstakingly began to draw Scooby Doo *(Drawing 43)*.

On a third sheet of paper, Davey was asked to draw how his problem would look "all better." He closed his eyes for a moment, then opened them wide and with enthusiasm drew his third picture *(Drawing 44)*.

Davey's parents were instructed to put paper and markers in his room. When he awoke at night, crying and afraid, they were to help

DRAWING 46
Davey's Present Dream

him employ the same drawing process. The parents were delighted to become a part of their son's healing process. They had anticipated many sessions of individual psychotherapy to "figure out" the problem. Instead, a total of nine sessions took place during which straightforward information about the stages of child development was provided. During the final session, Davey drew how his nightmares used to look *(Drawing 45)* and how his dreams looked in the present *(Drawing 46)*.

POST SCRIPT

In a follow-up call one month after therapy had been terminated, the parents reported no recurrence of the problem. Some six months later during a chance social encounter at a play one evening, Davey's parents again reported how well he was doing in school and that his sleep problems were "a thing of the past."

The Ice Man Cometh

Seven-year-old Peter had developed a number of fears following the birth of a brother and the changes in the family constellation that ensued. Most of these fears centered around the issue of separation. In the last few months, Peter had become more and more attached to his mother and continually demanded her attention. Although he was left in the care of a babysitter whenever his mother needed to leave the home, Peter would become extremely fearful and burst into tears. Seeing her son in such emotional pain created more guilt in the mother. Even at school, Peter found it difficult experiencing the transition from mother to teacher, and he was described by the teacher as distracted much of the time.

Peter was presented with crayons and drawing paper and asked to "draw that worry you have when Mommy is not with you." As he was drawing, he spontaneously began to talk about it, providing a kind of running narration of the picture's unfoldment *(Drawing 47)*.

Peter was then asked to introduce into his story a cartoon character who could change his feelings of aloneness and fear into a happy ending of safety and security. As he talked, Peter began drawing Ice Man and The Hulk. His selection and drawing of these cartoon characters

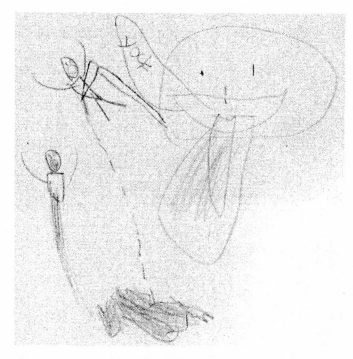

DRAWING 47
Peter's Worry

carried the unconscious implication that security and safety were available to him when he was not with his mother *(Drawing 48)*.

As he drew, Peter continued talking about how powerful Ice Man and The Hulk were, describing in detail how they always overcame the "bad guys" (the bad feelings). Once again he was encouraged to draw as many examples as he wished to describe the abilities and strengths of Ice Man and The Hulk.

On the third piece of paper, Peter drew how his worry would look all better now that Ice Man and The Hulk were on the scene. He eagerly drew, continuing to tell his story which contained many different sources of resolution *(Drawing 49)*.

For the first time in recent months, Peter was no longer stuck in his painful experience of fear. He had created his own resources (Ice Man and The Hulk) and his own solutions (security and safety). Now, whenever he became distracted about his separation from his mother,

DRAWING 48
Peter's Cartoon Friends, Ice Man and The Hulk

DRAWING 49
Peter's Worry Looking "All Better"

he had positive thoughts available (his verbal story) and positive pictures (the Inner Resource Drawings of his cartoon helpers). These new therapeutic creations helped to interrupt his previous painful feelings about separation by blending in the new feelings of safety and security.

No More Pockets

Nine-year-old Suzie, our friend from the hospital who created her own "Pain Getting Better Book," discovered yet another important use of our three-stage drawing process. Her dog, Pockets, was dying and she was struggling with her fear and sadness about this serious loss. As an aid in coping with her feelings, she was asked to draw how her fear and sadness looked (*Drawing 50*).

DRAWING 50
Suzie's Fear and Sadness

She was then asked to draw a cartoon character who could help her feel better while she was dealing with this experience. She chose Fred Flintstone, and drew him (*Drawing 51*).

DRAWING 51
Suzie's Cartoon Helper,
Fred Flintstone

DRAWING 52
Suzie's Fear Looking "All Better"

She was then asked to "draw the fear feeling all better" *(Drawing 52)*. Afterwards Suzie stated, "I was drawing pictures of what it feeled [sic] like when my dog died. Then I drew Fred Flintstone; then me and Fred together so I would feel better after my dog died." Some weeks later Suzie called to tell me that Pockets had died. She spoke about her sadness but added that she was "okay" because whenever she thought about "no more Pockets," she imagined Fred and that made her feel less alone.

With a Little Help From My Smurfs

When eight-year-old Erica, whom we first met in The Resource Board Game (page 192) and then again in The Magic Puppet Theater (page 199), came in for her initial session, her foster mother described her as "crying all the time." She showed frequent and dismaying mood shifts and wanted to be with the foster mother incessantly.

We naturally felt that Erica's behavior was directly related to her painful losses. After establishing a good rapport with her, she was asked about her favorite cartoon characters and told to select one that made her feel happy. She readily talked about Smurfette and the other Smurf characters. A story was then created which used these cartoon characters to depict similar losses—thereby matching the child's problem—and to depict ways of dealing with loss in a healthy way—thereby stimulating the child's own inner resources and strengths to do the same.

After a few sessions using this approach, Erica was asked to draw a picture of her cartoon friend. She drew a picture consisting of a

DRAWING 53
Erica's Cartoon Helper, Smurf, with the Rainbow

rainbow, a Smurf character holding a ball with a happy face, and a few raindrops *(Drawing 53)*. When asked about the raindrops she said, "There are only a few raindrops now because the rainbow is coming out." This indicated to us that the story utilizing the Smurf character had successfully evoked her strengths (the rainbow), and had established a positive association which eventually could clear up all the raindrops (tears), as the rainbow came out fully.

Cartoon Therapy in Society: A Metaphorical Approach to Child Abuse

The individual, familial, and social issues of child abuse have continued to be a national subject of investigation by therapists, physicians, educators, and parents alike. Intervention and prevention of this grave problem has extended from the therapist's office into the classroom and courtroom, and throughout the media. Parent support groups, children's homes, and foster placement agencies have been developed in an effort to ameliorate this heart-wrenching situation.

When we were requested by Childhelp USA to design an intervention in the form of a comic book for the purpose of helping abused children, we felt challenged to expand the Ericksonian model to fit this request. The comic book we created, *Gardenstones: Fred Protects the Vegetables,* was intended to help these children better understand and cope with the court and protective custody procedures they would be encountering. It would be distributed without cost to foster parents, social workers, childcare agencies, and to any individual requesting it.

We initially received a three-and-a-half page, single-spaced outline of the numerous points Childhelp USA wanted somehow included in the story (see Appendix). Clearly it would not be possible to create a captivating storyline that also literally covered each and every item on the Childhelp USA prospectus. As we saw it, our task was to take all the specific requests and transform them into a unified metaphorical *gestalt:* The story had to suggest indirectly, not provide a dot-to-dot picture of the material. Above all, the story would have to walk the finest of metaphorical lines: Where could it be more difficult than in cases of child abuse to portray a painful reality in ways real enough to evoke connection yet symbolic enough to maintain a sense of security?

Gaining the generous permission of Hanna-Barbera Productions, we utilized the Flintstone characters as the therapeutic wizards to deliver the important messages within the comic book format. Each character and plot development was carefully chosen for its potency and relevancy to the issues being addressed.

We submitted the following original storyline to Hanna-Barbera's artists, who then created the illustrations to match our descriptions.

Gardenstones: Fred Protects the Vegetables*

1. One day while Pebbles and Bam Bam are taking a walk, they pass by a garden and overhear a conversation between a tomato and a carrot.

2. With an ashamed look on its face the tomato says to the carrot, "Look what the gardener did to me," pointing to its bruises where it had been poked by the gardener. The carrot looks down with a tear in its eye and says, "You're not the only one." Turning to the side,

---

* Each number correlates with an illustration.

the carrot reveals a long mark on its wilted body and explains, "The gardener did this with the hoe."

3. The carrot continues to say, "I'm so afraid to go back there to be hurt again."

4. The tomato retorts, "And I don't like that ickey feeling I sometimes get inside when I'm around the gardener!"

5. At that point, Pebbles and Bam Bam pop up from behind a bush exclaiming excitedly: *[Pebbles]* "My daddy, Fred," *[Bam Bam]* "and my daddy, Barney," *[back to Pebbles]* "can help you because they know people who can protect you from being hurt again!"

6. The carrot and the tomato get a scared look on their faces. The tomato says adamantly, "The gardener told us never to tell anyone about what's been going on in the garden because he said it's a secret."

7. Pebbles reassures them, "My daddy knows of other gardens with gardeners who really know how to take good care of their vegetables." "Sometimes," Bam Bam adds, "even good gardeners hurt their vegetables because no one ever taught them how to take care of them in the right way."

8. Fred and Wilma are dressed in some kind of official garb as they go to the gardener's house and knock on the door. The gardener (gardener is an asexual type of character) opens the door and Fred says, "We're here to help with the problem in the garden." The gardener says in an angry voice, "There is no problem in the garden!"

9. But Fred tells them, "I have seen the bruises and poke marks on the carrot and tomato. My job is to take those vegetables that need help right now and transplant them in another garden where it is safe and secure. It's against the law for anyone, even a gardener, to hurt their vegetables."

10. Looking at the gardener, Wilma says, "And you also need help right now to learn what nobody ever taught you—how to take good care of the vegetables in your garden."

11. The next frame is a split frame in which the gardener is going off to gardening school while the vegetables are going with Fred and Wilma.

12. Fred and Wilma take the carrot and tomato to the new garden. The new gardener opens the door and greets them with a big smile.

13. Before Fred and Wilma leave, Fred tells the carrot and tomato, "You will be staying here with the new gardener for a short period of time." Wilma adds, "Then you will go on a journey in a boat

where you will meet many people who will ask you many questions in order to help you feel more secure and protected."

14. The new gardener is showing the carrot and tomato their new beds in the garden. *[It's a very warm atmosphere.]* The gardener notices that the tomato has a tear of sadness and the carrot has a look of fear.

15. This well-trained gardener tells each vegetable respectively: "Use your imagination to see what sadness looks like when it is *all better* [looking at the tomato], and what fear looks like when it is *all better* [looking at the carrot]. Take your time pretending the color and shape of sadness and fear can be magically changed into a new color and shape that you can call *all better*."

16. After a period of time, the tomato and carrot both smile. The gardener comments, "And there may be other times when your imagination can make those feelings look *all better*." [Note: Have picture of carrot and tomato smiling with a star containing the words *ALL BETTER* floating above their heads.]

17. A few days later there is a boat ride in which Fred is at the helm and the passengers include Wilma, the tomato and carrot, the new gardener, Pebbles, Bam Bam, and Dino the pet Dinosaur.

18. As the boat ride progresses, there are many booths along the shore which they stop to visit. There is a *Booth of Weights and Measures* where both vegetables get weighed and measured by funny characters [this is a pleasurable experience.]

19. Then there are the *Question and Answer Booths*. The vegetables enter one of the booths and as they exit, one vegetable looks sad and the other looks confused.

20. Another *Question and Answer Booth* is entered and this time one vegetable emerges mad, while the other one comes out scared. These booths are run by funny yet friendly characters whose intention is really to help the vegetables rather than upset them.

21. Barney and Betty are in the last *Question and Answer Booth*. Barney tells the vegetables, "Maybe you can remember a favorite thing you enjoyed playing with sometime in the past." *[Pause]*

22. Betty comments, "Maybe you can remember a special time that you know can bring a smile to your face." *[Pause]*

23. Betty adds, "And you can continue to hold on to all those pleasant memories whenever you need to feel that *all better* feeling." The vegetables nod with a smile and say, "Yes!"

24. Barney and Betty join the group on their journey. They are all back in the boat again except for Fred. There is a picture of Fred leaving the boat unnoticed while Barney takes over at the helm.

25. As the boat continues, it approaches two huge doors in the form of ears. The vegetables say, "What are those big ears for?" Barney replies, "Those are for hearing; those are the HEARING doors." [Above the huge doors/ears is the word *HEARING*.]

26. The ears open and the boat begins to go through the doors. At this point, the vegetables get scared.

27. Betty reminds them, "Hold on to all those past pleasant memories and watch how you can feel all better now." [After Betty reminds them to "feel all better," the earlier picture of the carrot and tomato remembering the *all better* feeling is recreated within the symbol of a star in the form of a thought over their heads.]

28. After the boat passes through the doors, all the passengers get out and find themselves in a large room with many unknown characters.

29. The vegetables notice a person behind a big desk with his back to them, wearing the special hat Fred wears at his lodge. Also, some of the official characters in the room are wearing hats from the lodge. [Create other characters' hats having a "sameness," such as the same color or shape, yet each one is a little different from the other.]

30. As the person behind the desk turns around, the vegetables are delightfully surprised and breathe a sigh of relief when they see that it is Fred.

31. Overall picture depicts all the characters included in the court-room scene. The new gardener, the old gardener, all the Flintstone characters and lodge characters, the carrot and tomato, along with a number of other vegetables as background in the section where the tomato and carrot are sitting. They are all listening intently to Fred.

32. Fred shuffles papers in front of him and begins to make his speech. "Some gardeners have learned very well how to care for their vegetables. And in a period of time, some of you may return to your gardens. Other gardeners must remain in gardening school until they learn more ways to help vegetables feel safe. Some vegetables have found their new gardeners to be pleasant; they may decide to stay with them for a longer period of time. Other vegetables might be transplanted until they are placed in the best soil and climate for them to grow up healthy and happy. Whatever happens to each of you, you can be certain that there are many people who will protect you

now and in the future." The story ends with the carrot and tomato looking content.

The children are now given the opportunity to integrate and anchor the unconscious resource messages within the comic book into their own lives. Fred Flintstone gives specific instructions for carrying out the three-stage drawing process described in the Artistic Metaphor:

Fred: "Sometimes we all have things that make us feel scared, bad, or mad. You can use this page to draw how that feeling of yours looks when you feel scared, bad, or mad." (Page 1)

Fred: "Now draw how that feeling you just drew looks *ALL BETTER*." (Page 2)

Fred: "Very Good! Now draw anything you like that can make that *all better* feeling happen. Maybe a toy makes it feel all better, or a smile and a hug, or perhaps a happy day like a birthday or holiday. Take your time to draw it."

Gardenstones: Fred Protects the Vegetables incorporated many of the theories and healing strategies we have discussed in relation to the storytelling and artistic metaphors. This project provided us with the rewarding challenge of expanding Erickson's influential methods of metaphorical intervention from the individual level into a broader social perspective. From this experience we have become convinced of the important role metaphor can play in mediating an evolution in societal awareness and human relatedness.

Epilogue

Peace and Beauty

On a delightful summer day, four of us sat enjoying a snack in an open gazebo within the Japanese gardens of San Francisco's Golden Gate Park. After a while an oriental family consisting of a father, mother, child and grandparents passed us by. Their little daughter of about four years wandered near our table as she played and looked inquisitively at us. Her father was nearby and we asked him if we could share some of our food with his child and family. He smiled and graciously accepted our offer.

As the little girl began to eat some cheese, I asked her father for his daughter's name. Softly he replied, "Wrong."

With a surprised tone in my voice I echoed, "WRONG? Could you please spell that?"

"R-O-N-G," he answered.

I repeated, "RONG" and commented, "That's very interesting. Does her name have a special meaning?"

He replied, "Yes. When translated, its meaning is close to *peace* and *beauty*."

My friends and I sat back for a moment and looked at each other as we shared in the brightened awareness of a new learning. We commented later how nice it would be, whenever we are worried about being "wrong" in trying something new, to simply remember this experience and perhaps exchange the worry for a feeling of *peace and beauty*. It is all a matter of translation.

Appendix

Childhelp USA Prospectus

Brothers and Sisters Emergency Care Program

COMIC BOOK PROJECT

Purpose:

The comic book is planned for use with children who have experienced serious physical or sexual abuse and have been removed from their homes. The book can help a child understand what is happening and how the process is intended to protect the child's interest. This knowledge should cause the protective custody and court experiences to be less frightening to the child.

The comic book is not intended to be exhaustive, technical, or specific to any one court jurisdiction or agency. It is to help foster parents or other adults explain to children what has happened and what to expect.

Content:

1. Good people, such as parents, relatives, friends and other adults sometimes do things that hurt children.

2. A child may think he is the only one who is ever hurt by a parent, relative, family friend, but there are many others. The child may feel hurt, unwanted, alone, sad, guilty, scared, helpless, or anxious.

3. Children are hurt in many different ways:

   — Hitting (fist, object such as stick, belt, or extension cord)
   — Pushing (down or against wall)
   — Throwing (baby in air—against wall)

— Pinching
— Shaking
— Biting
— Burning (with fire, cigarette, hot water)
— Not getting enough to eat, not having the right things to eat
— Not being clean
— Not getting medical care when not well (not seeing doctor, dentist, not having medicine)
— Not having suitable clothing (not enough clothes, only worn-out clothes, only dirty clothes or clothes that do not fit)
— Sexual molestation (fondling, touching of private parts, intercourse, sodomy, oral sex, pictures, etc.)
— Left alone, no adult taking care of children.

4. A policeman is a friend.

— If a child is being hurt at home, the policeman will take the child to a safe place.
  — The child may be taken to a large place where there are many other children.
  — The child may be taken to a hospital or doctor if hurt.
  — The child may be taken to a home where foster parents take care of children who cannot live at home.
— A policeman needs to ask many questions to find out who hurt the child and how.
— A policeman often asks a social worker to help the child and to tell the Judge at Court what is happening.
— The policeman will go to Court and talk to the Judge.

5. The Juvenile Court is the place where people go to talk to a Judge, Commissioner or Referee when a child has been hurt. It is an important place where decisions are made. The Juvenile Court is usually in a large building with many separate courtrooms.

6. The meeting at the Court is called a "hearing." The Judge will hear what everyone has to say about how the child was hurt and what can be done about it.

7. Going to Court can be scary because the child does not understand what is going on.

8. The child is often afraid, nervous, worried about what is to happen.

— Sometimes the child cannot sleep before the Court hearing—has nightmares—wets the bed—is restless.
— Sometimes the child withdraws or refuses to form new attachments.
— Sometimes there is crying, vomiting, thumb sucking, head banging, lying, compulsive eating, refusal to eat, distrustfulness, or lack of trust.
— Sometimes it is difficult to eat or to concentrate.
— Sometimes brothers and sisters cling to each other and try to comfort each other.

9. The Judge is a helping person.

— He wants to see children safe and not being hurt.
— He does not punish parents or children.
— A child can ask to speak with the Judge privately if he does not wish to talk in front of his parents or others. They will talk in the Judge's private office.
— The Judge decides where a child is to live. The child may tell the Judge where he wants to live or where he does not want to live. The Judge does not always let the child live where he wants to.
— The Judge tells the parents what they must do before their children can live with them.

10. There may be more than one hearing. The first hearing is usually so the Judge can decide where the child will live for a short time until everyone is ready to make a full report to the Court. This is called a Detention Hearing. If a child is ordered detained this means the child cannot go home. He must stay with a relative or in a shelter care or family foster home until the next hearing which is held within a few weeks.

11. When there is to be a juvenile court hearing, many people are involved. Some of the people who will try to help the child or take part in the hearing are:

a. Foster family—This is a family that shares its home with children who cannot live at home. The foster parents will see that the child has food, clothing, a comfortable place to sleep, and interesting things to do. The foster parent understands the child may be upset and afraid. The foster parent will provide comfort and try to explain what is happening. The child can help by telling the foster parent how he feels, what he likes to eat, his favorite play activities, and by asking questions.

b. Social Worker—The social worker is responsible for helping the child and his family. The child will probably see several social workers who do different things.

— One social worker will get all the facts about how the child was hurt and will prepare a report for the Judge recommending a plan for the child and the family. The social worker will talk to the child, the parents, relatives, neighbors, the police, the schools, the doctors, friends— anyone who might know something important. The child should tell this social worker how he was hurt, who hurt him, and where he would like to live. This social worker is sometimes called an "investigator."

— One social worker will find a place (foster home, relative, shelter care facility) for the child to live until the Judge decides what should be done. Then the social worker will help the child and his family do whatever the Judge tells them to do. This social worker can help the child with all kinds of problems; troubles at school; can't talk to parents; bad feelings about self or others; not sleeping well, unhappy, etc.

c. Attorney-lawyer—This is a person who knows the laws and gives advice about matters of the law and speaks for someone else in Court. Lawyers are called by different names depending upon who their employer is: Counselor, County Counsel, District Attorney.

— If a child does not like what his social worker is recommending to the Judge, he may ask for his own attorney.

— Attorneys do most of the talking to the Judge in Court. They understand how the Judge wants things done and they know the law.

d. Marshall—This is a person, usually in a uniform, that keeps order in a courtroom so a hearing can be held. He calls people to come into the courtroom when the Judge is ready to have the hearing. He stops any trouble that might start in a courtroom.

e. Guardian ad litem—This is a special adult the Court sometimes asks to be a good friend to the child and to help the child throughout the Court proceedings.

f. Transportation Worker—This is the person who will pick up the child on the day of the Court hearing, take him to Court, and if the Judge does not let the child go home with his parents, a relative, or someone else, will return the child to the foster home.

12. Law—A law is a rule or regulation made by a county or state for all the people who live there. It is against the law for anyone, even a parent, to physically hurt a child badly.

13. Court Order—This is an order issued by the Court Judge telling someone to do something or to stop doing something. The Judge will give an order about where a child is to live and what the parents must do before the child can go home to visit or live. Everyone should do what the Judge says.

References

Abrams, J. (1980). Learning disabilities. In G. Sholevar (Ed.), *Emotional Disorders in Children and Adolescents*. New York: SP Medical & Scientific Books, pp. 483–500.

Adams, C., & Chadbourne, J. (1982). Therapeutic metaphor: An approach to weight control. *Personnel & Guidance Journal, 60*(8), 510–512.

Allan, J. (1978). Serial storytelling: A therapeutic approach with a young adolescent. *Canadian Counsellor, 12*(2), 132–137.

Amira, S. (1982). Figurative language and metaphor in successful and unsuccessful psychotherapy. *Dissertation Abstracts International, 43*(4-B), 1244.

Andersen, H. (1965). *The Ugly Duckling*. Translated by R. P. Keigwin. New York: Charles Scribner's Sons.

Arden Press. (1978). *Imagine*. Huntington Beach, Calif.

Arnott, B., & Gushin, J. (1976). Film making as a therapeutic tool. *American Journal of Art Therapy, 16*(1), 29–33.

Axline, V. (1955). Play therapy procedures and results. *American Journal of Orthopsychiatry, 25*, 618–626.

Axline, V. (1969). *Play Therapy*. New York: Ballantine. (Originally published in 1947)

Ayres, A. (1971). Characteristics of types of sensory integrative dysfunction. *American Journal of Occupational Therapy, 7*, 329–334.

Bandler, R., & Grinder, J. (1975). *The Patterns of the Hypnotic Techniques of Milton H. Erickson, M.D. Vol. I*. Palo Alto, Calif.: Behavior & Science Books.

Barber, J. (1982). *Psychological Approaches to the Management of Pain*. New York: Brunner/Mazel.

Bassin, D., Wolfe, K., & Thier, A. (1983). Children's reactions to psychiatric hospitalization: Drawings and storytelling as a data base. *Arts in Psychotherapy, 10*(1), 33–44.

Some references for Milton H. Erickson and Carl G. Jung contain two dates: the first date is the original time of publication; the second refers to the publication used for this volume. (For Erickson: *The Collected Papers of Milton H. Erickson on Hypnosis;* for Jung: *The Collected Works of Carl G. Jung*)

239

Baum, L. (1900). *The Wonderful Wizard of Oz*. New York: G. M. Hill. Reissued as *The Wizard of Oz* by Rand McNally; numerous editions available.

Beck, C., & Beck, E. (1984). Test of the eye-movement hypothesis of Neurolinguistic Programming: A rebuttal of conclusions. *Perceptual & Motor Skills, 58*, 175–176.

Becker, R. (1972). Therapeutic approaches to psychopathological reactions to hospitalization. *International Journal of Child Psychotherapy, 1*(2), 65–97.

Bettelheim, B. (1975). *The Uses of Enchantment*. New York: Alfred Knopf.

Bishop, B., & Stumphauzer, J. (1973). Behavior therapy of thumbsucking in children: A punishment (time-out) and generalization effect: What's a mother to do? *Psychological Reports, 33*(3), 939–944.

Brink, N. (1982). Metaphor creation for use within family therapy. *The American Journal of Clinical Hypnosis, 24*(4), 258–265.

Brody, M. (1976). The wonderful world of Disney. *American Imago, 33*(4), 350–360.

Burnett, P. (1983). A self-concept enhancement program for children in the regular classroom. *Elementary School Guidance & Counseling, 18*(2), 101–108.

Cameron-Bandler, L. (1978). *They Lived Happily Ever After*. Cupertino, Cal.: Meta Publications.

Campbell, J. (1956). *The Hero with a Thousand Faces*. Cleveland: World Press.

Cantwell, D. (1980). The treatment of minimal brain dysfunction. In G. Sholevar (Ed.), *Emotional Disorders in Children and Adolescents*. New York: SP Medical & Scientific Books, pp. 457–482.

Capacchione, L. (1979). *The Creative Journal*. Athens, Ohio: Swallow Press.

Condon, M. (1983). Symbolized and desymbolized figurative language: A psychological case study. *Dissertation Abstracts International, 44*(2-B).

Copp, L. (1972). A projective cartoon investigation of nurse-patient role perception and expectation. *Nursing Research, 20*(2), 100–112.

Crowley, R., & Mills, J. (1982). Therapeutic metaphors for children. Paper presented at the 25th Anniversary Meeting of The American Society of Clinical Hypnosis. Denver, Colorado.

Crowley, R., & Mills, J. (1983). A theoretical and clinical differentiation between "unconscious" and "out-of-conscious" systems. Paper presented at the Annual Scientific Meeting of The American Society of Clinical Hypnosis. Dallas, Texas.

Crowley, R., & Mills, J. (1984a). Innovative approaches for behavioral and communication problems with children and their families. Workshop presented at the California Association of Marriage and Family Therapists, 20th Annual Meeting. Los Angeles, California.

Crowley, R., & Mills, J. (1984b). Interrupting adult psychosomatic symptomatology: An integration of right-brain phenomena and multisensory metaphor. Paper presented at the Annual Scientific Meeting of The American Society of Clinical Hypnosis, San Francisco, California.

Crowley, R., & Mills, J. (1984c). The multisensory metaphor: Innovative dissociative techniques for children. Paper presented at the Annual Scientific Meeting of The American Society of Clinical Hypnosis, San Francisco, California.

Crowley, R., & Mills, J. (1986). The nature and construction of therapeutic metaphors for children. *British Journal of Experimental & Clinical Hypnosis, 3*(2), 69–86.

de Saint-Exupery, A. (1943). *The Little Prince*. New York: Harcourt, Brace & World.

Dilts, R. (1983). *Roots of Neuro-linguistic Programming*. Cupertino, Cal.: Meta Publications.

Dilts, R., Grinder, J., Bandler, R., DeLozier, J., & Cameron-Bandler, L. (1979). *Neuro Linguistic Programming I*. Cupertino, Cal.: Meta Publications.

Edinger, E. (1973). *Ego and Archetype*. Baltimore: Penguin Books.

Edward, B. (1979). *Drawing on the Right Side of the Brain*. Los Angeles: Tarcher.

Ehrlichman, H., & Weinberger, A. (1978). Lateral eye movements and hemispheric asymmetry: A critical review. *Psychological Bulletin, 85*(5), 1080–1101.

Elkins, G., & Carter, B. (1981). Use of a science fiction-based imagery technique in child hypnosis. *The American Journal of Clinical Hypnosis, 23*, 274–277.

Ellis, G., & Sekyra, F. (1972). The effect of aggressive cartoons on the behavior of first-grade children. *Journal of Psychology, 81*(1), 37–43.

Erickson, M. (1944/1980). The method employed to formulate a complex story for the induction of an experimental neurosis in a hypnotic subject. In E. Rossi (Ed.), *The Collected Papers of Milton H. Erickson on Hypnosis. Vol. III. Hypnotic Investigation of Psychosomatic Processes*. New York: Irvington, 336–355.

Erickson, M. (1952/1980). A therapeutic double bind utilizing resistance. In E. Rossi (Ed.), *The Collected Papers of Milton H. Erickson on Hypnosis. Vol. IV. Innovative Hypnotherapy*. New York: Irvington, 229–232.

Erickson, M. (1954a/1980). Pseudo-orientation in time as a hypnotherapeutic procedure. In E. Rossi (Ed.), *The Collected Papers of Milton H. Erickson on Hypnosis. Vol. IV. Innovative Hypnotherapy*. New York: Irvington, 397–423.

Erickson, M. (1954b/1980). Special techniques of brief hypnotherapy. In E. Rossi (Ed.), *The Collected Papers of Milton H. Erickson on Hypnosis. Vol. IV. Innovative Hypnotherapy*. New York: Irvington, 149–173.

Erickson, M. (1958a/1980). Naturalistic techniques of hypnosis. In E. Rossi (Ed.), *The Collected Papers of Milton H. Erickson on Hypnosis. Vol. I. The Nature of Hypnosis and Suggestion*. New York: Irvington, 168–176.

Erickson, M. (1958b/1980). Pediatric hypnotherapy. In E. Rossi (Ed.), *The Collected Papers of Milton H. Erickson on Hypnosis. Vol. IV. Innovative Hypnotherapy*. New York: Irvington, 174–180.

Erickson, M. (1959/1980). Further clinical techniques of hypnosis: Utilization techniques. In E. Rossi (Ed.), *The Collected Papers of Milton H. Erickson on Hypnosis. Vol. I. The Nature of Hypnosis and Suggestion*. New York: Irvington, 177–205.

Erickson, M. (1962/1980). The identification of a secure reality. In E. Rossi (Ed.), *The Collected Papers of Milton H. Erickson on Hypnosis. Vol. IV. Innovative Hypnotherapy*. New York: Irvington, 507–515.

Erickson, M. (1964a/1980). Pantomime techniques in hypnosis and the implications. In E. Rossi (Ed.), *The Collected Papers of Milton H. Erickson on Hypnosis. Vol. I. The Nature of Hypnosis and Suggestion*. New York: Irvington, 331–339.

Erickson, M. (1964b/1980). The "surprise" and "my-friend-John" techniques of hypnosis: Minimal cues and natural field experimentation. In E. Rossi (Ed.), *The Collected Papers of Milton H. Erickson on Hypnosis. Vol. I. The Nature of*

Hypnosis and Suggestion. New York: Irvington, 340–365.

Erickson, M. (1966/1980). The interspersal hypnotic technique for symptom correction and pain control. In E. Rossi (Ed.), *The Collected Papers of Milton H. Erickson on Hypnosis. Vol. IV. Innovative Hypnotherapy.* New York: Irvington, 262–278.

Erickson, M. (1980a). A therapeutic double bind utilizing resistance. In E. Rossi (Ed.), *The Collected Papers of Milton H. Erickson on Hypnosis. Vol. IV. Innovative Hypnotherapy.* New York: Irvington, 229–232.

Erickson, M. (1980b). An indirect induction of trance: Simulation and the role of indirect suggestion and minimal cues. In E. Rossi (Ed.), *The Collected Papers of Milton H. Erickson on Hypnosis. Vol. I. The Nature of Hypnosis and Suggestion.* New York: Irvington, 366–372.

Erickson, M. (1980c). Notes on minimal cues in vocal dynamics and memory. In E. Rossi (Ed.), *The Collected Papers of Milton H. Erickson on Hypnosis. Vol. I. The Nature of Hypnosis and Suggestion.* New York: Irvington, 373–377.

Erickson, M. (1980d). Respiratory rhythm in trance induction: The role of minimal sensory cues in normal and trance behavior. In E. Rossi (Ed.), *The Collected Papers of Milton H. Erickson on Hypnosis. Vol. I. The Nature of Hypnosis and Suggestion.* New York: Irvington, 360–365.

Erickson, M. (1980e). *The Collected Papers of Milton H. Erickson on Hypnosis.* Edited by Ernest L. Rossi.

Vol. I: *The Nature of Hypnosis and Suggestion*
Vol. II: *Hypnotic Alteration of Sensory, Perceptual, and Psychophysical Processes.*
Vol. III: *Hypnotic Investigation of Psychodynamic Processes*
Vol. IV: *Innovative Hypnotherapy*
New York: Irvington.

Erickson, M. (1980f). Visual hallucination as a rehearsal for symptom resolution. In E. Rossi (Ed.), *The Collected Papers of Milton H. Erickson on Hypnosis. Vol. IV. Innovative Hypnotherapy.* New York: Irvington, 144–148.

Erickson, M., & Rossi, E. (1976/1980). Two-level communication and the microdynamics of trance and suggestion. In E. Rossi (Ed.), *The Collected Papers of Milton H. Erickson on Hypnosis. Vol. I. The Nature of Hypnosis and Suggestion.* New York: Irvington, 430–451.

Erickson, M., & Rossi, E. (1977/1980). Autohypnotic experiences of Milton H. Erickson. In E. Rossi (Ed.), *The Collected Papers of Milton H. Erickson on Hypnosis. Vol. I. The Nature of Hypnosis and Suggestion.* New York: Irvington, 108–132.

Erickson, M., & Rossi, E. (1979). *Hypnotherapy: An Exploratory Casebook.* New York: Irvington.

Erickson, M., & Rossi, E. (1981). *Experiencing Hypnosis: Indirect Approaches to Altered States.* New York: Irvington.

Erickson, M., Rossi, E., & Rossi, S. (1976). *Hypnotic Realities.* New York: Irvington.

Freud, A. (1946). *The Psychoanalytic Treatment of Children.* London: Imago.

Freud, S. (1923). *The Ego and the Id.* In J. Strachey (Ed.), *The Complete Psychological Works of Sigmund Freud.* (Standard Ed., XIX) London: Hogarth.

Freud, S. (1936). *The Ego and the Mechanisms of Defense.* (Published in English in 1946.) New York: International Universities Press.

Freud, S. (1962). Creative writers and daydreaming. In J. Strachey (Ed.), *Jensen's "Gradiva" and Other Works. Vol. IX. The Complete Psychological Works of Sigmund Freud.* (Standard Edition). London: Hogarth.

Fung, E., & Lazar, B. (1983). Hypnosis as an adjunct in the treatment of von Willebrand's Disease. *International Journal of Clinical & Experimental Hypnosis, 31,* 256–265.

Galin, D. (1974). Implications for psychiatry of left and right specialization. *Archives of General Psychiatry, 31,* 527–583.

Galin, D., & Ornstein, R. (1973). Individual differences in cognitive style—I. Reflective eye movements. *Neuropsychologia, 12,* 367–376.

Gardner, G., & Olness, K. (1981). *Hypnosis and Hypnotherapy with Children.* New York: Grune & Stratton.

Gardner, R. (1968). The mutual storytelling technique: Use in alleviating childhood oedipal problems. *Contemporary Psychoanalysis, 4*(2), 161–177.

Gardner, R. (1970). The mutual storytelling technique: Use in the treatment of a child with neurosis. *American Journal of Psychotherapy, 24*(3), 419–439.

Gardner, R. (1971). *Therapeutic Communication with Children: The Mutual Storytelling Technique.* New York: Science House.

Gardner, R. (1972a). Mutual storytelling: A technique in child psychotherapy. *Acta Paedopsychiatrica, 38*(9), 253–262.

Gardner, R. (1972b). The mutual storytelling technique in the treatment of anger inhibition problems. *International Journal of Child Psychotherapy, 1*(1), 34–64.

Gardner, R. (1973). *Talking, Feeling, Doing Game.* Cresskill, N. J.: Creative Therapeutics.

Gardner, R. (1974). The mutual storytelling technique in the treatment of psychogenic problems: Secondary to minimal brain dysfunction. *Journal of Learning Disabilities, 7*(3), 135–143.

Gardner, R. (1975). Techniques for involving the child with MBD in meaningful psychotherapy. *Journal of Learning Disabilities, 8*(5), 272–282.

Gazzaniga, M. (1967). The split brain in man. *Scientific American, 217,* 24–29.

Gilligan, S. (1986). *Therapeutic Trances.* New York: Brunner/Mazel.

Gindhart, L. (1981). The use of metaphoric story in therapy: A case report. *American Journal of Clinical Hypnosis, 23*(3), 202–206.

Goldstein, M. (1983). The production of metaphor in poetry therapy as a means of achieving insight. *Arts in Psychotherapy, 10*(3), 167–173.

Gordon, D. (1978). *Therapeutic Metaphors.* Cupertino, Cal.: Meta Publications.

Greelis, M., & Kazaoka, K. (1979). The therapeutic use of edited videotapes with an exceptional child. *Academic Therapy, 15*(1), 37–44.

Grinder, J., DeLozier, J., & Bandler, R. (1977). *Patterns of the Hypnotic Techniques of Milton H. Erickson, M.D.* II. Cupertino, Cal.: Meta Publications.

Gross, R., & Gross, B. (1965). Let the child teach himself. *New York Times Magazine,* May 16, p. 34.

Haley, J. (1963). *Strategies of Psychotherapy.* New York: Grune & Stratton.

Haley, J. (1967). *Advanced Techniques of Hypnosis and Therapy: Selected Papers of Milton H. Erickson, M.D.* New York: Grune & Stratton.

Haley, J. (1973). *Uncommon Therapy.* New York: Norton.

Haley, J. (1985). *Conversations with Milton H. Erickson. Vol. III. Changing Children and Families.* New York: Triangle Press.

Hapkiewicz, W., & Roden, A. (1971). The effect of aggressive cartoons on children's interpersonal play. *Child Development, 42*(5), 1583–1585.

Hapkiewicz, W., & Stone, R. (1974). The effects of realistic versus imaginary aggressive models on children's interpersonal play. *Child Study Journal, 4*(2), 47–58.

Hariman, J. (1980). An exploration of group procedures in the management of mentally retarded and psychotic patients. *Australian Journal of Clinical Hypnotherapy, 1*(2), 67–72.

Hawkey, L. (1951). The use of puppets in psychotherapy. *British Journal of Medical Psychology, 24,* 206–214.

Heller, S., & Steele, T. (1986). *There's No Such Thing as Hypnosis.* Phoenix: Falcon Press.

Hilgard, J. (1970). *Personality and Hypnosis: A Study of Imaginative Involvement.* Chicago: University of Chicago Press.

Hoff, B. (1982). *The Tao of Pooh.* New York: Dutton.

Hoffman, L. (1983). Imagery and metaphor in couples therapy. *Family Therapy, 10*(2), 141–156.

Jaynes, J. (1976). *The Origins of Consciousness in the Breakdown of the Bicameral Mind.* New York: Houghton Mifflin.

Jung, C. (1911–12/1956). *Symbols of Transformation, Parts I and II. Vol. I. The Collected Works of Carl G. Jung.* Translated by R.F.C. Hull. Bollingen Series XX. Princeton, N. J.: Princeton University Press.

Jung, C. (1916/1960). *The Structure and Dynamics of the Psyche. Vol. III. The Collected Works of Carl G. Jung.* Translated by R.F.C. Hull. Bollingen Series XX. Princeton, N. J.: Princeton University Press.

Jung, C. (1921/1971). *Psychological Types. Vol. VI. The Collected Works of Carl G. Jung.* Translated by R.F.C. Hull. Bollingen Series XX. Princeton, N. J.: Princeton University Press.

Jung, C. (1934/1959). A study in the process of individuation. In *The Archetypes and the Collective Unconscious. Part I. Vol. IX. The Collected Works of Carl G. Jung.* Translated by R.F.C. Hull. Bollingen Series XX. Princeton, N. J.: Princeton University Press.

Jung, C. (1958). *Psyche and Symbol.* New York: Doubleday.

Jung, C. (1959). *The Archetypes and the Collective Unconscious, Parts I and II. Vol. IX. The Collected Works of Carl G. Jung.* Translated by R.F.C. Hull. Bollingen Series XX. Princeton, N. J.: Princeton University Press. (Jung's first article on the archetypes ["Archetypes of the Collective Unconscious"], which became the basis of this volume, was published in German in 1934.)

Jung, C. (1961). *Memories, Dreams, and Reflections.* New York: Vintage Books.

Jung, C. (Ed.) (1964). *Man and his Symbols.* Ljubljana, Yugoslavia: Mladinska: Knjiga.

Kagan, R. (1982). Storytelling and game therapy for children in placement. *Child Care Quarterly, 11*(4), 280–290.

Katz, G. (1983). The noninterpretation of metaphors in psychiatric hospital groups. *International Journal of Group Psychotherapy., 33*(1), 53–67

Kelley, M., Jarvie, G., Middlebrook, J., McNeer, M., & Drabman, R. (1984). Decreasing burned children's pain behavior: Impacting the trauma of hydrotherapy. *Journal of Applied Behavior Analysis, 17*(2), 147–158.

Kinsbourne, M. (1972). Eye and head turning indicates cerebral lateralization. *Science, 58,* 539–541.

Kocel, K., Galin, D., Ornstein, R., & Merrin, E. (1972). Lateral eye movement and cognitive mode. *Psychonomic Science, 27*(4), 223–224.

Kopp, S. (1971). *Guru: Metaphors from a Psychotherapist.* Palo Alto, Cal.: Science & Behavior Books.

Kramer, E. (1971). *Art as Therapy with Children.* New York: Shocken Books.

Kreitler, H., & Kreitler, S. (1978). Art therapy: Quo vadis? *Art Psychotherapy, 5*(4), 199–209.

LaFleur, N., & Johnson, R. (1972). Separate effects of social modeling and reinforcement in counseling adolescents. *Journal of Counseling Psychology, 19*(4), 292–295.

Lakovics, M., Becher, E., Goldstein, D., Kruger-Weisberg, S., Towle, S., & Walker-Wessells, B. (1978). Expressive psychotherapies: Administrative considerations. *American Journal of Art Therapy, 17*(4), 141–144.

Lamb, S. (1980). Hemispheric specialization and storytelling: Implications and applications for longstanding problems. Masters thesis, University of California, Los Angeles.

Lankton, S. (1980). *Practical Magic.* Cupertino, Cal.: Meta Publications.

Lankton, S., & Lankton, C. (1983). *The Answer Within: A Clinical Framework of Ericksonian Hypnotherapy.* New York: Brunner/Mazel.

Lawrence, D. H. (1969). *Sons and Lovers.* New York: Viking. (Originally published in 1913 by Thomas Seltzer.)

Levine, E. (1980). Indirect suggestions through personalized fairytales for treatment of childhood insomnia. *The American Journal of Clinical Hypnosis, 23,* 57–63.

Loomis, E. (1957). The use of checkers in handling certain resistances in child therapy and child analysis. *Journal of the American Psychoanalytic Association, 5,* 130–135.

Lowen, A. (1965). *Love and Orgasm.* New York: Macmillan.

Lowen, A. (1967). *The Betrayal of the Body.* New York: Macmillan.

Lowen, A. (1975). *Bioenergetics.* New York: Coward, McCann & Georghegan.

Lowitz, G., & Suib, M. (1978). Generalized control of persistent thumbsucking by differential reinforcement of other behaviors. *Journal of Behavior Therapy & Experimental Psychiatry, 9*(4), 343–346.

Luria, A. (1973). *The Working Brain.* New York: Basic Books.

Manoly, B. (1980). A clinical validation study of Ramsden's cartoon listening test for interpersonal communication. *Dissertation Abstracts International, 41*(11), 4688-A. The Medical College of Pennsylvania, Pennsylvania.

Mazor, R. (1982). Drama therapy for the elderly in a daycare center. *Hospital & Community Psychiatry, 33*(7), 577–579.

Mills, J., & Crowley, R. (1983). Positive effects of cartoon images. *Telemedia, 1*(2), 11–16.

Montessori, M. (1914). *Dr. Montessori's Own Handbook*. New York: Frederick A. Stokes.

Naso, R. (1982). Metaphor and clinical interpretation: A critical discussion and exploratory study of selected issues in a psychoanalysis. *Dissertation Abstracts International, 43*(2-b), 530.

Nathanson, D. (1977). Designing instructional media for severely retarded adolescents: A theoretical approach to trait-treatment interaction research. *American Journal of Mental Deficiency, 82*(1), 26–32.

Naumberg, M. (1958). Art therapy: Its scope and function. In E. Hammer (Ed.), *The Clinical Applications of Projective Drawings*. Springfield, Illinois: Charles C. Thomas, pp. 511–517.

Nebes, R. (1977). Man's so-called minor hemisphere. In M. Wittrock (Ed.), *The Human Brain*. Inglewood Cliffs, N. J.: Prentice-Hall, 97–106.

Neyer, J. (1976). Community based art therapy. *Creativity and the art therapist's identity: Proceedings of the 76th Annual Conference of the American Art Therapy Association*. Baltimore, Maryland.

Nickerson, E. (1973). The use of art as a play therapeutic medium in the classroom. *Art Psychotherapy, 1*(3–4), 293–297.

Oaklander, V. (1978). *Windows to Our Children*. Moab, Utah: Real People Press.

O'Connell, W. (1979). The demystification of Sister Saint Nobody. *Journal of Individual Psychology, 35*(1), 79–94.

Olness, K. (1978). Little people, images, and child health. Presidential address, Northwestern Pediatric Society, Minneapolis, September 28.

Ornstein, R. (1978). The split and whole brain. *Human Nature, 1*(5), 76–83.

Owens, L. (1977). An investigation of eye movements and representational systems. *Dissertation Abstracts International*, 4992-B.

Papp, P. (1982). Staging reciprocal metaphors in a couples group. *Family Process, 21*(4), 453–467.

Pardee, J. (1984). A cognitive model of psychotherapeutic insight: The effects of insight statements and figurative language on subjects' comprehension and recall of psychotherapy dialogue. *Dissertation Abstracts International, 44*(9-b), 2904.

Pearce, J. (1977). *Magical Child*. New York: Bantam.

Pelletier, K. (1978). *Toward a Science of Consciousness*. New York: Delta.

Perlowski, S., & Reisman, J. (1974). The existential significance that injustice in human relationship has for the neurotic. *Social Behavior & Personality, 2*(1), 97–103.

Perls, F. (1969). *Gestalt Therapy Verbatim*. Lafayette, Cal.: Real People Press.

Piaget, J. (1951). *Play, Dreams, and Imitation in Childhood*. New York: Norton.

Poore, M. (1977). Art therapy in a vocational rehabilitation center. *The American Journal of Art Therapy, 16*(1), 55–59.

Reich, W. (1949). *Character Analysis*. (3rd Ed.) New York: Orgone Institute Press.

Remotique-Ano, N. (1980). The hidden agenda of story-making therapy. *American Journal of Psychotherapy, 34*(2), 261–268.

Ritterman, M. (1983). *Using Hypnosis in Family Therapy.* San Francisco: Jossey Bass.

Robertson, M., & Barford, F. (1970). Story-making in psychotherapy with a chronically ill child. *Psychotherapy: Theory, Research, & Practice, 7,* 104–107.

Rogers, A. (1983). Use of metaphors in the treatment of bedwetting. *Dissertation Abstracts International, 43*(10-b), 3373–3374.

Rogers, L., TenHouten, W., Kaplan, C., & Gardner, M. (1977). Hemispheric specialization of language: A EEG study of bi-lingual Hopi Indian children. *International Journal of Neuroscience, 8,* 1–6.

Rossi, E. (1982). Hypnosis and ultradian cycles: A new state(s) theory of hypnosis? *The American Journal of Clinical Hypnosis, 25*(1), 21–32.

Rossi, E. (1983). Personal communication.

Rossi, E. (1984). Unpublished written communication.

Rossi, E. (1972/1985). *Dreams and the Growth of Personality.* (2nd Ed.) New York: Brunner/Mazel.

Rossi, E. (1986a). Altered states of consciousness in everyday life: The ultradian rhythms. In B. Wolman (Ed.), *Handbook of Altered States of Consciousness.* New York: Van Nostrand.

Rossi, E. (1986b). *The Psychobiology of Mind-Body Healing: New Concepts of Therapeutic Hypnosis.* New York: Norton.

Rossi, E., & Jichaku, P. (1984). Therapeutic and transpersonal double binds: Continuing the legacy of Gregory Bateson and Milton H. Erickson. Paper presented at the Annual Scientific Meeting of the American Society of Clinical Hypnosis. San Francisco, October.

Rossi, E., & Ryan, M. (Eds.) (1985). *Life Reframing in Hypnosis. II. The Seminars, Workshops, and Lectures of Milton H. Erickson.* New York: Irvington.

Rossi, E., & Ryan, M. (Eds.) (1986). *Mind-body in Hypnosis. III. The Seminars, Workshops, and Lectures of Milton H. Erickson.* New York: Irvington.

Rossi, E., & Ryan, M. (Eds.) (In preparation). *The Seminars, Workshops and Lectures of Milton H. Erickson. IV.* New York: Irvington.

Rossi, E., Ryan, M., & Sharp, F. (Eds.) (1983). *Healing in Hypnosis. I. The Seminars, Workshops, and Lectures of Milton H. Erickson.* New York: Irvington.

Rubin, J. (1981). Art therapy in a community mental health center for children: A story of program development. *The arts in psychotherapy, 8*(2), 109–114.

Rule, W. (1983). Family therapy and the pie metaphor. *Journal of Marital & Family Therapy, 9*(1), 101–103.

Russo, S. (1964). Adaptations in behavioral therapy with children. *Behavior Research & Therapy, 2,* 43–47.

Schienberg, P. (1979). Therapists' predictions of patients' responses to humor as a function of therapists' empathy and regression in the service of the ego. *Dissertation Abstracts International, 40*(8), 4501-A. California School of Professional Psychology, Los Angeles.

Schooley, C. (1976). Communicating with hospitalized children: The mutual story-telling technique. *Journal of Pastoral Care, 28*(2), 102–111.

Scott, R. (1978). "It hurts red": A preliminary study of children's perception of pain. *Perceptual & Motor Skills, 47*(3, Pt. 1), 787–791.

Sperry, R. (1968). Hemispheric disconnection and unity of conscious awareness. *American Psychologist, 23,* 723–733.

Spiegel, H., & Spiegel, D. (1978). *Trance and Treatment.* New York: Basic Books.

Stirtzinger, R. (1983). Storytelling: A creative therapeutic technique. *Canadian Journal of Psychiatry, 28*(7), 561–565.

Tebecis, A., & Provins, K. (1975). Hypnosis and eye movements. *Biological Psychology, 3*(1), 31–47.

Ungame Company. (1975). *Ungame.* Anaheim, Cal.

Whitney, J. (1983). Art therapy training for counselors in a community mental health center. Unpublished doctoral dissertation. International College, Los Angeles.

Wildgen, J. (1975). "Once upon a time . . ." or how to teach retarded children to tell stories—toward conversational speech. *Dissertation Abstracts International, 36*(2), 899-B. University of Kansas.

Xianyi, Y., Yang, G. [Trans.] (1981). *Chinese Ancient Fables.* Beijing, China: Foreign Language Press.

Yampolski, P. [Trans.] (1971). *The Zen Master Hakuin: Selected Writings.* New York: Columbia University Press.

Yapko, M. (1981). The effects of matching primary representational prediates on hypnotic relaxation. *The American Journal of Clinical Hypnosis, 23,* 169–175.

Zeig, J. (1980). *A Teaching Seminar with Milton H. Erickson.* New York: Brunner/ Mazel.

Index

Page numbers in **boldface** type indicate major topics of chapters or chapter sections. A lowercase *n* after a page number indicates that it is in the References.

249